LIBERALISATION AND GLOBALISATION

LIBERALISATION AND GLOBALISATION

Dr. P.R. Dubhashi

GYAN

Liberalisation and Globalisation

ISBN: 978-81-212-1135-2

Published in 2012 in India by
Gyan Publishing House
23, Main Ansari Road, Daryaganj,
New Delhi-110002
Phone : 23282060, 23261060
Fax : (011) 23285914
E-mail : books@gyanbooks.com
Website : gyanbooks.com

Leser Type setting : Lucky Graphic, Delhi
Printed at : Chowla Offset Printer, Delhi

"For my
grand children
Archana, Vinu and Minu
who represent the 21st Century"

CONTENTS

Preface

This book brings together my articles on Liberalization and Globalization, most of them published in leading journals and newspapers, over the period of fifteen years from 1995 to 2010. The articles have been divided into three parts (1) Liberalization (2) Globalization (3) Critique of the theory of neo-liberalism.

1991 marked a watershed, almost a U-turn, in Indian economic policy pursued over forty years from 1951 to 1991, often described as a Nehruvian model of economic policy. The major features of that model included what came to be known as the 'socialist pattern' of society, a planned economy, emphasis on public sector enterprises and heavy industries which were expected to gain the commanding heights of the economy, autarchy, import substitution and self-reliance. The new economic policy introduced in 1991 by the Narsimharao minority government was a shift from planning to marketization, from public sector and co-operative sectors to private enterprise, from command and control economy to de-regulation, from autarchy to inter-dependence of an open economy, and from progressive taxation to moderate taxation on the high income groups and corporates.

The genesis of this policy has to be traced to the economic and political crisis with which the country was confronted and which was a big challenge faced by the Narsimharao Government which came into power in 1991. He appointed as finance minister in his cabinet Dr. Manmohan Singh, an erstwhile civil servant, who had held high positions in economic administration. On his appointment, he immediately entered into discussion with the World Bank and International Monetary Fund who agreed to provide a standby loan and further assistance, subject to the conditionality of India's acceptance of Structural Adjustment Program. The policy of liberalization and globalization initiated by Dr. Manmohan Singh reflected all the elements in the structural adjustment programme which included fiscal discipline requiring heavy cut in public expenditure, incurred in the name of the welfare of the common people. It also reflected the theory of 'the minimal state' i.e. a state which has no direct role in economic activities and gives free scope to the private enterprise.

The first three articles in this book deal with the genesis, working and aftermath of the new economic policy. The new policy was always described as a policy of economic reforms. But the Government did not show courage to state that it has consciously and deliberately rejected the Nehruvian model. It's approach was somewhat timid and cautious so as not to invite criticism. Those who did not quite agree with the so called economic reforms raised larger issues relating to the pattern of growth to which the economic reforms gave birth namely unequal distribution of the fruits of the liberalization, growing disparities between the rich and the poor, rise of consumerism, and the growing influence of the multi-nationals in the economy and the erosion of national sovereignty.

As the five year term of Narsimharao government was coming to an end, it decided to slow down the new policy lest it should alienate the common people. Despite this the Congress lost power in 1996 general elections. But the non-Congress governments from 1996 to 2004 of which six years were of the BJP Government led by Atal Behari Vajpayee continued the policy of liberalization. The rate of economic development accelerated and BJP made 'Shining India' as its election slogan. But the BJP was in for a shock. In 2004 general elections the Congress emerged as the largest party and formed government with outside support of the leftist parties on the basis of the 'common minimum programme'. This put constraint on the reformist agenda of the Prime Minister Manmohan Singh (the chosen candidate of Sonia Gandhi) and P. Chidambaram, as Finance Minister, who could not undertake large scale disinvestments of the public enterprises and opening up of Banking and Insurance to the multinationals. The first three articles in the book deal with the various aspects of the policy of liberalization and globalization pursued with the ambiguity of approach.

The articles that follow raise a number of issues relating to the effect of these policies on the common people. The article 'Reforms can't afford to ignore the common man' states that no attempt has been made to explain the policy of liberalization to the people nor has the new policy improved the lot of the common people. Rather it let to the neglect of public investment in social sectors and agricultural and rural development. It, therefore, states that the Central Government should get over the euphoria of liberalization and pay attention to the implications of the new economic policies in term of the welfare of the people and introduce necessary corrections.

The same theme is carried further in subsequent articles. The policy of liberalization has led to rural-urban divide. The economic reforms has overlooked the need for spatial planning, industrial dispersal and provision of public service in rural areas. Rural and agriculture economy suffered comparative neglect. Its extreme manifestation was the tragic phenomenon of nearly two lakh farmers committing suicide in the era of liberalization. The farmers were forced to commit suicide when they fell in a debt trap. While the cost of agriculture inputs increased, the prices of the agriculture produce fluctuated widely. The agricultural extension services got weakened and failed to provide necessary guidelines to the farmers. Institutional credit both by cooperatives and commercial banks failed to meet the credit requirements of the farmers who were forced to go to the money lender, despite the usurious rates of interest. What was required was a comprehensive policy including large public investment in irrigation and rural infrastructure, rejuvenation of co-operative credit, marketing and processing system, strengthening the agricultural extension services and sympathetic administration closely working with the farming community. Unfortunately, no such policy was formulated either by the Congress led government or the BJP led government. The larger aspect of the policy should have been strengthening the natures' life supporting system by widely dispersed projects of soil and water conservation which would have provided ample employment opportunities if they had been taken up under the 'Right to employment program'.

The policy of liberalization has also led to continuous inflationary pressure with the result the prices of essential commodities have gone up from time to time putting them beyond the reach of the common people. The public distribution system went into disrepair and the chief economist of the Finance Ministry, Kaushik Basu has recently admitted that the Government has been left without any instrument to control inflation.

The policy of liberalization and globalization has also led to exclusive emphasis on profits by the private enterprise at the cost of public interest. The tendencies of grabbing and acquisitive mentality has filtered down throughout the society. Instead of liberalization leading to reduced corruption because of the end of "license permit raj" has instead led to new opportunities of corruption in a use of public resources in which the private entrepreneurs like builders and unscrupulous businessmen joined hands with unscrupulous politicians in power. The fall in ethical standards has gone hand in hand with liberalization in other countries like China, Russia, Italy and even Japan. No wonder era of liberalization in India has witnessed financial scams and scandals of huge proportions. The high traditions of public life laid down by the leaders of India's freedom movement have all been forgotten. The corporate sector which talked of high standards of 'Corporate governance' has also been thoroughly exposed by the Satyam episode. The cancer of corruption has spread throughout the economic and social system and needs drastic measures to curb it. This has been discussed at length in the article under the caption 'Fighting the Cancer of Corruption'.

India's economic growth is often compared with that of China. China has progressed much faster but it has an authoritarian government. On the other hand India has a democratic system and therefore, Indian economic growth, it is said, would be enduring and democracy would provide a mechanism for preventing corruption and financial crisis. Unfortunately this has not happened. Indian democracy is flawed and the mechanism of automatic correction of abuse of power leading to misuse of resources does not function.

Swadeshi which was the watchword of great leaders like Lokmanya Tilak and Mahatma Gahdhi has often been decried by the advocates of neo-liberalism. Swadeshi needs to be dynamically interpreted in the present context. Interdependence which is implied in globalization should not degenerate into dependence on dominant countries, nor should the state go down under the pressure of mighty multinational companies. It should not give up its role to give a sense of direction to the economy in public interest.

Liberalization means that we have accepted the free market economy but free market economy should not mean complete abandonment of planning. The market is not always rational, and needs to be corrected, it works under the pressure of those who command more resources at the cost of the common man. We should rather follow the example of countries like Japan which plans on the basis of macro economic forecasting and France which has system of indicative planning. The Planning Commission should concentrate on the formulation of the long term policies, planning has to be multi-level and decentralized.

The first article in the second part on globalization states that the imperial powers had created a global system under which the economies of the colonized countries were tied to the apron strings of the economies of the imperial powers over a period of five hundred years of imperialism from 1498 onwards. The ample raw materials in those colonized countries were fully exploited by the colonial powers. The colonized countries emerged to freedom after the world war–II. The erstwhile colonial powers took a lead in creating a new international order through establishment of the global institutions like the UNO and its subsidiary bodies, the World Bank, the IMF and more recently in 1995 the World Trade Organization.

After the collapse of socialism and disintegration of the Soviet Union, USA remained the unchallenged super power which has been trying to shape the world system according to its own design and for promoting its own interest. The present system of globalization is a product of the efforts of the super power. The US Secretary of State the Madelaine Albright had once boasted that US is only indispensable country in the world, it, therefore, does not hesitate to make a disproportionate claim on the available natural resources and disproportionate use of energy without any regard for pollution and global warming. The so-called inter-dependent economy based on free flow of goods and services, capital and finance entrepreneurship and management and technology, in fact, works in the interest of the US and other dominant economies. The World Bank, The International Monitory Fund and WTO work under the dominance of the USA and follow policies which have come to be known as Washington consensus. This distorted system of globalization has often led to instability and has also led to growing in-equalities. The structural adjustment policies imposed by the World Bank on countries in Latin America and Africa have led to disastrous consequences as in Argentina and Brazil. The one sided approach of the World Bank and the IMF was also seen in course of what came to be known as 'East Asia Crisis' of 1997-98. No wonder that people's movement against global capitalism have emerged for mobilization against globalization to create a more humane and equitable economic and social order.

While the Chicago School under Milton Friedman asserted that the capitalist market economy is self correcting, the collapse of giant American Financial institutions in 2009 gave a serious setback to the claims of unbridled capitalism. The collapse of American institutions had a cascading impact on Britain and other European countries as well as Japan. President Bush had to introduce a huge plan to bail out the American Financial Institutions. He was criticized for preaching capitalism to the ordinary people while promoting socialism to protect the huge financial institutions. America has not yet come out of the recession. It will not do so unless the systemic defects which have crept in to the capitalist economy are overcome. On assuming the post of President of USA, Barak Obama attributed the financial crisis to the insatiable greed of the CEO's of American Companies but he has not yet not been able to overcome the systemic defects of American Capitalism.

A more benign aspect of globalization relates to free flow of knowledge and cross cultural cooperation. The TRIPS introduced by WTO is no doubt a hindrance to the free flow of knowledge. In addition, in the worldwide dissemination of knowledge and culture, the local social and cultural ethos of different countries of the world should not be overlooked.

The last part deals with the theoretical foundations of neo-liberalism. After World War the II Keynesian economics drew attention to the factors behind unemployment in the capitalist countries and emphasized the importance of public investment and redistribution of income to overcome the same. Also a new body of economics known as "development economics" was formed which emphasized the importance of 'big push' to be given by the State to enable the people of the developing countries to get out of the poverty. However, the ascendancy of the Chicago School banished both these new schools of thoughts and restored the primacy of the neo-classical economics and its backing of a totally free market economy with no role for the State. This thinking is at the core of what has come to be known as Washington Consensus which is at the back of today's liberalization and globalization. But a critical examination of the propositions of the neo-classical economics shows that its foundations are not sound. The market is never perfect and human beings are not rational economic entities. There are different motivations behind the economic transactions. A number of economists including those who have been Nobel prize winners have shown the need for re-examination of the basic propositions of free market economy and liberalization and globalization based on it. The reality of capitalism is far different from the myths of capitalism propagated by the Chicago School. If socialism has failed, capitalism has not succeeded in solving the problems of the humanity. There is need for the search of alternatives. One alternatives is 'Participative Economics' as propounded by Michael Albert. The other is the Gandhian philosophy which has emphasized that the blind pursuit of material achievements is not the be all and end all of life. It is at the root of conflict and violence which we witnessed in the world in our competitive pursuit of economic interests. The essential propositions of Gandhian ideology are of great relevance today in the era of liberalization and globalization.

PART- I
LIBERALIZATION

1

THE NEW ECONOMIC POLICY – GENESIS, WORKING AND AFTERMATH

The New Economic Policy which was ushered in the year 1991 is rightly described as water-shed in Indian economic evolution after independence. A Recently, in the gathering of the World Economic Forum, Dr. Manmohan Singh, the Finance Minister announced that there will be no more economic reforms till the elections. That does not mean that the process of economic reforms has come to an end. Indeed it must go on with full national determination and efforts. Since there is an all party consensus on economic reforms, the process of reforms, hopefully, will be resumed, no matter which Government would come in office. This is only a temporary pause, a lull and is, therefore, perhaps the right time to take stock of what happened during the last four years, make an assessment and suggest the future course of action.

The Genesis

The new economic policy was a response to the economic crisis of 1991. The proximate manifestation of the economic crisis in 1991 was the critical balance of payment position. Despite borrowing from IMF, the country's total fo eign exchange resources fell precipitiously – August 1990 Rs. 5000 Cr; March 1991 Rs. 4300 Cr; and June 1991 Rs. 2300 Cr; i.e. one billion dollars – hardly adequate to meet the requirements of a week's imports, and this in the face of a negative flow of external resources. Looking at this precarious situation, the NRI's were rapidly withdrawing their foreign exchange deposits and the country was faced with international bankruptcy. India had never defaulted in the past and had an unblemished record of international financial rectitude. Now suddenly a country of high credibility had reached the rock bottom.

The RBI which had the responsibility to maintain the record had no alternative but to push the panic buttons. It imposed savage compression on imports but even this proved inadequate. Twenty tons of gold in the vaults of the RBI had to be mortgaged to the Zurich Bank, and later 46 tons to Bank of England to salvage the situation. Shri. I.G. Patel then described this as a mater of national shame.

But the crisis did not develop all of a sudden. It was in the making. The country had for long been living beyond its resources as reflected in the immense internal and external deficits. The country's external debt had risen to a high level of $ 70 billion. There was persistent deficit in the balance of payments which soared to $6 – 7 billion. The country had lost its credibility. Moody's international Investor service downgraded India's credit rating. India slipped to the bottom of investment grading.

India had a long tradition of conservative fiscal management. For such a country to fall in Latin American type of debt trap was indeed an unprecedented calamity. How did this happen? How and when did economic conservatism degenerate into economic profligacy? It was in the 80's that the seeds of economic profligacy were sown. In order to break through the situation of economic stagnation, the Government of Shri. Rajeev Gandhi, the then Prime Minister, started transforming a policy of import substitution into a policy of export promotion. In order to promote export, floodgates were opened for import of capital, synthetic and electronic goods, and crude oil imports soared by 1990-91 because India's oil production fell from 33 million tons to 28 million tons. While exports increased by 17.5% in 1990-91, imports increased by 21.9%, trade deficit increased by 3% from Rs. 7738 cr. In 1989.90 to 10644 Cr. cn 1990-91. This imbalance rapidly depleted the foreign exchange reserves. In order to fill up the gap, the country resorted to short term commercial borrowing at high market rate. Outstanding debt to private creditors in 1970 was only $ 330 million. In 1989 it was $ 4689 million. High interest commercial borrowing increased by leaps and bounds and such became the burden of payment of interest and amortization of debt that the debt service ratio zoomed to 27 from the traditional 10%. The burden of servicing external debt (Rs. 4000 Cr.) was more than the fresh commercial debt (Rs. 3050 Cr.). India was truly in a debt trap.

The external deficit was in a way a reflection of internal fiscal deficit. While the public expenditure was mounting up year after year, the resources generation was not keeping pace. Successive budget left huge deficits. Between 1983-84 and 1990-91 the gap between government expenditure and current revenue increased annually by 16.2%. The budget deficit increased from Rs. 1470 Cr. in 1983-84 to Rs. 11430 Cr. In 1990-91. Most of the government expenditure was on non-development heads. Out of Central Government expenditure of Rs. 106717 Cr. In 1990-91, Rs. 21850 Cr. was spent on interest payment on accumulated public debt. Rs. 15750 Cr. on defence and Rs. 12120 Cr. on subsidy and deficit of public enterprises. The expenditure on these three heads increased annually by 21.7%, 14.2% and 21.2% respectively. The national debt was 55% of the gross domestic product and burden of interest payment on the accumulated debt became very heavy. The public expenditure on defence, subsidies and interest payment was inelastic and could not be curbed. The country came to such a pass that capital surplus had to be diverted to revenue expenditure instead of revenue surplus being used for capital expenditure and building up of assets.

No wonder, this has let loose a spiral of inflation which reached 17 Percent.

The New Government And The Sap

The new Government which took office under Shri. Narasimha Rao in 1991 had to tackle this severe economic crisis. He found his man for fire-fighting in Dr. Manmohan Singh who was for long in Government as an Economic Adviser; Secretary, Economic Affairs; Secretary, Planning Commission and Governor of the Reserve Bank of India and in all these capacities had developed personal contacts with the senior functionaries in the international financial institutions viz. World Bank and International Monetary Fund. He immediately got into touch with the heads of both these institutions who reposed trust in his financial statesmanship and having regard to the importance of India agreed to privide immediat and long term support to overcome the crisis but this was contingent on the conditionality of India accepting the 'Structural Adjustment Programme' (SAP). The World Financial Institutions had developed the SAP to bail out the Latin American and African Countries in the 80s and they wanted to administer the same medicine to India also. Indeed in two of their reports on the Indian economic situation they had worked out both the dignosis and the remedies.

These two reports of the World Bank were – 'India – an industrializing economy in transition', 1987 and 'India – a strategy on Trade Reforms' 1990. Both these reports recommended that sustained high rate of economic growth alone can create productive employment and reduce poverty. This can be accomplished by replacing India's restrictive discretionary and complex system of regulatory control – difficult to understand and administer with an allocative mechanism that relies on market signals and internal and external competitions.

The Reports found fault with the 'false', concept of self-reliance which led to import substituion regardless of cost, emphasis on heavy industry and a regime of protection and control. The Reports recommended replacement of high tariffs and quantitative restrictions on imports with moderate and uniform tariffs. The former had provided Indian industry a high level of protection from international competition. As a result of the sheltered economy, much of the industrial sector became inefficient, high cost and technologically backward. This led to a declining share in the world market. The Reports recommended phased implementation of trade reforms and appropriate fiscal and exchange rate policies for the creation of efficient, dynamic and internationally competitive economy. The new economic policy based on such structural reforms recommended by World Bank and IMF was expected to lead to an efficient allocation and utilization of resources and faster rate of economic growth.

India had developed a control and command economy. Internal and external controls had imprisoned the impulses of economic growth. The picture of Indian economy was in sharp contrast to the East Asian countries like South Korea, Hong Kong, Taiwan, and Singapore who had followed the footsteps of Japan to develop a pattern of development based on exports promotion and had 10% cumulative growth. Other countries of East Asia like Indonesia, Malaysia and Thailand had also started showing a high growth rate. On the other hand, thanks to the stifling regulations of a controlled economy, Indian economic growth rate had stunted to around 3.5% per annum. With a more than 1% per capita growth and with unequal distribution of fruits of growth, the economic conditions of the poor had deteriorated.

In the sheltered market, industry and trade exploit the consumer because goods could be sold in the sheltered market regardless of quality. The Indian consumers were deprived of the benefits of goods of high quality which were products of advanced technology. The static and the stagnant Indian economy was, therefore, the result of a sheltered market and the regulated economy.

India's isolation from the world economy had yet another consequence. India attracted only $280 million net private foreign investment as against a much higher amount attracted by other Asian Countries.

Indonesia	$	542 million
Malaysia	$	649 million
Philipines	$	986 million
Thailand	$	1093 million
China	$	2344 million

Indian economy needed to be integrated with the global economy. Globalisation, it was felt, would bring new opportunities for India. Globalisation is based on interdependence. In a globalised world, yarn may be supplied from Java-Indonesia, converted into cloth in Rajasthan, India, tailored in Bangkok, Thailand, according to fashions designed in Taipei, Taiwan and eventually sold in Duseldorf Germany.

In the absence of globalisation, India's position in the world market declined. In 1960 India's manufactured exports exceeded combined total of diverse countries like South Korea, Singapore or Taiwan, or Brazil, Mexico, Argentina or Columbia. By 1973, India accounted for only 10% of aggregate manufactured export of these countries.

India's share in the world market declined from 2% at the time of independence to .2% in 1991. Asian dragons – South Korea, Singapore, Hongkong, Taiwan followed aggressive exports strategies and gained enormously. In 1962 South Korea had the same per capita income as India. After three decades, it was ten times higher.

Abandoning Nehruvian Model

Indeed, accepting the World Bank's prescription of SAP meant a total change from what came to be known as the Nehruvian Model. It had to undergo a complete transformation. India had to take a 'U' turn from planning to marketisation, from the dominance of the public sector to privatization, from the command and controlled economy to free economy and from autarchy and a closed economy to globalisation and open economy. This alone could make India a dynamic and vibrant economy with a cumulative growth rate of to 7 to 8 per cent.

India had embarked in the year 1951 on a system of planned economic growth. At that time, India felt that the economic fortunes of the country could not be left to the vicissitudes of the market forces and planned and deliberate efforts had to be made to mobilize human and national resources of the country to reach predetermined objective of growth with equity.

In this model of planned economic growth, the State had to play a major role, especially to develop basic and heavy industries and to produce machines to make machines. The Mahalonobian second five year plan fully reflected this approach, Nehru was very fond of the public sector in basic and heavy industries and described them as 'commanding heights of the economy.'

Even the private sector had to work within the framework of planning, which could not be allowed to indulge any wasteful use of economic resources for 'non-priority' purposes. The private sector too had to follow the plan priorities. The industrial policy resolutions of the years 1948 and 1956, the Industrial Development and Regulation Act, the Monopoly and Restrictive Trade Policy Act, the Foreign Exchange Regulation Act, the control over capital issues and controls over export and import setupmany legal and administrative institutions to regulate the private industry.

While all these components of economic policy were well meant, they had a disastrous impact on the economy. This led to a stagnant and static economy. An economic administrator the late Shri. Bhoothalingam who in his long career dealt with many of these control mechanisms has in his posthumously published Autobiography mourned in retrospect, that these controls, a legacy of World War II, were allowed to continue so long.

What is worse, the controls gave rise to the generation of unearned income. The manipulation of machinery of government for getting all kinds of permits and licences under the various rules and regulations led to the generation of black income and black market dominated the economy of the country. It become a parallel economy.

The economic power which politicians and bureaucrats gained as managers of a controlled economy led to illegal gains. Those with economic powers in the shape of disbursement of permits and licences started using them for their own private gains. The public sector far from being allowed to be autonomous and work on a commercial basis as was originally contemplated became a milch cow of the politicians. Contracts were awarded and appointments made to serve the purposes of politicians. The commanding heights of the economy became the breeding ground of corruption. It is only now that through the disclosures of the Hawala racket and other scams and scandals that the country has come to know the extent of the harm done by the command and control economy. It has been estimated that India has lost more than $ 4 b. through Hawala transactions. The nexus between politicians, businessmen and criminals led to criminalisation of politics and economics of the country.

Part of World Wide Change

In a way the abandonment of Nehruvian model of the economy which come to be known as the 'socialist pattern of the economy' may be looked upon as a part of world wide change in the economic outlook. In Britain, Margaret Thatcher, systematically dismantled the whole facade of the Welfare State set up by the labour government of Attlee to take care of the citizens from womb to tomb. Japan also denationalized several economic enterprises. But most cataclysmic changes took place in the erstwhile Soviet Russia and East European countries. All the glory of the October revolution vanished with the collapse of Socialism in USSR and the East European countries Socialism became, as Heyek predicted, became 'a road to selfdom' – It meant long queues of the ordinary consumers for bread and butter but dachas and luxury goods for the rulers. Brehznev years became a long era of economic stagnation and corruption. Reforms became inevitable. The beginning was made by Gorbachev with his Glassnost and Perestroika. But in implementing his reforms, the situation went out of his hands till he lost power and the Soviet Union disintegrated. Socialism vanished from the face of the earth perhaps never to return. While Communist parties have been elected back into power, they have sworn not to go back to static model of the past.

In China under Deng Zoo Peng radical reforms were introduced in the year 1978 to get the China's economy out of the shackles of communism. The farmers were allowed to sell private products free from the control of local communists. The communist party hegemony was dismantled. The party could not dominate government and government could not strangle private enterprise. Free economic zones were created to rival Hongkong.

However, compared to the erst-while communist economies, the task of economic change is much easier in India. The Indian pattern of mixed economy has not destroyed the market and the market institutions. Private ownership of means of production, private entrepreneurship, contracts, banks and a host of market institutions were available as also entrepreneurs and operators to work in these market institutions. It was, therefore, much easier to bring above transformation of the economy in India as compared with the erstwhile communist countries.

Working of Economic Reforms

The Start was made in the very first budget of Dr. Manmohan Singh in 1991. It was meant to be a turning point in fiscal history. It aimed at putting back on rails the crisis ridden economy by correcting fiscal and balance of payment disequilibrium which had landed the country in a debt trap. He took the first three steps viz devaluation of rupee, reduced fiscal deficits from 8.3% of GDP to 6.5% and deregulation of the economy. He abolished export subsidy and reduced food, fertilizers and sugar subsidies, and the budgetary support to public sector enterprises which were actually expected to generate their own resources. But the most important reform was for liberalization through deregulation by removing a maze of controls.

In the 'ancient regime', the greatest obstacle to India's industrial and external growth reposed in the office of the Controller of Imports and Export which issued import licenses and determined whether something could be classified as capital goods, restricted goods, special import goods, banned goods, canalized goods, limited permissible or appendixed goods. Minister of Commerce issued over 150 custom exemption notifications annually making tariff opaque. SIA adjudicated whether a potential contract was to be barred under MRTP, FERA or Capital Goods Imports. DGTD bureaucrats decided whether a particular technology was good for the nation. Civil servants of these organizations had devised forms which ran into 15 pages of which 13 copies had to be submitted. All these government controls on the economy had to be loosened. Major reforms were needed to scrap regulations which had become barriers to entry and investment. Some reforms were introduced in 1980s but they were ad-hoc and half-hearted and did not deal with the fundamental problem of a highly restrictive trade regime.

Amongst the deregulation measures introduced in the very first budget were, removal of industrial licenses except for 18. The scope of Monopoly and Restricted Trade Practices Act was reduced so as not to discourage the size but only regulate the misuse of monopoly powers. It was announced that the tariff barriers would be reduced progressively from 100 or 300 per cent to 50 or 60 per cent. Tariff and excise on capital goods had raised the prices of manufactured goods. The Finance Minister also undertook fiscal reforms bringing down rates of corporate and individual taxation so that greater incentives would be available and evasion of taxation minimized.

Assessment of Reforms

How far have the reforms introduced so far been successful in reaching their objectives? Has the economy of the country gone in the right direction? This has been a matter of continous assessment in the country and elsewhere. Let us first consider the measures of devaluation of the rupee, fiscal discipline, deregulatory, stepping of the rate of savings and investment and then the outcome in terms of higher growth rate.

Devaluation of The Rupee

The devaluation of Indian rupee by 22% in the year 1991, was intended to bring the rupee to its correct international value and to stimulate exports and restrict imports. But it will be a mistake to assume that devaluation alone can reduce the gap in the balance of payment. Devaluation may be ineffective, if import and export are inelastic. The imports of an inevitable nature such as Petrolum are inelastic. Export can be inelastic because of inability to overcome the competition of developed countries in the West and newly developed countries in the East. Real productivity is required to produce goods of quality such is expected in cash rich but discriminating market of the developed countries.

Devaluation also cannot be once and for all measure. Consistent with free market economy and globalisation, the rupee was allowed to float (except for the capital flows) and find its own value vis-a-vis dollar and other currencies. For quite some time, the rupee was able to hold its own. But the recent months saw a precipitous fall in the value of the rupee from Rs. 31 to Rs. 38 per Dollar. Such was the outcry in the country that the R.B.I. and Minister of Finance were perforce required to take some strong interventionist measures to bolster the rupee. This incidence has shown that free working of foreign exchange market is indeed not all that feasible all desirable. It is a thin market in which exporters by delaying the receipt of their foreign exchange earning and importers by making advance payment in foreign exchange, can put the rupee in a jeopardy though the fundamentals of the economy may be allright. But what constitutes proper value of Rupee is always mater of doubt. Finance Minister feels that 36 rupees per Dollar is the right value. But others feel that it should be 34. In any case, as Keynes pointed out long back, Cassinos (i.e. speculation) can not be allowed to decide the course of economic development.

Fiscal Discipline

Fiscal discipline is considered to be the corner stone of SAP. However, attempt to reduce the fiscal deficit has not been very successful. Fiscal deficit after some improvement seems to have crawled back to 1991 level. With growing burden of interest payments, attempts to control the expenditure only meant reduced availability of resources for the social sector and for agricultural development. Even the latest interim budget has saddled the country with a fiscal deficit of Rs. 62404 Cr. The major factor responsible for persistent deficit is the high nonplan expenditure on interest payment on accumulated debt. Borrowing by Government during 1996.97 alone is estimated at Rs. 6000 Cr. On the other hand, there is short fall of Rs. 31000 Cr. in targeted capital expenditure for the VIIIth five year plan which may hurt long term economic growth. As the election drew near, the Government brought back populist measures for rural development and poverty alleviation. There has however been no systematic examination of the pattern of public expenditure. Government should have taken steps for a comprehensive view of public expenditure so that obsolete structures and programmes could be scrapped. Without such an exercise, considerable saving in public expenditure would hardly be a reality.

Inflation and Price Control

In the absence of control over public expenditure and continuing fiscal deficits, prices have continued to rise. The

Government have been putting up bulletins, day in and day out, on the television that the double digit inflations has been a thing of the past and rate of inflation has come down from 17% to 5%. But the common man still seems to groan under the burden of inflation because what has taken place, is not actual fall in prices but only fall in the rate of inflation and this increase is taking place week after week over and above the cumulative inflation of the past.

Moreover, while the rate of inflation in India cumulatively has been above 5% in India, in USA and in the European countries it is about 3% or less. This has increasingly put the price level in India out of alignment with the relative prices elsewhere, thus justifying the devaluation of rupee taking into account the purchasing power of currencies.

The budgetary control is not the only aspect of the price rise in a globalised economy. There is bound to be a continuing pressure on the price level in India to approximate the world prices. The multinationals are introducing new brands of sophisticated products but these are high price products and while they find a ready market of the creamy layer of the Indian consumer, they have the effect of pushing prices for the Indian brands as well. Also the multinationals are paying their employees at internatinal rates thereby increasing the pressure on the consumer market. Without an income policy, such pressure has become inevitable.

India has been singularly fortunate in having seven successive good monsoon. Even though there has been substantial rise in support prices, yet the abundant availability of food-grains has certainly had the effect of keeping the prices under control. However, food-grains reserves of the order of 30 million tonnes should be used to soften the impact of inflation on the common man.

In more recent months there has been fall in the rate of inflation from 10% to 5%. It has been pointed that one reason for this is deliberate effort on the part of the Government, as Elections drew near, not to resort to increase in 'Administered Prices' of petroleum products and their cascading effect on Railway and

Transport Tariffs. Soon after the elections, pent up pressure of delayied rise on the administered prices will assert itself and there would be inevitable dose of increased administered prices and push up in the rate of inflation.

Rate of Savings and Investments

The critical factor in a high rate of growth are saving and investments as a proportion of national income. Over years it had gone down from 25% to 20% though the latest budget shows that it has come back to nearly 25%. However, it is still low as compared with the saving rate in China where it is nearly 40%. No wonder the rate of growth of the national product in China is 13$ as compared with 5 to 6% in India. This only shows that amount of effort that we have to put in to compete with China and other countries in stimulating economic growth. Moreover investment should be efficient. This requires sustained improvement in productivity. Capital, labour and technology should be used more efficiently. This is absolutely basic.

There are many ways by which the resources can be mobilized. One way is to widen the tax base. In a country in which 154 million belong to middle class, the total number of income tax payers is 90 lakhs i.e. less than 1 percent.

Yet another way particularly in the wake of the new policy of privatization would be selling away shares of public enterprises and raising resources through such sales. No major privatization has taken place so far. The economic reforms did not include a wholesale denationalization of public setor enterprise or dismantling of public sector. Only leas than 1% of the assets of public sector undertakings have been sold away so far. Thus, the scale of disinvestments or dis-investment has been very limited. Nor has it been conspicuously successful. The Controller and Auditor General of India found fault with the manner in which the shares of public sector enterprises were sold away at throwaway prices.

The recent budget shows that at against expected recept Rs. 7,5000 Cr., the sale of public sector shares has brought only Rs. 358 Cr. to the public exchequer. Two explanations were given for this. First that the shares market was bearish and it was not the right time sell of public enterprises. Secondly the tax yields proved to be buoyant and put additional Rs. 6900 Cr. In the coffers of the public exchequer.

The other way of raising resources is for public sector enterprises to raise world deposit receipts. The attempt of Videsh Sanchar Nigam proved to be a flop since the buyers in the international market were not forthcoming to buy the shares at the minimum prices expected by government. The efforts of the private enterprises to raise the world deposit receipts have been more successful. They raised $ 3 billion. through issue of GDRs.

Privatization was a strategy of resource mobilization in the private sector and saving public resources for public purpose like education, health, roads and other infrastructure. Overseas private banks like Standard Chartered Bank, City Bank and Grindleys Bank opened their branches. However, insurance continues to be in the private sector and Malhotra Committees recommendations for privatisatino of insurance business are yet to be implemented.

As the rate of investing in the private sector has been stepped up, the resource constraint is being acutely felt. Businessmen and industrialists have been complaining about severe liquidity crunch though the Governor of RBI has denied that such a crunch exists. But the business feels that the money market has not been able to provide resources for an accelerated pace of economic development. One of the reasons given for the liquidity crunch are the measures taken by the RBI to maintain the stability of the rupee by selling dollars in the foreign exchange market. The high rates of interest also make it difficult for industry to borrow. In response to the liquidity crunch, the RBI reduced the cash reserve ratio to enable banks to realize additional resources for trade and industry.

Investment by Multinationals

As compared to India, China, was able to attract enormous amounts of investments. India is now trying to attract investment by multinationals. The multinationals can either make direct investment or pick up portfolio investment in the share market.

Direct investment is preferred since portfolio investments tend to be volatile. With the advent of the new economic policy, India has started attracting foreign investment. The climate has brightened. 225 foreign financial institutions here started operating in India bringing investment of the order of $ 2.5.

There is a great deal of controversy as to what kind of investment multinationals should make. One point of view is that multinationals should be encouraged to go in for high tech investments of infrastructure and not in low tech investments like manufacture of consumer goods such as potato chips, corn flakes, Coca-cola, Pepsi Cola or fast food like MacDonald and Kentucky Fried Chicken. Investment of this sort has evoked resistance and even violence. Government is pointing out that multinationals have come forward to invest in infrastructure sector as well – power generation, highways etc. But on what terms? The Enron controversy showed that unless there is transparency and professional assignment, the terms of contract could be excessively tilted in favour of the multinationals.

Balance of Payment, Foreign Exchange Reserve and External Debt

In order to get over the crisis situation of 1991, a substantial improvement in foreign exchange reserve position was necessary. It had gone down to $ 1 million. Through the timely assistance of the World Bank and the IMF it was possible to build up substantial reserves of the order of $ 20 billion. Following recent RBI intervention to support the rupee, these reserves have come down by $ 4 billion.

An encouraging feature has been that the exports have stared zooming with a growth rate of more than 20% per year. However, the imports have grown even faster resulting in the increase of the trade gap to more than $ 4 billion. The export growth rate has to be maintained in the face of growing competition and protectionist measure by developed countries despite the WTO.

As against this, external debt during the reform period has increased from $ 70 billion to $ 100 billion. Despite the decline of debt, GDP ratio from 40% to 35.3% by March 1994 and debt service ratio from 30.6% to 25.1% and decline in short term debt from 7% to 4%, total size of external debt is very high and will prove burdensome in the years to come.

Limited Success of Reform Measures

The above review would show that the reform measures had so far had only limited success. Fiscal deficits persist. Fiscal discipline needs to be tightened. Gap in balance of payment continues and exports need to be stepped up. Rate of inflation has fallen but prices continue to rise. Foreign reserve position is no longer precarious but external debt is mounting up. No doubt, number of steps have been taken to deregulate the economy. But the process of deregulation has to continue in every field of economic activity. Moreover, deregulation process has to percolate at the state level. Procedures for allotment of land, sanction of power connection, water supply, environment clearance and giving various approvals and clearances have to be simplified. Single window system should be introduced to save private investment from going from pillar to post. Institutional structures should be reviewed and institutional capabilities should be improved. Inspection Raj must go.

Unfinished Agenda of Reforms

Several financial sector reforms are yet to be taken on hand. Insurance has not yet been opened to the private sector.

Comprehensive national labour policy has not yet been evolved. Unification of labour laws should be taken on hand. Much has to be done on the field of human resources development to create productive labour.

Infrastructural bottlenecks are going to be the biggest bottlenecks in attaining our goal of 7% growth rate. Private sector has to come in a big way in the field of power, transport and telecommunications.

Urban land reforms for relaxing land ceiling and rent act have not been taken up.

As the same time the sate has to develop the Social Sector and halt long term decline in investment in agriculture.

The Outcome – Increasing Economic Growth Rate

The measures taken to deregulate the economy, to step up the flow of private and foreign investment and to stimulate exports were aimed at stimulating the rate of economic growth. This has been accomplished to some extent. The economic growth rate stagnant at 3.5% for several years has been stepped up and according to the National Council of Applied Economic Research, the economy is likely to register rate of growth of about 5.8% in the real gross domestic product.

Moreover, there are signs of continued high rate of growth of industrial production despite the current liquidity crunch and high rate of interest. Impulses of growth, according to the Finance Minister, are widely distributed throughout the economy. In his recent pre-budget election speech, the Finance Minister exuded confidence that the Indian economy will soon reach a growth rate of 7%, if the present policy of economic reforms continued – as he thinks indeed it would be – by the new government. The British Chancellor of the Exchequer Mr. Keneth Clerk said during his visit to India in 1995, "There is not a shred of doubt that by the turn of the century India would become a major economic power."

Larger Issues

Larger issues have been raised in the context of the consequences of the pattern of growth – rise of consumerism, unequal distribution of the fruits of liberalization, aggravating contrast between the filthy rich and the appallingly poor and the influence of the multinationals on our economy and society, erosion of national sovereignty and setback to Swadeshi.

Crass Consumerism

The economic reform era has created a bizarre situation where city consumers thronged Auto Epo 1996 recently held in Delhi to make a choice amongst expensive cars of latest degisn but our roads are pot holed and public transport is in a wretched state. Distributive justice and social needs are forgotten in the frenzy of consumerism.

Poverty

It has been pointed out that reforms period has seen increased rather than reduction of poverty. Dr. S.P. Gupta, Director, Indian Council for Research on International Economic Relations has pointed out that while a fairly sharp reduction in poverty levels took place between 1987-88 and 1990-91 it fell from 29.9% to 18.3% across the country – there has been a sharp increase to 20% in 1992. Though this came down to 19% in 1993-94 it is still higher than in 1990-91. With rise in food prices both in market and PDS, there has been increase in rural poverty. Real wages of unskilled agricultural labour declined by 2.5%. Dr. C. Gopalan in his article 'Towards food and nutritional scarcity'. (*Economic and Political Weekly*, December 30, 1995) has pointed out that the recent gains that may have accrued at the macroeconomic level through policies of globalisation and liberlisation have yet to be reflected in better nutritional status of the poor.'

Influence of Multinationals

The multinationals cannot be expected to be supporters of Swadeshi. They are there for profitable investment. They have enormous financial resources, a great amount of staying power and world wide network of marketing and they are bound to pose a challenge to the Indian enterprise. Some Indian entrepreneurs have complained that they do not have a level playing ground. The multinationsls are using their enormous clout to claim and obtain concessions not available to domestic enterprise as happened in the case of the Enron Contract. It is feared that multinationals would obliterate Indian brands and assimilate Indian Companies and Indian enterprise will start playing a subordinate role. What is worse, they would have undue influence on India's policy makers and ultimately obliterate India's cultural identity and way of life. Mr. Leequan Yew, the elder statesman of Singapore has characterized such fears as entirely unwarranted and unfounded. However, it is as well that such fears should make us develop our own strength and use our association with the multinationals to assimilate world class standards of technology and management. Indian companies can be competitive if they restructure themselves and become world class companies.

Swadeshi

Swadeshi had been the philosophy of our fight for freedom. After independence, Nehru made 'Self Reliance' the bedrock of our planning. But nor SAP has made Swadeshi and self reliance the culprits which held back our economic progress. In the SAP outlook Swadshi is an obsolete concept in the age of globalization and in the context of interdependence. On the other hand, there is a strong point of view that the country must be self reliant though not self sufficient in respect of every commodity. In particular it should develop technological self reliance. But world multinationals are reluctant to pass on uptodate technology to the Indian enterprises.

Multinationals – Front Runners of Usa and Developed Countries

It is said that with the multinational on the world stage of business, national boundaries have been obliterated and indeed the concept of nation itself has become out of date in the era of globalisation. But multinationals, as Chomsky has pointed out, are the front runners of the developed nations and represent the philosophy and strategy of the developed nations. USA and other developed nations have introduced the doctrine of 'dual technology'. According to this doctrine, technology even for peaceful purposes would be denied to the developing countries, if there is a possibility of that technology being used for military purposes.

Indeed India has to be careful while dealing with USA and other developed countries and the International Organisations where they play a dominating role. India had to join World Trade Association after accepting the proposals of GATT Negotiations. They provide for the protection of intellectual property rights but at the same time do not envisage free international movement of labour, of which India and under developed countries have abundance.

The USA and WTA also insist on amendment of Patent Laws to provide protection of process as well as products. Patents on Neem are an example of how our own biodiversity would be exploited by such patents.

There are many cases where US has enforced quotas in export from developing countries, while talking all the time of free trade. They are insisting on clauses of labour welfare and environmental standards to create problems for exports from developing countries.

In developing technological self reliance, India can follow the example of Japan which assimilated technology from developed countries and then improved upon it on their own, making their products superior to those of USA and Europe. That is how Japanese cars and computers were able to capture markets in USA and Europe. India has to pay much greater attention to R & D. Investment in R & D should be stepped up substantially.

All these should make us realize that Swadeshi is not an out of date concept even in the era of liberalization and globalisation. What we need is to build of our own technology, organization and management to world class standards to survive and succeed in a competitive world.

Follow Japanes Advice And Model

It this context, Indian reformers will do well to pay heed to the advice of Yoshihito Karibe, a leading intellectual and Chairman of the Research Institute of Self Government, a think tank of Japan's liberal democratic party, 'India has chosen the wrong path in its liberalization efforts by opening its market to all and sundry. Indians have not learnt from their experience with the British East India Company. Let foreign direct investment come but do not welcome merchants or fortune hunters. I would not be surprised to see a repitition of their experience in India if the present trend continues. India should not allow itself to be a dumping ground for Western Consumer products and obsolete technology. Instead it should go in for production tie ups in core areas which would enable it to become self sufficient. India with its rich natural resources continus to remain poor whereas Japan has carved a niche for itself in the comity of nation only through its man made resources.'

What Kind of Society?

India should follow the model of development of Japan, South

Korea, Taiwan, Hong Kong and Singapore where real and solid economic performance has led to rapid export promotion, improvement in the rate of economic growth and improvement in standard of living of their people which has brought them in the category of newly developed nations.

Finally a word about the kind of society, the new policy of liberalization and its concomitants in the form of advertisements and other programme in the electronic media would be ushering in. Noam Chomsky, in his recent visit to India, has warned that multinationals with their huge budget of advertising especially foreign commodities can overwhelm anything that India can have and make Indians addicts to a life style of artificial wants. Even the conservative economist Klaus Schwab has warned that 'globalised economy must not become synonymous with 'free market' economy on the rampage – a breakless train wreaking havoc.'

The era of liberalisation and globalisation can let loose a wave of materialism completely submerging the traditional spiritual values of India. This has happened elsewhere. For example, the economy in Taiwan has climbed so high that it has delinked itself from the society and its cherished values. This is what the Taiwanese intellectuals regret.

This can happen in India as well not only to city societies but also in towns and villages. Every where, the creamy layer has appeared, flourishing on the philosophy of 'each for himself and Values of compassion, humility simplicity, helpfulness and social commitment seem to have all but vanished. If this is true, then India would have materially progressed but lost her spiritual soul.

(T M Joshi Memorial Lecture delivered at Fergusson College Pune in 1996)

2

RESTRUCTURING OF THE INDIAN ECONOMY–PENUMBRA OF AMBIGUITY

The Finance Minister has made statements on his economic reforms – both on the floor of the Parliament and in the recent Congress Session at Tirupati. These have been characterized, not without reason, as examples of double think and double talk. Certainly, the Finance Minister has the responsibility to explain the rationale of his economic reforms to the nation, and to obtain for it as a wide measure of agreement as possible in all sections of the society. But this cannot be accomplished by projecting partisan or one sided versions, nor by creating ideological ambiguities which might well serve to confound rather than clarify.

In the first instance, the Government should not be in a hurry in claiming success for the new economic reforms. To be sure, the Government has gained temporary reprieve and has been able to save the country from external bankruptcy. But at the same time, the Government must make the entire nation realize that the real task only lies ahead because it is yet to be accomplished; The foreign exchange reserves which had reached an all time low of Rs. 2,3000 crores in June, 1991 have no doubt climbed to Rs. 15,000 crores. But this has been accomplished by increasing India's debt from $ 70 billion to $ 80 billion. This would only increase the liability of the nation in the years to come. Nobody can vouch safe for the nation's ability to service or repay the huge debt in the years to come with the present level of economic performance.

The real challenge before the nation is whether the nation's capacity to repay such a heavy burden of external debt could be built up in the years to come. This would be the crucial test of the new economic policies.

In meeting this grave challenge, we must understand why the foreign exchange crisis in June 1991 assumed such serious proportions that resort had to be had to the transfer of gold from the vaults of the Reserve Bank of India to the vaults of Bank of England and Banks in Zurich. Economist I.G. Patel described this even as a matter of shame. This was followed by a savage compression of imports by the Reserve Bank imposing 200% cash margin for foreign exchange required imports. The third step was the devaluation of Indian rupee by more than 20% in two stages.

While emergency measures had to be taken by the government to stall imminent bankruptcy, the bankruptcy itself was building up for quite sometime in the eighties, and was the result of policy changes introduced in the second half of the last decade. In a hurry to take India in the 21st century, the past policy of economic self reliance based on imports substitution was abandoned in favour of export led growth. The new policy encouraged imports in order to promote exports. The import of capital goods, electronics and synthetic goods led to the rapid rise in imports from Rs. 14,000 crores in 1984-85 to Rs. 35,000 crores in 1989-90. While imports increased by 21% exports increased only by 17%. This was inevitably reflected in the soaring trade deficit of Rs. 7,700 crores in 1989-90 and Rs. 10,600 crores in 1990-91. This was against the background of cumulative external debt of $ 70 billion and debt service ratio of 27%.

Faced with such a situation, instead of introducing financial discipline and reducing indebtedness, the Government resorted to short term commercial See the gap between borrowing and repayment of outstanding debt. This led to a massive increase of private credit from $ 330 million in 1970 to $ 21000 m. in 1989 and $ 54000 m. in 1991. For 40 years India was living beyond its means by getting aid on concessional loans and NRI to finance over consumption.

During 1991, while commercial borrowing was of the order of Rs. 3050 crores, servicing of debt was of the order of Rs. 4,600 crores i.e. a negative balance of Rs. 956 crores. This a sure sign that the country was indeed caught in a debt trap.

Despite this history, instead of candidly admitting facts, an attempt to place the entire burden of responsibility of crisis on the government or the opposition, parties may appear to be only a political exercise. Such an approach would not enable the nation to draw a proper lesson from the past experience.

The change in our policy from import substitution to export promotion was based on the facile assumption that increased imports by themselves would lead to adequate increase in exports. We must know that the latter would depend on competitive price of our products and our ability to satisfy a demanding and discriminating consumer market of cash rich economies requiring high uniform quality, and timely deliveries, not to mention our ability to counter the lobbies even in these markets in favour of domestic producers, despite their preaching of benefits of free market economy to the developing countries.

Nor is it correct to assume in a facile manner that devaluation by itself would lead to improvement in the trade balance. Already, the exports price advantage of devaluation has been washed away by increasing domestic prices. All that has resulted from devaluation is that our country is required to pay more in terms of rupees for all its imports of essential commodities like petroleum and edible oil, further fuelling the fires of inflation.

It has also been realized that the external debt crisis moves in a tandem with the internal debt crisis caused by a phenomenal increase in deficit financing and public debt. The latter again is the result of economic profligacy in the latter half of the last decade. Between 1983-84 and 1990-91, the gap between government expenditure and current revenue increased totally by 16.2%. Most governmental expenditure came under non-development heads. In 1990-91, 72% of the Central Government expenditure of Rs. 106,717 crores was spent on non-plan heads. The budget deficit during 1983-84 was of the order of only Rs.

1470 crores. It increased to Rs. 3745 crores in 1984-85 and to whopping deficit of Rs. 10,982 crores in 1989-90 and to Rs. 11,430 crores in 1990-91. The growth in inflexible commitments to interest payment, defence expenditure and subsidies were given as the main reasons for increase in deficit financing. The interst payment rose by 1.7% annually, defence by 14.2% and subsidies by 21.2% reaching by 1990-91 to Rs. 21,850 crores, Rs. 15,750 crores and Rs. 12,121 crores respectively. The increasing interest payments reflected rapid increase in domestic public debt which reached 55% of Gross Domestic Products.

The large fiscal imbalance has led to excessive liquidity in the economy. This has inevitably generated severe inflationary pressure, leading to double digit inflation.

The Finance Minister claims that the fiscal deficit has been reduced from 8.3% to 6.5%. But it is not quite clear how this has been accomplished. No doubt, abolition of exports subsidy as also reduction in fertilizer subsidies has provided substantial savings in public expenditure. But while the Finance Minister has appealed to the public to tighten the belt, there has been no major attempt to do this in Government itself. Over the years, many white elephants and holy cows have flourished in the domain of public expenditure in India. The government has been carrying the burden of expenditure due to organizational obsoloscence. The government must learn from what Mrs. Margaret Thathcher did in U.K. to reduce public expenditure. She undertook an extensive exercise of 'value for money analysis throughout the entire gamut of public expenditure. Recently, there has been a report on the substantial savings in expenditure on defence established in United Kingdom which nevertheless has not reduced the efficiency, but has enhanced it. The Finance Minister has tried to assure the public employees that economy in public expenditure would not result in retrenchment of staff but only redeployment. But redeployment must be such to improve the productivity and performance of government. Our government would do well to follow the 'scrap and build technique' of Japan, where old organizations in Government which do not serve the purpose any longer or have become disfunctional are scrapped and replaced by new organizations for performing new tasks which have become relevant in the new context. Here again a comprehensive approach is needed. Many organizations in the central government have lost their relevance in the context of the new policy like DGTD, Chief Controller of Imports and Exports, many portions of the departments of Industry and Commerce dealing with licensing and the Planning Commission itself.

In England the unpleasant task of pruning public expenditure was performed by Sir Dennis Rainer, Joint Director of Marks and Spencer. Government of India must find her own agent to undertake this unpleasant but necessary task.

Instead of undertaking such a comprehensive exercise for pruning public expenditure on a rational basis, the Finance Minister, in a hurry to bring down deficit from 8.3% of GDP to the predetermined figure of 6.5% of GDP has chopped allocations to 'soft' social sectors like prevention and control of pollution, rural 'sanitation and water supply, waste land development, promotion of non-conventional energy sources, bio-mass development, etc.

Devaluation and reduction in public expenditure were only the initial measures which have been followed by many others which constitute the new economic policy. These other measures include reduction of the scope of public sector to only 8 areas as against only 17 so far, elimination of industrial licensing except for list of 18 items, shift of emphasis of MRTP from controlling the size of investment by large business houses to controlling unfair or monopolistic practices, reforms of the financial system, and removal of the clause by which financial institutions could convert their loans into shareholding, automatic approval for foreign technology agreements in list of high technology areas, automatic approval to import of capital goods where their cost is covered by foreign equity and permission to foreign direct investment up to 51% in a list of high priority industries. These are all the measures for deregulation of industries and the globalisation of the economy.

The Finance Minister asserted on the floor of the Parliament in his reply to the debate on the budget that all the measures which constituted the new economic policy stemmed from the manifesto of the Congress Party rather than the prescriptions of the World Bank and the International Monetary Fund. At the same time, he also stated that India as a founder member of these institutions has a right to approach them during times of stress and when a country avails of financial support of these two institutions they have to accept the conditionalities attached to loans given by these institutions. The acceptance of these conditionalities, Government claimed, does not amount to an abridgment of the sovereignty of the country, as alleged by some of the opposition parties. It was also argued that there was nothing wrong in the acceptance of such conditionalities if they were necessary for the economic and financial turn around.

It is now well known that all the recent economic reforms have been based on the 1987 World Bank Report 'India, an industrializing economy in transition' and the November' 90 Report "India's strategy on trade reforms". The first report cited above suggested economy wide improvement in efficiency in resource allocation by gradually replacing restrictive, discretionary, opaque, complex and 'difficult to understand and difficult to administer' system of regulatory control and protection with an allocative mechanism that relies on the market system of external and internal competition. This report has also recommended replacement of high tariffs and quantitative restrictions on imports with moderate and uniform tariffs. The report conceded that such reforms would no doubt upset macro economic balance and render a significant portion of domestic industry uncompetitive but the reports assured that the phased implementation of trade reforms and approapriate fiscal and exchange rate policies would assure restoration of macro economic balance.

The economic policies of the past had created a situation in which despite high level of investment, growth of the industrial sector was disappointing, India's share in the world market was declining, and parts of the industrial sector were inefficient and technologically backward, thanks to the sheltered market in which they functioned. The creation of a dynamic, efficient and internationally competitive industrial sector, the report suggested, required replacement of the protective regime with one based on moderate uniform tariff of average of 20% and elimination of quantitative restrictive imports on all items. The report also recommended restructuring of enterprises and removal of impediments to such restructuring of enterprises. All firms should be allowed to rationalise and impose restrictions on exit and labour displacement should be removed. The report also recommended devaluation of the order of 22%. The report criticized the 'false concept' of self reliance of the past based on import substitution regardless of cost. Emphasis on heavy industry, protection and control led to a high cost economy.

The close congruence between the prescriptions of the World Bank and the International Monetary Fund and the new package of economic reform is evident and yet to deny the connection between the two and to insist on an entirely domestic origin of the new policies would only put in jeopardy the very credibility of the pronouncements of the government. A candid admission of the influence of the World Bank institutions, obviously under the control of the only surviving super power, would prepare the nation much better to put the effort required to get the country out of the situation which has made it inevitable for the country to accept the conditionalities.

Of the same category is the insistence of the Congress Party in Parliament and at the recent Tirupati Session that the Government has not deviated from the Nehruvian Model, while at the same time abandoning every single component of the model. Nehru, throughout his 17 years as Prime Minister always insisted on non-doctrinaire and pragmatic approach to policies, and it is doubtful if, were he to be alive, would follow the 'Nehruvian Model'. Nehru himself would have asked the country to change the model if such a change served the national purpose and delivered the goods.

While swearing by the Nehru Model, an impression is created that the Nehruvian model has failed to deliver the goods. This again is not true. As explained above, the present crisis is not the result of following the Nehruvian Model. Rather it is result of the abandonment of the model in the late eighties. The Nehruvian model had given the country slow but steady growth based on self-reliance, though in course of its implementation it finally led to the emergence of the 'low growth economy'. But all this was the result of the rigidities of the complex controlled economy. However, the controls were not a necessary part of the Nehruvian model. Controls were only the means and never the objectives.

It is necessary for the country to clearly and dispassionately reflect on what went wrong with the Nehruvian model, and to what extent its various components have or have not served the national purposes. This would be a much better exercise than what is happening today, namely, giving up the essentials of Nehruvian model but swearing by it on the public platforms, all the time.

Nehru wanted development and abolition of poverty through planning in which the state would play a leading role. Nehru did not want the economic fortune of the country to be left to the vicissitudes of the market forces but rather be the result of deliberate and conscious planning for the optimum use of the natural and manpower resources of the country. He felt that such planning resulted in a faster rate of economic growth, its equitable distribution and greater self-reliance. Planning achieves many things which the market cannot. Firstly, planning stands for purposive arrangements of the future. It is based on an attempt to forecast the future trends in relation to predetermined objectives. Secondly these objectives are defined not in terms of the present level and distribution of purchasive power, but in terms of what is needed by the nation as a whole and by the masses of the people.

Thirdly, it stands for collective decision making of the nation. Behind it is the concept of 'India incorporated'. It reflects the common determination of all the components of the nation. All these ideas canot be dismissed as unfriendly to the market and therefore deserving summary rejection. In Japan there have been planning for many years based mainly on forecasting. The role of Ministery of International Trade in Japan in forging 'Japan incorporated' is also well known. Japan's spectacular economic performance has been the result of the combined efforts of the government, business, and workers in Japan. There is no reason why these time tested ideas relating to the growth of a nation should be totally abandoned. In this context it is pertinent to take note of Japan's view that 'the World Bank and IMF should encourage more developing countries to engage in government backed industrial planning, in other words to emulate some of the policies that Japan used in the 1950, 1960s and 1970s to attain its dominating economic presence'. (Indian Express – April 28, 1992)

For many years, the concept of 'indicative planning' has been projected as one which does not replace market, but rather works with it. Such a system of planning has been tried in France with advantage. It also exists in Japan. In his address to Indian Merchants Chamber, Bombay, Dr. Saburo Akita pointed out that 'Planning in Japan was not the exclusive work of Government economists but included participation by a broad spectrum of people including representatives from industry, labour, media and academia'.

Economists like Amartya Sen have emphasized that the institution of market is not appropriate in fields like education and health. Secondly, market does not lead to optimization unless certain preconditions are fulfilled, and these include, among others, perfect knowledge and innumerable buyers and sellers of products and services. Several economists have emphasized that these conditions do not obtain even in developed countries much less so in India. It, therefore, cannot be assumed that free market by itself can lead to efficient allocation of resources. As Dr. Akita pointed out in his lecture cited above 'It is not true that market economies are necessarily superior to centrally controlled economies. Market mechanisms are not infallible'.

Nor is it correct that private sector is necessarily efficient. There are any number of examples of thoroughly inefficient private enterprises and efficient public and co-operative public enterprises.

Moreover, how do we measure efficiency ? Profit is not the only measure of efficiency; nor can any one say that social benefit counts for nothing. The issue has recently been raised by Dr. Kurien of NDDB. If availability of liquid milk to consumers in the country is a desirable objective, then it makes little sense to insist that private milk enterprises should also be allowed entry in the milk sector. As has rightly pointed out, such an entry would lead to diversion of milk to manufacturing of milk products rather than to the consumption of the poor in the cities. Profit is not always synonymous with social benefit.

Attributing economic efficiency to market alone also overlooks the fact that efficiency is a product of human resources development. The connection between markets and efficiency is stated in abstract at the macro level. It is based on the concept that in market economy any organization which is less efficient than the optimum, will incur losses and will be pushed out of the market. Only those firms with efficiency higher than the average would survive. But large firms use the resources for controlling and manipulating the market and hold it to ransom.

Efficiency is the product of ability to work and willingness to work. Ability is the result of education and training and attitude to work is the result of system of incentives and motivation and culture of a people. It is true that the examples of erstwhile Soviet Russia and Eastern European countries show that even after 70 years of so called socialist incentives motivation, they do not really work. Pursuit of self interest is the dominant motive and the incentive system in the economy should encourage such pursuit in the interest of an efficient performance of the economy. Yet to rule out all non pecuniary motivations and replacing them by hedonistic motivations alone, is unlikely to be the right prescription for a developing society.

The public sector, no doubt, has failed to come up to the expectations of Pandit Jawaharlal Nehru. Instead of being at the commanding heights of the economy, they have come to depend on budgetary support. But the condition for efficient performance of the public sector enterprises was operational autonomy. If the condition is not fulfilled, public sector enterprises cannot be expected to perform efficiently. Unfortunately, the politicians and the bureaucrats have not always stood by the autonomy of the public sector enterprises. Loan melas and write off of loans are two clear examples of meddling with the public sector banks with disastrous results. Planning without excessive control regime and public enterprises without erosion of their autonomy would still deliver the goods.

In hurrying with liberalization, it would be hazardous to overlook the role of the state and its agencies. The Government will have to play a crucial role in building up physical and social infrastructure of development. It also has to create a climate in which the private sector could act, remove any barriers that may arise and to indicate general directions. (M.V. Kamath – India and Japaniess Lessons to Learn – *Gomantak Times*, April 24, 1992).

The Nehruvian model envisaged that the State would play a leading role in the process of development. It would be 'a welfare state in action'. It would set up a machinery of development administration which would be an agent of change. If these expectations were not fulfilled, it was because of deterioration in political standards way below what existed soon after independence. The State became, in the words of Gunner Myrdal, a 'soft state', what is worse, precipitous fall in moral standards. Corruption, black economy and criminalisation of politics raised there ugly head in the post Nehru era. Even Nehru had noticed deterioration in moral standards only a few years after he assumed office as Prime Minister and drew pointed attention of the Chief Minister to this phenomenon in his fortnightly letters. He appointed a Committee under K. Santharam to suggest measures to stem the tide of corruption. But when Indira Gandhi publicly declared that corruption is a world wide phenomenon, corruption gained a new legitimacy in India. And now ugly shadow of Bofors looms large on the public life of the country. The State cannot play its role unless there is a tradition of clean public life and those who control the leveas of power are held accountable to those who place them in power in the first instance. Officers of the IAS, the highest Civil services of the country, were considered above corruption in the early days after independence. Today many of them as well as members of even the higher judiciary in the country have become suspect in the eyes of the people. How can the State in such conditions play the role assigned to it in the Nehruvian model?

The combination of a command economy and corrupt machinery of the State can be disastrous. That is why liberalization of the economy has been hailed as a liberation from the tentacles of the State machinery.

Nor is the idea of self reliance to be faulted per se. Indeed it should continue to be the sheet anchor of our policy, if India is to escape the strangle hold of the new economic imperialism. The Finance Minister wants to forget about the East Indian Company. But the new Multi national Companies are not necessarily different from the erstwhile East Indian Company in terms of their attitudes as is shown by the attitude of the Union Carbide Company notoriously connected with the Bhopal Gas tragedy. The attitude is the same to make use of the raw materials and the market of the backward countries and exploit the backward people. The multinational companies would bring capital and technologies, but only if these subserve their interest. If they import capital ands technology for producing soft drinks and potato chips, the country may not benefit at all. Here again the concept of profit may not be in consonance with social benefit.

It is necessary for India to bear in mind the experience of Latin American countries in following the prescriptions of the World Bank and International Monetary Fund. Countries like Brazil and Turkey which followed the World Bank prescription, had to undergo very painful process of adjustment which involved the fall of their standard of living by 10 percent. People of India, already with a low level of living, might not be able to survive such a fall. If India suffers from stagflation in the wake of the new policies or if already a low standard of living of the people is further sacrificed at the alter of the free market, the result may be disastrous. It is necessary, therefore, for the nation to be on the guard and continuously monitor the impact of the new policy.

The nation was gripped in financial crisis despite the fact that there was no real economic crisis. The nation had the good fortune of three successive good monsoons. This was an extraordinarily lucky circumstance. However, such good luck cannot continue for all time. In a country where climatology has six years of seasonal cycle, drought years are bound to follow good monsoon years. Already the shadow of drought has loomed large on the vast areas of the country in states of Maharashtra, Gujarat, Madhya Pradesh and Rajasthan. This will not only worsen the economic scenario, but put severe pressure on public expenditure at a time when government is keen to reduce it as a part of the package of economic reforms. Drought management cannot be left to the market. The British followed the *laisez faire* policy resulting in mass starvation. Here is yet another example of the inadequacy of the market mechanism dealing with serious socio-economic problems.

The real task of the country is to develop its own productive capacity and not getting some loans from the World Bank or the International Monetary Fund. This would require much greater efficiency in production in fields, factories and offices and a wide spread dissemination of work ethics. These must have a place of priority in the new package of economic policy reforms. The nation is capable of making any sacrifices provided it is confident that those who are at the helm of affairs mean what they say and make sacrifices first before they ask the nation to tighten the belt. Unfortunately, this is not happening. The recent event of a vast amount of Rs. 600 crores of bank money being placed at the disposal of a stockbroker shows how carelessly public money is being utilized.

The nation must get out of the ideological ambiguities and must be shown the clear path of self-reliant economic growth.

3

RECESSION – CAUSES AND CURES

Economic diagnosis and prescription are never easy. Neither the World Bank nor the IMF nor any of the leading economist or reputed economic journals could predict the 'Asian Meltdown' or 'Asian flu' which afflicted in 1997 succession economies which hitherto had shown commendable growth and had come to be known as Asian Tigers viz. Thailand, Malaysia, Indonesia and even South Korea, Hong Kong and Japan. The IMF later laid the blame at the door of "Crony Capitalism". We in India started congratulating ourselves that we did not follow the policies of these countries in completely opening our economies to globalization and saved ourselves from flight of currency and capital and consequent drastic fall in the external values of currencies, corporate failures and fall in national incomes.

India has never shown during 50 years since independence the dynamics of the economies of these countries. India had followed the model of 'Import substitution' instead of 'export promotion'. If preferred 'self-reliance' to 'integration' with the economies of the developed countries. It developed a 'controlled' and a 'planned economy' with large public sector rather than free, open and predominantly private sector economy.

As a result of these policies, while India developed a base of a wide ranging industrial economy, it showed a rather slow annual rate of growth of 3.5% which the well known economist, the late Dr. Raj Krishan, described as 'Hindu Rate of Growth'. The phrase stuck and was indiscriminately repeated though it should have rather been called a 'Socialist rate of growth'.

As decades passed, the reasons of the slow rate of growth were traced to the 'license and permit raj' which came in the wake of our 'command and control economy' and which throttled the forces of economic dynamism. Hence a beginning was made in the eighties to relax controls, to reform the public sector and to open the economy. The rate of growth increased from 3.5% to 5%. But in the process, India incurred a huge short term commercial debt and while exports looked up imports increased even faster, leading to a mounting adverse balance of payments. This rapidly eroded the foreign exchange reserves of the country, leading to the crisis of 1991 when India had hardly the reserves needed for a week's imports. India was on the verge of external bankruptcy. The confidence in the Indian economy was lost and NRI's withdrew funds. It was in such a desperate situation that India had to approach the World Bank and the IMF to bail out the Indian economy.

The IMF gave immediate facility to tide over the situation but insisted on India adopting the 'Structural Adjustment Programme' – the same kind of programme introduced in Latin American countries which in the eighties had been caught in a debt trap. The SAP required a series of economic reforms viz. fiscal discipline to eliminate deficits, devaluation of the currency, deregulation of the economy, disinvestment of the public sector, promotion of privatization, replacement of the model of 'Planned Economy' with a 'Market economy' and free entry to foreign capital, both direct and portfolio and the multinationals.

These economic reforms were introduced with vigour in the first three years and the results were encouraging. The fiscal deficit was reduced from 8.6% of GDP to 6.5%, the external value of the rupee was reduced by more than 20%, the rupee was made freely convertible on the current account, though not on the capital account, industry was substantially delicensed, the Monopoly and Restrictive Trade Practices Act was amended to allow large enterprises to function and entry of foreign capital and multinationals was encouraged.

However, as the general elections drew nearer, the Narasimha Rao government changed track. The reforms had not greatly benefited the common man. Despite Narasimha Rao's repeated statements that the economic reforms were irreversible, he turned away from reforms, in the direction of populist measures. However, this did not help the Congress which lost the 11th general elections.

The UF government which came in power in 1996 had two PMs in a short period of two years. It was a coalition government in which the communists also participated. They were opposed to many elements of reforms like dismantling of the public sector and the free entry of multinationals. As a result, while the Finance Minister P. Chidambaram was enthusiastic about economic reforms, he façed internal opposition. As a result of these 'inner contradictions', despite the Common Minimum Programme, not much progress was made with economic reforms. On the other hand, the government went down before the demands of the employee's unions of the Fifth Pay Commission, saddling the public exchequer with the huge additional burden of more than Rs. 18000/- crores. The state governments had to concede to the corresponding demands of their own employees. This saddled the public finance of both the centers and the states with a staggering bill of Rs. 90,000/- crores.

After the fall of UF Government, BJP led coalition came into power. Shri. Yashwant Sinha even before his appointment as FM identified industrial and economic slow down as the main economic problem before the new Government about to be sworn in and talked of measures for 'kick starting' the economy. It adopted the national agenda which involved economic reforms,. Faced with criticism in Parliament and outside, the Finance Minister Yashwant Sinha was compelled to withdraw many of the proposals in his first budget such as increase in urea price and added to the reputation of the Government as 'roll back Government' unsure of itself, Shri Sinha went on publicly stating that from September onwards the economy would start recovering.

When this did not materialize, even several months after September, he started getting ridiculed as 'Come September' Minister. The unprecedeted rise in the prices of onions, potatoes and tomatoes led to public outrage and the popularity of BJP reached the nadir. The ruling party lost the elections in Rajasthan, Delhi, and even Madhya Pradesh. The survival of the Central

Government, itself become doubtful and the shadow of political instability Government gave a further set-back to the economy. The hurriedly introduced first budget of 1998 could not do anything in the direction of improving the economic performance.

But things gradually improved. The bumper rains gave a bountiful Rabi harvest. Foodgrains production reached 200 million tonnes. Rate of growth of agriculture exceeded 5% giving hope for better agricultural output. Demand in the market for the industrial economy continued to remain sluggish. The supplies of agricultural commodities which included onions and tomatoes, substantially improved even leading to conditions of glut compelling the Government to permit export of onions. The much harassed consumer got some relief when rate of inflation climbed down from more than 8% to less than 5%.

But the problem of sluggish industrial economy remained to be tackled. The rate of industrial growth remained low at 2 per cent and exports declined. The Economic Survey 1998-99 preceding the budget painted a very gloomy picture. It candidly admitted that "the economic condition today is not significantly better than in 1991-92'. This despite the fact that the economy as a sequel to the reforms since 1991 is more open today. The average rate of custom duty was halved from 47% in 1990-91 to 29% in 1998-99.

Cheap imports made exports more competitive. The average rate of excise duty was reduced from 28% in 1990-91 to 18% in 1997-98. But this did not boost industrial production significantly. The pursuit of fiscal discipline did not lead to a curb in consumption expenditure of government. It only led to a steady fall in Government investments in sectors like power plants, road construction, transport and other infrastructure. These used to be the engines of economic growth. In their absence, there was sluggish growth in core industries like steel, and cement. The Public Sector Disinvestments Programme did not make much headway between 1991-92 to 1997-98. The Economic Survey called for the second generation of economic reforms.

In addition to the fall in public investment as a cause of

industrial recession, other factors also should be mentioned. First, there was over investment in durable consumer goods industry including cars, Colours TVs, Refrigerators, etc. The over investment was the effect of the excessively optimistic view of the middle class consumer market whose size and purchasing capacity was grossly overestimated. The size of the consumers middle class was estimated to be 250-300 million. Actually it turned out to be much smaller, about 100 million. Also the demand of this class was price sensitive.

When in response to such overestimated figures, over-investment took place, there was bound to be a corrective in the shape of restraint on investment in the sector. Secondly, the foreign direct investment expected in the infrastructure sectors like power generation and highways did not materialize. The foreign investor took a less optimistic view than during the early years of reforms. Various administrative bottlenecks, high real estate prices and rigidities in the labour market were said to be responsible for this change.

Thirdly, domestic industrialists started complaining that they did not have a 'level playing field' and hence could not compete with the multinationals. Fourthly the primary investors shied off from the stock market having burnt their fingers in the initial boom period of economic reforms which turned out to be speculative in character. Fifthly the Asian recession had a depressing effect on the Indian economy. The exports to these countries shrunk and their increased competitiveness following depreciation of their currencies displaced the Indian goods in the export market.

It was against such a gloomy background that Shri. Yashwant Sinha presented his second budget. He had wanted a tough budget but had preempted much of the toughness by pre-budget increase in the prices of commodities supplied through the PDS, cooking gas, diesel and urea. Consequently, the budget proposals turned out to be less tough than feared. As a result the stock market responded with unprecendented enthusiasm. It simply zoomed. Even the industrial circle received the budget with subdued optimism. The incentives to the processing sector, information software industry, housing and rural development all contributed to the optimistic response.

Even an economist of the ruling party Shri. Jai Ram Ramesh could not but appreciate some of the budget proposals viz.

1. Rationalisation of the excise and custom duty structure.
2. Phasing down custom duties to Asian level by 2004.
3. Scheme to make productive use of private gold.
4. The incentive to equity oriented mutual funds.
5. Long term capital gains tax halved to 10%.
6. The write-offs to facilitate corporate mergers.
7. Incentives to promote housing.
8. Increased allocation to agricultural and allied activities.
9. Proposal for 'strategic sales' of public sector shares.
10. Proposal to constitute expenditure reforms commission and intention to downsize government – the only real measure to curb fiscal deficit which had touched Rs. 103,737 or 6.5% of GDP. Shri. Sinha has promised to reduce fiscal deficit to 4.4% of GDP.

In addition several other measures were in the pipeline viz.

1. A new company bill.
2. The insurance regulatory bill – opening door to investment by foreign insurance companies.
3. Bill to replace FERA.
4. Reducing Government equity in the banking sector to bring it below 50%.
5. Amendment of the Industrial Dispute Act.
6. Ceiling on public debt.

Industry which was disappointed at 10% surcharge on

corporate and industrial income tax, saw in the budget no major effort to revive trade and industry but was encouraged by the following RBI announcements on 1 March, 1999 – two days after the budget.

The bank rate was slashed by one percentage point to 8%., the repo rate (the rate at which RBI redeems treasure bill) was down to 6 per cent from 8 per cent and the cash reserve ratio (CRR) was reduced by 0.5 per cent from 11per cent to 10.5 per cent freeing over Rs. 34,00 Cr. to be circulated in the economy.

With the above measure the money supply was expected to increase by Rs. 55,000 cr. With interest rates coming down, deposit rates and lending rates were expected to decline, bringing down production costs of companies and increasing corporate profits encouraging manufacturing and leading ultimately to industrial revival which had witnessed downward spiral during the first nine months of 1998-99.

Both the Economic Report and the Budget spoke of second generation reforms 'removing the last mile barricades' and extending the reform process to a much wider arena. Some of these include:

1. Completing the unfinished task of decontrol and debureaucratisation eliminating remaining price and distribution controls, and reservation for small scale sector.
2. Reforms in agricultural sector – decontrol and delicencing with reference to transport, storage, and processing of agricultural goods, export-import control.
3. Reform in infrastructural sectors like electricity, and road transport – removing investment controls and promoting innovative financing.
4. Improving the legal system – simplifying laws, rules, regulations, rules and procedures.
5. Promoting R & D.
6. Comprehensive examination of labour laws.

7. Improving quality of governance both at the Centre and in the states – in areas like sanitation, health, drinking water. To these must be added the basic task of improving law and order situation which had seriously deteriorated even in metropolitan centers including national capital Delhi and the commercial capital Mumbai.

4

REFORMS CAN'T AFFORD TO IGNORE THE COMMON MAN

The massive rebuff suffered by the Congress Party in the elections would undoubtedly make the Prime Minister and his advisors undertake an agonizing reappraisal of the new economic policy of liberalization which was initiated three years ago.

For some time, the World Bank and the IMF as also several economic experts and advisors have developed the feeling that the policy of liberalization has somewhat slowed down, that there are still miles to go and so the pace of liberalization should be stepped up and economic reforms vigorously followed up to their logical conclusion.

However, the success of the policy would depend upon the understanding and the support of the people. Encomiums of the World Bank and experts from abroad and awards from Europe and Japan to the Finance Minister for his outstanding performance are not enough. The policy must earn the appreciation of the people of India.

The people through their verdict in the 1996 elections, have shown that they cannot be taken for granted and they would defeat the party in power at the Centre with a vengeance unless the consequences of the economic reforms on their well-being are taken into account.

Unfortunately, no attempt has been made to explain the liberalization policy, its dimensions and the implications to the common man. For example, there has been no discussion of the policy at the local levels like Panchayat Samitis or Panchayats. Economists may argue that the economic policy is technical in nature and is beyond the understanding of the common people. However, it must be realized that economic policy is too important a matter to be left to economists alone.

The logic of the new policy of liberalization is based on the sanctity and efficiency of the market – on the belief of the economists that market alone provides for a rational allocation of resources. A free market enterprise whose market costs are less than market prices will enter, survive and succeed, whereas those whose market cost exceed market prices have to suffer exit. Everything should be decided by the calculus of profit and loss, says the logic of the free market.

All decisions as to what to produce? How much to produce? For whom to produce? Where to produce? And when to produce have to be determined by the market signals. This does not take into account the fact that the market reflects the existing distribution of purchasing power, and if it is inequitable, the market will not produce and supply essential goods and services which are required by a large majority of the people, many of whom are below the poverty line.

The beginning of the new economic policy was the imposition of fiscal discipline, which was a good idea. The habitual tendency of budgetary deficits had to be curbed. The Finance Minister had made a commitment that fiscal deficits will come down from 8.6 per cent to 6.5 per cent of GDP. The deficit can be reduced by cutting down public expenditure and mobilizing public revenue. The World Bank way of cutting down public expenditure was by abolishing subsidies and raising the price of public utilities and services.

While in the name of fiscal discipline. People have bene made to pay more for railway, power supply and banking services, there is a steep deterioration in the quality of these services. On the other hand, those in power have not shown the slightest consideration for people suffering from sustained inflation by cutting down their extravagant expenditure.

They have not abandoned conspicious standard of living and enormous expenditure incurred on the maintenance of these public functionaries including the expenditure on their security. There has been no detailed and comprehensive exercise for curbing public expenditure of the sort undertaken by Raja Cheliah for reforming the tax structure.

In the command and control economy which emerged in the wake of planning, deregulation was no doubt long overdue. It was stifled by a jungle of permits and licences. Rajaji had asked long back for the end of the license permit, but Nehru gave short shrift to his call. While in the wake of the new economic policy, the Centre had taken a bold initiative in removing licensing for most of the industries, there are still all sorts of hassles and impediments at the state and municipal level as for example in acquiring land or power supply which are essential prerequisites for setting up of enterprise. The small industry feels that the era of inspector Raj has not yet ended.

Similarly, while the danger of international bankruptcy has been obviated with foreign exchange reserve spectacularly rising from $ 1 billion at the time of economic crisis of 1991 to $ 20 billion now, this has been to a substantial extent, the result of inflow of portfolio funds in the stock market and is accompanied by a rise of foreign debt from $ 70 billion to $ 90 billion which is bound to create problems of payment of interest and repayment of debt in the years to come. The fundamental improvement in the shape of sustained and sustainable increase in exports has yet to materialize. That would depend on improvement in productivity and quality which should be a conscious objective of the economic reforms. This cannot just be left to the spur of competition.

The people have so far hot enjoyed the fruits of deregulation and globalization in the shape of conspicuous increase in the rate of growth of industry. The progress of industry has not been such as to provide gainful employment opportunities to the educated unemployed which has left a sense of frustration among the educated youth of the country.

The Prime Minster and the Finance Minister have given figures which show boost given to the flow of foreign investment in the country. But people are yet to get the fruits of foreign investment. The multinational enterprises have been producing soft drinks like Coca Cola and Pepsi Cola or potato chips. Or if they are in the infrastructure sector like power, the investment is conditional on a government guarantee of an assured return. Domestic industries have complained that they do not have a level playing ground.

Nor have the people any particular reason to be enthusiastic about privatization of public enterprises. Privatization is not proper just to raise budgetary resources and fill up fiscal deficit. However, under the pressure of the need for raising resources, privatization of public enterprise has been carried out in such a manner that even CAG has castigated the Government for sale of shares at throw away prices causing a loss of crores of rupees to the Sate exchequer.

The new economic policy seems to have been concentrating only on the private enterprise. The preoccupation of the government with the liberalization policy has led to the neglect of public investment in social sectors and in agriculture and rural development despite steep increase in anti poverty programmes by way of what the World Bank calls the 'safety net'. Seven successive good monsoons have undoubtedly come as a god sent and helped the government in cushioning the effects of inflation. But one drought can cause havoc, and the nation will have to pay a heavy price for the neglect of agriculture and rural development.

Finally, in the wake of marketisation and economic liberalization, planning has become a thing of the past. Planning has no doubt to change its character. Planing has to be more of indicative planning, planning of the public investment and micro planning in rural areas, but of late in the quest for market, planning of even this nature has taken a back seat.

The time has, therefore come for the Central Government to get over the euphoria of liberalisatoin, understand the implications of the new economic policy in terms of the welfare of the people and introduce necessary corrections. India cannot forget the hardship caused by the World Bank sponsored structural adjustment programmes in Brazil and Mexico. While reforms to make the economy vibrant and efficient should be pursued, they should come along with austerity and productivity of public expenditure, curb or luxury expenditure, elimination of corruption and extravagance in public expenditure and attention to the social sectors.

5

THE RURAL-URBAN DIVIDE:NEED FOR POSITIVE ACTION

Fifty years ago when India attained Independence, it was categorised as an underdeveloped country whose economy was characterized as a 'dual economy' with a big divide between a few metropolitan centers like Bombay (now Mumbai), Madras (now Chennai) and Calcutta (know Kolkata) and five thousand village communities plunged in the darkness of a vast hinterland of backwardness.

As distinguished from the 'dual economies' of underdeveloped countries of Asia and Africa, the developed economies of Europe and the USA had a homogenized economy with hardly any distinction, in terms of level of living or availability of modern facilities, between urban and rural settlements. It was expected that as India transformed itself from an underdeveloped to a developed country, the vast divide between urban and rural India would be bridged.

Towards Rural Development

But when India in 1951, embarked on the planned process of economic development, bridging the divide was not the express goal of planning. It was rather to improve the quality of life in the rural areas and make the life of the rural people richer, fuller and better through a programme of rural development. Many years before Indian Independence, the leader of India's fight for freedom,

Mahatma Gandhi had told his fellow Indians that India lives in villages. 'Go back to the villages' was his clarion call. He himself was directly involved in the constructive programme in a village which he called 'Sevagram'. The great poet Rabindranath Tagore had also his programme of village improvement at Shriniketan. There were other experiments of rural development like the Baroda or the Martandam experiments.

The State sponsored nation-wide programmes of rural development have gone through many phases during the four and a half decades of planning in the country. In the initial phase, the programmes were community development, national extension service, co-operation and land reforms. From the middle of the sixties, there was preoccupation with and concentration on increasing food and agricultural production. This resulted in a visible shift from the generalized programmes of the fifties to more focused programmes of agricultural development like the intensive agricultural development programme and command area development programme. But in the seventies, Indira Gandhi's 'Garibi Hatao' call gave birth to a variety of antipoverty programmes like rural employment programmes, small farmer, marginal farmer and landless farmer development programmes and opening of the brnaches of nationalized banks in rural areas, etc.

Through all these phases, varying attention was paid to evolve the Panchayat Raj institutions. The Constitution did not embody Mahatma Gahhi's concept of Gram Raj. As an after thought, Article 40 was introduced as a Directive Principle of the Constitution stipulating that Panchayats shall be promoted as institutions of self-government. In 1956, following the report of the Balwantrai Mehta Study team, a three-tier set up of Panchayati Raj institutions was setup in different States; following the Asoka Mehta team report (1977), Mandal Panchayats were set up in Andhra Pradesh and PR institutions were given a new lease of life. And the recent 73rd Amendment Act gave a constitutional status to PR institutions.

Bridging The Gap

Through all these programmes, evolved the following strategy of bridging the rural-urban divide:

(1) Create a sense of consciousness amongst the rural people and motivation for better level of living. For centuries, Indian agriculture had been a gamble in rain. This created a sense of fatalism. Periodic droughts and famines impoverished the rural community and led to mass starvation and death. Rural communities came to terms with mass poverty with little hope for getting out of the vicious circle of poverty. A confidence had to be generated amongst the rural people, that through effort, life can change for the better.

(2) Create institutions conducive to development. The traditional structure of landlordism (in some parts of the country) and of tenure and tenancy created disincentive and had to be changed to give land to the tiller, give tenants a security of tenure and limit rent. Also since arable land was limited, land ceiling laws had to be passed. All these land reforms aimed at creating a new institutional structure of land property rights.

During the British rule, rural development administration was extremely weak. The administration merely consisted of revenue and police administration. In the wake of the community development programme, a new system of block development administration headed by a block development officer assisted by eight subject matter extension officers and ten village level workers came into existence. The traditional role of the collector also underwent a change. He became a district development officer.

The village communities needed vigorous institutions of local self-government. The traditional institutions of caste Panchayats was unsuitable to promote all round development. The new setup of PR institutions consisted of village Panchayats, Panchayat Samities at block level and Zilla Parishads. They had to be endowed with adequate devolution of powers and functions to initiate a decentralized process of development.

Co-operatives were found to be suitable institutions for the organization of the economic life of the rural communities through a variety of programmes of agricultural credit, supply of input, marketing, agricultural processing, dairy development, etc. Regional Rural Banks and rural branches of the commercial banks supplemented the efforts of the cooperatives.

(3) Provide basic services and facilities : The rural urban divide manifested itself in the form of a lack of basic services and facilities in rural areas such as accessible primary schools with suitable buildings, basic health facilities, clean potable water, and approach roads had to be made universally available in rural areas.

(4) Transfer of technology and information : No programme in any aspect of rural life was possible without transfer of modern technology. From 1951 onwards, a network of National Extension Services was established throughout the length and breadth of the country to convey technical services and know how to reach the doors of the rural families.

Later, after the establishment of Agricultural universities, the extension service was linked up with the research in the universities. The expansion of radio and TV network has made it possible to communicate information to the rural people regarding new techniques of the agricultural and allied activities and new ways of living. Above all, it raised the expections of the rural people and broadened their mental horizons.

(5) Promotion of economic development and creation of employment opportunities : A variety of programmes for modernization of agriculture and allied activities like dairy and fishery development, irrigation, agro-processing, all helped to improve production and productivity in rural areas. For the landless falling outside the mainstream of production, employment opportunities were created on the works programme for creation of rural assets like tanks and roads.

The following diagram shows the links between various schemes and the strategy to reduce the rural-urban divide :

Schemes V/l Romen

National Extension Service	Co-operation	Panchayati Raj	Land Reforms	Anti-Poverty Programme

Strategy

Transfer of techn--ology	Provision of public services	Institutional Development	Eronomic development and generation of Employment opportunities Motivation

While the programmes were of an all-India character, the success of the strategy was in different parts of the country. While the rural areas in the BIMARU region (Bihar, Madhya Pradesh, Rajasthan and Uttar Pradesh) have generally lagged behind in all respects, States like Kerala, Punjab, Haryana and even West Bengal have forged ahead for different reasons, creating the need for formulation of differentiated strategies and programme of rural development for different parts of the country according to the stage of their development. A recent study, 'Indian Development – Selected Regional Perspectives' edited by Jean Dreze and Amartya Sen (Oxford University Press, 1977), clearly brings this out.

Human Development : A Comparative Study

The following table shows the vast difference between quality of social and human development in rural areas in UP compared with those in South Indian States.

Quality of Human Development (Rural)

Educational Achievement and Participation

	Literacy Rate 1990		Age 7+
		Male	Female
Rural	UP	52	19
South Indian States		63	41
Urban	UP	70	50
South Indian States		83	68
Rural Urban combined UP		56	25
South Indian States		68	49

	Literacy Rate 1987-88	Age	10-14
Rural	UP	68	39
South Indian States		84	72
Urban	UP	76	69
South Indian States		90	85

Proportion of Children		Never Enrolled in a School 1986-87	
Rural	UP	27	68
South Indian States		14	28
Urban	UP	19	39

Thus, if UP countryside has remained backward, it is because of the poor services in rural areas owing to the inertia of the government.

Even those facilities which do exist in rural area are not up to the mark. Schools do exist but teachers are frequently absent. Health care facilities are provided but they are used to promote only female sterilization. Poverty alleviation programmes are launched but have degenerated into instruments of patronage of the rural life.

A typical example – The Sunday *Times of India* Review (August 10, 1997) carries in article on Dharmapur village in UP. A mere one hour journey from Aligarh. Little has changed in this village over the four hundred years of existence – not even during the last fifty years of Independence. It is swatched in isolation. Wolves still carry away sleeping children and dacoits continue to storm the village and loot its meager riches. The Thakurs continue to 'soil' lower caste women at will. 'Latrine' needs to be performed in the fields in ankle deep slush. For villages like Dharmapur in UP, all talk of 'development', 'liberalisation' or even 'governance' is a cruel joke.

Unsatisfactory state of public services in rural areas in UP is closely connected with the character of administration and institutions in rural areas. Public services are poor because of the failure of implementation of development programmes and failure of implementation is the result of lack of accountability in public administration.

While UP has failed to utilize various rural development strategies to improve conditions in villages, West Bengal has shown that agrarian reforms and democratic decentralization through PR institutions can have a favourable impact on the implementation of rural development programmes.

The Kerala Model

Attention also must be drawn to the alternative Kerala model of development launched by the Kerala State Planning Board a year ago. Over 50 lakh people have, under this approach, participated in Gram Sabhas spread over 990 Gram Panchayats. 152 block Panchayats and 14 district Panchayats to translate the aspirations of the people into development plans including schemes for drinking water, health and sanitation, roads, irrigation, dairy farming and employment generation. It has become a grass roots level mass movement. The MPs and MLAs who were initially opposed to the grass roots planning have now accepted it.

Kerala leads the country in better quality of life – highest life expectancy (male 68, Female 74), high literacy (male 94.5, female 87), low infant mortality (17 per 1000 in rural Kerala, 13 in Urban area), low death rate (6.1 per 1000 as against 9.8 for the country) This must be attributed to greater political and social consciousness amongst the people leading to greater accountability in administration and better public service. There are no great disparities between urban and rural areas.

This lack of rural urban divide has however to be attributed to the periculiar pattern of human settlement in Kerala where there is a rural urban continuum. Households are scattered and not clustered in a village bahitation as in the rest of the country. The average size of a village in Kerala is 16,867 persons per village according to 1981 census as against 911 persons per village in the country as a whole. Because of the peculiear pattern of human settlement, the Kerala model of urbanization cannot be reflected in other parts of the country.

However, Kerala's high level of human development is not accompanied by commensurate economic development., Kerala has low or no growth economy. Keıala has to translate the high level of education and health standards into higher production through dissemination of entrepreneurship and work ethics; otherwise Kerala would continue to suffer from a high level of unemployment specially amongst the educated.

Compared with Kerala, Punjab, Haryana and Western UP have done much better in terms of modernization and intensification of agriculture and generation of employment opportunities.

Focus on Spatial Planning

India has been undergoing urbanization which is much faster in the western States of Maharashtra and Gujarat, Mumbai, Pune, Nasik, Aurangabad and Kolhapur and Ahemadabad and Vadodara have emerged as growing centers of industrialisation and urbanization. The growing sprawl of these urban conglomerations has absorbed in continuously widening circumference a large number of villages whose agricultural land has been converted into urban sites. But this growth has been haphazard. Greater attention needs to be given to spatial planning which so far has been neglected. Our approach to planning has been sectoral and not spatial. Urban agglomeration has taken care neither of the villages which are absorbed nor of the cities which absorb them. Both have suffered.

Cities have been continuously under the pressure of immigration of the unskilled rural people in search of livelihood. They leave their villages despite the abominable conditions of living in urban slums and shanties or even on pavements because there are no gainful employment opportunities in rural areas. Agricultural land is limited. The number of farming families has gone beyond one hundred million, two thirds of whom are marginal farmers. The population of landless families has soared. Cottage and Village industries have been on the decline all the time. District industries centers or schemes of Khadi and Vilalge Industries Commission have been unable to sustain them or to revive them. Rural employment schemss are not properly implemented nor are they linked with plans for integrated development of local resources. Thus, they do not provide for economic security and migration to the cities is the only alternative for the landless and the poor in the rural areas. Thus, it is that rural poverty spills over in the cities and takes the form of urban poverty.

Backward regions : There is the larger problem of backward regions. The impulses of economic development have escaped them. Schemes for incentive to setup industries in backward areas have not led to industrial dispersal because of stronger forces in favour of industrial agglomeration. The National Committee for development of backward areas 1991 has recommended special initiative to tap the potential of backward areas. In this respect, agro-industrialization has led to striking results. The co-operative dairies on Amul pattern and co-operative sugar factories in Maharashtra have shown how even in rural areas growth centers can improve the quality of life and bridge the rural urban divide.

As a part of spatial planning we should promote interlinked clusters through market mechanism and technology with strong multiplier effect. The policy of liberalization and marketisation does not mean that the State must abdicate its role in spatial planning, industrial dispersal, and provision of public services in rural areas. Development means elimination or at least reduction in rural-urban divide through positive action, or else we will have an unbalanced economic growth which will be difficult to sustain and will create social tension and strife.

6

NEGLECT OF RURAL AND AGRICULTURAL ECONOMY IN THE ERA OF LIBERALIZATION

Following the advent of the new policy of economic liberalization, the attention of policy makers has been concentrated on the deregulation of the private enterprise and the industrial sector and the dismantling of the public sector, while rural and agricultural economy seems to have suffered from comparative neglect. Vital issues related to that sector seem to be on the back-burner. The neglect of agricultural and rural economy has led to the emergence of several disturbing and disquieting developments. A few examples may be quoted :

The State of Andhra Pradesh is desperately trying to be at the forefront in information technology, but at the same time, reports have come of farmers being forced to sell away one of their kidneys to repay their debt to money lenders, incurred at a huge rate of interest in order to meet the rising cost of agricultural inputs. Obviously, the credit requirements of farmers have not adequately been met by the cooperatives or other banking institutions. In several other states too farmers had committed suicide and in the absence of the bread earner, their families are left without economic security.

It has been reported that, today, the institutional credit meets hardly 4 per cent of the requirements of agricultural credit which is only a percentage more than what was reported by the Rural Credit Survey Committee Report, way back in the year 1951. Obviously, all the efforts for over four decades after independence to build up credit institutions for the agricultural sector seem to have failed, and we are back to square one with the farmers once again in the clutches of traditional money lenders.

Agricultural Marketing in Dire Straits

The Crop Loan Scheme introduced on the basis of recommendations of the Rural Survey Committee reports, 1952 envisaged close links between supply of agricultural credit, supply of agricultural inputs, agricultural marketing and agricultural extension. All these links appear to have been lost. It has been reported that commercial agents and salesmen of bogus marketing companies selling insecticides have misguided the farmers and made them buy insecticides which were either inappropriate or used in wrong doses leading to damage of crops. Farmers, unable to bear the loss, were driven to suicide.

The marketing of agricultural commodities is also in dire straits. Production and prices of onion have been widely fluctuating. The unprecedented rise in the price of onion a year ago, led to the electoral defeat of the National Democratic Alliance in elections to four states. Only a few months later, such was the glut of the same commodity, that huge quantities of onions had to be destroyed. In a bid to meet the desperate situation, the Government of Maharashtra, entered in to buy the commodity, and in the process, incurred huge losses. The Central Government belatedly raised the export quota, but only inadequately. There are inadequately arrangements to provide ventilated godowns needed for stocking onions. There is no organised attempt for marketing by Co-operative Marketing Institutions, nor is there a linkage between the Marketing Cooperatives and Consumer Cooperatives. The stop-go policy of the Government has caused grave discomfort to consumers and producers alike. The same applies to other perishable commodities like tomatoes and potatoes. The farmers around Bangalore threw the freshly harvested tomato crops under the tyres of the trucks running on the highway.

There was also a glut in the production of cotton and sugarcane. Here again the State Government of Maharashtra had to step in to buy cotton at a big cost to the exchequer, when its own financial position was really difficult. For sugarcane, the

Government has asked for the extention of the crushing season, even then the glut is such, that the farmers are likely to incur losses. There seems to be no long-term policy and strategy but, only ad-hoc measures, which provide palliatives, not cure.

During the last ten years, there has been neither a clear cut enunciation of the agricultural policy, nor of cooperative policy or policy related to rural economy. After a decade of neglect, it has now become an urgent necessity to formulate a comprehensive macro-policy, related to agricultural economy. The policy of liberalization and globalization is bound to make a huge impact on rural economy. Bulk of the people of this country, earn their livelihood in the rural sector. It is necessary to take into account the impact of liberalization and globalization on their daily life. The regime of the World Trade Organisation is also creating an environment to which the rural economy may find it difficult to adjust. A deep study of this problem has to be conducted, and proper policies framed. Imports of agricultural commodities from the United States or Europe or other advanced economies with low import tariff may create difficulties for the survival of our agricultural economy.

Attention is drawn below to some specific points which are necessary to be addressed to in formulating the new policy on agricultural, rural and cooperative sector.

Technology, investment, incentives, and organisation are four strategic factors which have to be taken into account in dealing with rural economy?

Investement

Huge investment is required to build up the rural infrastructure, consisting of roads, irrigation and electrification. Whole new irrigation potential has to be developed, there is a huge gap between potential created and actually utilized. The irrigation water is not used in an optimum manner. Excessive usage in the higher reaches leads to water logging and inadequate water available at the lower reaches. Water users associations or cooperative may be a possible solution. There has to be a proper crop planning with encouragement to crops requiring less water input. Proper water rates have to be charged so that the opportunity cost of water is recovered.

Controversies regarding huge irrigation dams have persisted far too long. Also, inter-state water dispute have come in the way of a national perspective in the use of water resources.

Much attention has to be paid to the conservation of water and watershed management. While last year huge quantities of water had flown in the Narmada basin, this year, the same area is suffering from drought. Efforts have to be concentrated on water conservation, and recharging of ground water resources. Excessive and reckless exploitation of ground water resources has to be controlled.

Incentives. Great attention has to be paid to marketing of agricultural commodities. Cooperative marketing have not touched the fringe of the problem. Substantial parts of fruits and vegetables are wasted in the absence of capacity of storage and processing. A huge investment is required to undertake the programmes for storage, marketing, and export of agricultural commodity. Proper fiscal incentives must be provided for such investment.

Organisation. The sub-division and fragmentation of agricultural land have led to a large number of small and marginal farmers with uneconomic holdings. Some kind of cooperative or community farming has to be organized. On the other hand, the concepts of 'contract farming' and 'corporate farming' have also come up. Corporate farming is likely to turn the farmers into wage earners, handing over their land to commercial corporations. Contract farming will compel the farmers to grow commercial crops like mushrooms, or flowers, for export market. This may prove to be a grave national danger as it may threaten the food self-sufficiency of the country, as has happened in respect of several African countries.

7

FARMERS' SUICIDES, THEIR CAUSES AND REMEDIES

One of the most disquieting developments in the era of the neo-liberal policy in India has been widespread occurrence of farmers' suicides in different parts of the country including not only the drought prone areas of Andhra Pradesh, Karnataka and Maharashtra but also a State of heavy rainfall like Kerala, as also a State like Punjab with large areas under irrigation. With the preoccupation of the Government with the rate of economic growth and promotion of the private enterprise in the secondary and tertiary sectors, that is, industrial and service sectors, the agricultural sector and the sector of rural development were neglected. The government did not wake up for many years to attend to this phenomenon. The Finance Minister was disturbed by the fall in the stock exchange and elated when the stock exchange rose. The Reserve Bank, forgetting its responsibility for the agricultural and rural sector, started concentrating on what it considered to be its legitimate concern, namely, monetary policy and sound banking, mainly measured in terms of profit and loss. It is estimated that more than one-and-a-half lakh farmers committed suicide. This is indeed a black mark on the economic performance of the government.

Even though the phenomenon of farmers' suicides started assuming serious proportions, the then Chief Minister of Karnataka, S.M. Krishna, and the then Chief Minister of Andhra Pradesh, Chandrababu Naidu, looked upon themselves as the CEOs of their States and found a sense of achievement in making Bangalore the Silicon Valley of India and Hyderabad, a cyber city. While they thought that this was the touchstone of their achievement, the rural voters suffering from drought rejected them and both lost power. In Maharashtra, the government neglected the phenomenon which was most striking in the Vidarbha area, until the High Court got seized of it and asked the Tata Institute of Social Sciences to study the subject. The Government of Maharashtra then woke up and asked the Indira Gandhi Institute of Development and Research to make a survey and submit its findings. The Planning Commission also sent a team at the instance of the Prime Minister to study the causes of farmers' suicides and propose suitable measures and programmes. The State Government under pressure made some provisions and after the Prime Minister's visit, the Central Government provided a financial package. Both these failed to stem the tide of farmers' suicides, suggesting that the package was not based on a correct understanding of the causes of farmers' suicides. As the general elections were drawing near, the Finance Minister, in his Budget speech, made a dramatic announcement of the write-off of loans of small and marginal farmers and made a provision of Rs. 60,000 crores, later increased to Rs. 71,000 crores, to enable the banks to write off the loans. This still leaves out the farmers' debts to the private moneylenders, which are a substantial part of indebtedness. In the era of neo-liberalisation, since 1991, the nationalised banks started reducing their commitment below the prescribed 18 per cent, while the cooperative banks turned sick and failed to provide adequate credit. This forced the farmers to turn from institutional credit to the moneylenders, despite the usurious interest rates charged by them.

The problem cannot be solved unless the causes of farmers' suicides are properly pinpointed and comprehensive policies and programmes are formulated. This is what the book under review endeavours to do. It concentrates its research on the districts in the Vidarbha area, whose Yavatmal district is the epicentre of the phenomenon of farmer's suicide. The study, based on a wealth of statistics and case studies, shows that farmers commit suicides because they are driven to do so by the desperate conditions in which they find themselves. These farmers belong to different caste groups and not only small and marginal farmers but even those owning larger holdings, which in the context of dry agriculture are not enough to enable the farmers' families to eke out livelihood. The suicide of the breadwinner, whether young or old, leave the families desolate and disrupt family life. The causes of farmers' suicides are both economic and social. The economic causes are:

(i) growing expenditure, specially on bought inputs

(ii) low productivity

(iii) inadequate prices of agriculture produce

(iv) difficulties in marketing and marketing hazards

(v) natural hazards caused by drought

(vi) absence of proper crop planning

(vii) unsatisfactory agriculture credit

(viii) accumulated burden of debt.

Amongst the social causes are :

(i) the drinking habit which atrophies the productivity of the farmer

(ii) extravagant expenditure on marriages

(iii) bad health and illness and inability to meet the necessary expenditure on medicine and health services

The study rightly comes to the conclusion that unless all these causes are simultaneously dealt with the situation cannot improve. It requires large public investment in irrigation and rural infrastructure, rejuvenation of the cooperative credit, marketing and processing system, strengthening of the agricultural extension services and sympathetic administration working closely with the farming community.

(Reference - Farmers Suicide – Facts and Possible Policy Interventions, by Meeta and Rajiv Lochan, Publshied by Yashwantrao Chavan Academy of Development Administration, 2006).

8

VAGUE AND UNCLEAR AGRICULTURAL POLICY

Any policy document, if it is to be meaningful, must not contain vague generalities. It must have precise and concrete formulations. Does the document of the national agricultural policy fulfill these criteria? Unfortunately, a reading of the sixteen page document shows that it does not.

Without any such assessment, the policy fixes a growth rate – in excess of 4 per cent per annum in the agricultural sector. It is not clear on what basis such a growth rate is fixed nor is the growth rate disaggregated with reference to various sub-sectors like food crops, commercial crops, horticultural crops or auxiliary sectors like dairy and fishery. The contribution of various inputs like seeds, fertilizers and irrigation for the attainment of the predetermined growth rate have also not been worked out. Nor does the document take into account the risk factors which are inherent in Indian agriculture exposed as it is to the vagaries of the monsoon.

With all these shortcomings it is difficult to give any credence to 'growth rate in excess of 4 per cent per annum'. Nor does the policy document take any note of several disquieting features which have emerged on the agricultural scene in recent years. In a number of states, farmers have committed scucide because they have not been able to repay their debt to money lenders. Does it mean that the system of institutional credit built since Independence to liberate the farmers from the clutches of moneylenders has failed? In some other cases, the farmers were ruined by salesmen who lured them into purchasing wrong kinds of insecticides. Does it mean that the nationwide system of agriculture extension with the back up support of Krishi Vikas Kendra and agricultural universities has become non-functional? The policy seems to have adopted an ostrich like approach to these disturbing developments.

Over the last several years there has been a continous increase in the number of small and marginal farmers. The agriculture holdings have become progressively smaller and uneconomical. Some kind of community and cooperative approach not only in the supply of inputs and marketing of produce but also in the process of procuction through joint investment has become necessary. Instead of developing such an approach, the policy talks of land leasing and contract farming. This is the surest way of turning farmers into wage earners which could have disastrous economic and social consequences. This may also trigger off commercialization of agriculture of such a nature that it could be detrimental to the nation's food security.

Recent years have seen tremendous fluctuations in the prices of agricultural commodities, specially of a perishable nature like onions, tomatoes, oranges, bananas and sugarcane. Sometimes farmers have been forced to resort to distress sales or even destroy the crop. On some other occasions it is the consumer who has suffered because of acute shortages and zooming prices. One would have expected the policy document to come out with concrete measures for stabilization of agricultural prices which could give a measure of economic security to farmers and consumers alike. Even in respect of non-perishable food grins like wheat and rice, the country is saddled with embarrassing stocks of food grains rotting in the godowns of the FCI at grains cost to the exchequer. There has been complete confusion about the procurement prices in relation to prices of these commodities in the public distribution system, in the market and the import and export of these commodities. There has been cases where wheat and sugar have been imported despite the huge idle stock in the country.

The new phenomenon of globalisation and the regime of World Trade Organisation are bound to have a momentous impact on the fortunes of the Indian farmers. The import of agricultural commodities may totally destabilize Indian agriculture. The operations of multinational organisation and the patenting system may creat difficulties for the farmers. It is for the ministry of agriculture to closely analyse the consequence of globalisation on Indian agriculture and enable the farmers to face the new challenges. The policy document does not analyse the subject in depth and suggest measures so as to give a measure of confidence to the farming community.

The document fails to provide clear-cut policies to deal with the pressing problems. It seems to leave many things vague and unclear probably hoping that things would be worked out as and when we get along. If such is the cavalier approach what is the need of a policy document?

9

DUTCH LESSON FOR INDIAN FARMERS' COOPERATIVES DO NOT LOSE THEIR SOCIAL RELEVANCE WHEN THEY TURN BUSINESS LIKE

The rural cooperative movement in the Netherlands, as in other European countries was inspired by the Reiffeisen banks in Germany, which were established in 1844 to provide credit for small farmers, liberated from the yokes of the Prussian landlords, the 'Junkers' in the aftermath of the French revolution. In the second half of the 20th Century Dutch agriculture was in transition from subsistence farming to integration with market and money economy. In the 1880s it was in a state of crisis.

Market oriented agriculture had to be a specialized business dependent on chemical fertilizers, machines and new technologies, all of which required financial resources. But the commercial banks in towns and cities were not eager to help the farmers. The German example prompted the farmers union in the Netherlands to establish similar cooperative banks. Two umbrella central banks were established by the local cooperative banks in 1898, one in Utrecht for the center and north of the country and another in Eindhoven for the southern provinces.

The representatives of the two central banks travelled all over the country and by 1925 had established a nation wide network of 1,250 local cooperative banks. The two central banks were merged in 1972 to become Robotbank, 'Ra' and 'Bo' having been taken from the first two letters of the names of the original banks. In the 25 years that followed the merger, Rabobank continued to develop and extend its banking operations to cover the Dutch wholesale sector as well.

It established its presence in important trading centers for food and agro-business. A further expansion took place when the cooperative insurance company joined the Rabobank organization. The centenary year of 1998 saw the abolition of compulsory membership for business borrowers as well as the abolition of member loyalty. Rabobank still claims, though, that its cooperative principles were not diluted in the 100 years in which it grew in strength. It still has a strong customer base and a commited membership. This world class institution has simply adapted itself to the new economic and rural scenario.

Rabobank International places the bank's rich experience at the disposal of cooperative banks in developing countries. It offers strategy for promoting economic development in particular. Some of the papers talk of the manner in which cooperative principles and ideas slowly adapted to the changing economic environment and the preconditions that had to be fulfilled. The papers also dwell on the development of the cooperative movement in general and cooperative banking, in particular, in underdeveloped countries.

Cooperatives occupy a pride of place in agriculture and handle 50 per cent of the entire turnover of agro business in Europe. Cooperatives handle 95 per cent of the business in Denmark and Ireland. 90 per cent of the business in Austria and 84 per cent of it in the Netherlands. In other countries like France, Germany, Portugal and Belgium, the share of cooperatives in agribusiness is about 70 per cent.

Cooperatives also account for 87 per cent of the credit in Germany, Austria and Portugal. The share of cooperative in dairy business is 90 per cent in New Zealand and 60 per cent in Austria.

Coopperatives also play an important role in purchasing agricultural inputs, as in the United States, where they supply 25 per cent of the inputs to farmers and are responsible for 28 per cent of the processing and marketing. Cooperatives have, thus, made a substantial and sustainable contribution to the prosperity of developed countries over the last century and a half.

The cooperative movement owes its origin to the Rochdale consumer cooperatives born in North England in 1824 and to the Raiffeisen credit cooperatives in Germany started in 1944. They had their own sets of practices which were slowly elevated to the status of universal cooperative principles like democratic management, limited interest on capital and distribution of dividend in proportion to transactions. Cooperatives also believed in education and the vision of cooperative commonwealth based on the ideas of self-help and mutual help and cooperation among cooperatives.

As times changed, the cooperatives changed their objectives and management structures. With these changes cooperatives have begun to resemble capitalist firms. Some of the inevitable problems that have arisen as a consequence pertain to participation of members, their control over management and benefit to the primary producers ascompared to mere commercial profit, and preserving the original thinking which inspired cooperatives ideas. In the end though, cooperatives remain user oriented firms, which bring better returns to both producer members and consumers.

Developing countries like India can certainly draw inspiration from the cooperative experience in developed countries. The successful functioning of cooperatives require some definite preconditions. Firstly, cooperatives have to be looked upon as private business orgnisations and not as substitutes for states. In India the policy is just the opposite. Cooperatives are looked upon as agents or instruments of the state. They are required to undertake functions and activities without any regard for business considerations and called upon to work as agencies of the public distribution system, irrespective of the business prudence of such activities. An example is the use of NAFED meant for marketing farmers' produce at the best possible price for importing consumer goods.

This misplacement of functions hampers the working of cooperatives as business organizations. In some countries state cooperatives have been organized with the express purpose of monopolizing exports in order to generate state income. Such cooperatives have failed conspicuously.

Secondly, agricultural cooperatives can not function in a feudal environment, where farmers are controlled by absentee landlords. Land reforms have to confer elementary rights on the tillers of the soil before they qualify as members of cooperatives. Thirdly, cooperatives have to be protected from political interference. If cooperatives become a part of politics they become subject to illegal obstructions by politicians in power. Fourthly, cooperatives must have autonomy and freedom to work in an optimum manner in market conditions. Legislation on cooperatives should only provide a broad framework, leaving ample scope for members to regulate their own activities in a business like manner.

The tutelary legislations found in many developing countries is detrimental to the development of cooperatives. They have to be amended or removed Only with such preconditions could the success of cooperatives in Europe be transferred to cooperative institutions in developing societies. Cooperatives are business organisations and have to follow the laws of the market. Sound business behaviour is the sine quo non for their successful functioning. They should, moreover, be supported by enabling institutions in a global environment, with a wide range of functions from research to quality control and sales promotion.

Business like functioning of cooperatives does not rob them of their social relevance. Successful economic functioning of cooperatives do not have any indirect or long term impact on social objectives like equity and freedom either. The Rabobank publication is very timely and contains rich material, which can be of great educational value to managers of cooperatives and policy makers in India.

10
THE POOR NEED LEGALIZED ASSETS

Recently McKinzey and Company presented the Prime Minister a report, recommending steps for cleaning up land ownership titles which would free thousands of crores of dead capital and raise the rate of economic growth from 5.5 per cent 10 per cent.

The father of the concept of dead capital is the author of "The *Mysteres* of Capital – Why capitalism Triumphs in the West' and Fails everywhere else". Mr. Hermando D Sato is considered the principal architect of Peruvian economic reforms, focused on measures to activate dead capital. The book explores the whole subject of economic development in the United Kingdom and the United States in a historical perspective and underlines the need of underdeveloped countries to draw lessons from that experience.

The book has received critical acclaim from notable personalities like former British Prime Minister Margaret Thatcher, former British Foreign Secretary David Owen, Former Secretary general of the United Nations Javier Perez Cucellar, author of *The End of History* and *the Last Man Francis Fukuyama* and Nobel Prize winning economist Ronald Guase have.

They all considered the book a notable contribution to the thinking on economic development, with promising approaches to overcoming poverty in third World countries. Mrs. Thatcher felt that the book should be compulsory reading to all those who are in charge of the wealth of nations.

The author starts with the conviction that capitalism is the only rational way to organize a modern economy. Developing countries as well as former Communist countries are to introduce economic reforms to promote capitalism. The development of capitalism need not be based only on foreign investment. Capital can be generated from within developing countries if only they were to provide a rule that registers and protects private property.

At present, such a framework of the rule of law is absent and capitalism is unnecessarily blamed for being found wanting in promoting economic development. The Communist and Third World countries are coming in the way with entrepreneurs, in the absence of a proper legal framework which prevents them from having the opportunity to make profit even out of their meager assets, which remain dead.

The key to generating wealth in underdeveloped countries is to bring alive dead assets, abundant in what is called the unorganized sector of the economy. Every parcel of land, every building, every piece of investment and inventory in the unorganised sector, should be properly documented under law.

It is often forgotten that capitalism in the western countries and the United States could flourish only when documentation of assets was accomplished through proper property law. That was the beginning of the creation of capital. In the chapter titled "The Missing Lessons of US History", the author gives an account of how, over a long period, the law was modified to recognize ownership rights of the settlers, who had earlier been looked upon as squatters, occupying land extra legally.

The law only recognized what was already a fail accompli. The English Common Law was of no use. A new Homestead Act had to be passed in 1862. Often, people asserted their own rights and the law followed. The rationalization of the legal system, which was s major stumbling block for the settlers, was a long and arduous process.

Even the Congress took a long time to recognize the need for appropriate legislation. The recognition and integration of extra legal property rights was a key factor behind the United States becoming the most important market economy and producer of capital in the world. There was a kinerred connection between the legalisatoin of property rights and the creation of capital. The former released the aspirations and energies of the common people of the United States.

In contrast to the situation in the United States, developing and former Communist countries suffer from a bad legal and administrative system. Real estate is not legally held in these countries because they have not been properly surveyed, mapped and recorded and because the underground sector here takes cover under extra legal methods to avoid paying taxes. But ultimately, the people in the extra legal sector have to make higher extra legal payments to survive.

Urban planners and agronomists in the country must assign priority to mapping, surveying and computerizing property rights. Only when formal property rights are bestowed on people do they prosper in a capitalist society. Without an integrated formal property system, a modern market economy cannot flourish.

The author gives a number of examples of attempts made to legalise the assets of the poor in developing countries. In spite of such efforts, formal law is losing its legitimacy, as people continue to create property outside it and engage in extra legal social contracts on property in hundreds of scattered villages and city neighbourhoods.

The transition from extra legal relations to unified property law in advanced nations was accomplished through sustained efforts over many years. Similar efforts have to be made in developing countries.

In this respect, they are at a stage where the advanced nations were a couple of hundred years ago. The author makes the plea that heads of state in developing countries should recognize the importance of formal property rights and initiate steps in that direction.

To do this, they would have to overcome legal and administrative hurdles. Only after the assets of the poor are legalized can they have access to credit, which is crucial for the development of capital. Only when the poor know that their land and business are legally theirs will they gain confidence and be free from harassment by the police and other lower level administrative functionaries.

To bring about this transition, politicians, administrators and lawyers wil have to be reform minded. They would have to courageously end existing legal procedures which create insurmountable barriers to the economic progress of the poor. Before developing countries globalise their economies, they will have to globalise capital within their own countries. This should be a priority item in the agenda of macroeconomic reforms in developing countries.

In India, rural properties were surveyed and settled by the British administrators. A comprehensive land records system exists in Ryotwari areas. Such a system did not exist in the Zamindar areas, but efforts were made to create it through land reforms. Moreover, land rights once recorded have to be constantly updated through timely mutations. This task was entrusted to the traditional village accountants, known as Kulkarnis or Karnams during the British Raj.

After Independence, these hereditary offices were abolished and salaried staff appointed in their place. But they seldom stay in the villages and the mutation work is in arrears. Moreover the villagers must get ready access to land rights registered and obtain copies of relevant documents when needed. But often the villagers have to approach the accountant several times and even pay bribes to get copies. In recent years, land records have been computerized in several states. Hopefully, this modernization will help in updating land records and their accessibility.

In urban areas, vacant lands have been encroached upon by squatters, who are mostly immigrants from rural areas. In recent years illegal entrants from Bangladesh have joined their ranks. Slums and shanties come up overnight with the connivance of local authorities. '*Dadas*' or neighbourhood thugs extort money from poor squatters, which they share with the police and other lower level functionaries. This has become a big problem in all urban areas.

The property rights of the poor in urban slums and shanties need to be formaly recorded and registered. This is a big challenge before urban administrators in developing countries.

11

BOOST NATURE'S LIFE-SUPPORT SYSTEM

Haphazard urbanization has been a concomitant of economic development in this country as the consequence of the 'push and pull factors'. The 'pull effect' is created by the opportunities and facilities in urban centres while the push effect is caused by the shrinking economic and job opportunities in rural areas.

The latter phenomenon is explained by the fact that the per capita availability of resources for productive activities is diminishing. Arable land has remained constant while the number of farming households has gone up. The progressive sub-division and fragmentation, generation after generation, has created uneconomic holdings and triggered migration to cities.

The relentless migration has led to abominable conditions of living in towns and cities where infrastructural facilities have not been expanded and improved to accommodate the immigrating population. The immigrant rural population ekes out a livelihood in the so-called unorganized sector with low productivity and income. The cities are unable to bear the burden of rising population while the rural areas are deprived of productive human resources.

We require a more balanced pattern of spatial and sustainable development, possible if only we make a determined effort to enrich the production potential of rural areas. The potential for adequate income and employment opportunities exists but it has to be trapped through a sustained programme of soil and water conservation.

Year after year, soil is denuded through wind and rain erosion. Contour bundling can not only save the soil but actually help rebuild it. Soil conservation can bring so-called waste lands back to cultivation.

Conservation of water resources should go hand in hand with soil conservation. The whimsical monsoons are a fact of Indian agricultural life. But if whatever rainfall is available is harvested through watershed management and check dams, moisture stress for standing crops can be avoided. The stored water can even be used for irrigated crops.

Soil and water conservation can also lead to diversification of agriculture and the rural economy as a whole. Grazing lands can be upgraded and support livestock development. Horticulture can complement and re-enforce cultivation of dry land crops like millers. A thriving agricultural, horticultural and livestock economy can trigger non-farm employment. What is required are not so much of monetary resources as leadership and organisation, which can mobilise community development efforts.

In several villages in Maharashtra and Gujarat and Rajasthan, soil and water conservation projects have been successfully completed with the beneficent secondary and tertiary effects. Despair and pessimism have given way to hope and optimism. What is now required is large scale replication. This can take place not through stereotypes schemes but spontaneous and innovative efforts of self help groups. This is the path to sustainable development. India should follow the model of dispersal and decentralized development with the help of nature.

12

TACKLING INFLATIONARY SPIRAL

While prices of essential commodities like *dal*, potatoes, vegetables and sugar were, showing a sustained rise, over the last several months, putting them beyond the reach of the common people and making daily life difficult for them, the economist Prime Minister Manmohan Singh and his economist adviser Dr. Montek Singh Ahluwalia, Deputy Chairman, Planning Commission and the Finance Minister Pranab Mukherji, obsessed as they were with 'growth', were boasting that the rate of growth, was maintained in the year 2009 at 7% and will soon rise from 9 to 10% in the year 2010, even when the USA and other developed countries were still in the throes of recession. Some 'knowledgeable' people in government discovered the strange phenomenon, that while there was food price inflation, there was no general inflation. The folly of this discovery was soon realized when the rise in food prices started reflecting in the general index of prices. None in government were prepared to recognize that there was a serious problem on hand and had to be dealt with seriously. That only showed the priorities of government and their lack of concern for 'Amadani' the common man in whose name they got elected' for the second term. The Minister in charge of an omnibus Ministry covering several departments. like agriculture, food, civil supplies and consumer distribution who would be directly held responsible for the inflation of food prices washed his hands off saying that it was not his responsibility alone but the responsibility of the government as a whole ! When repeatedly asked when the food prices were expected to come down, he blandly stated that he was not an 'astrologer' to make prediction on food prices. The Finance Minister refused to tighten the monetory policy of credit liberalization and the fiscal policy of surge in public expenditure through deficit financing. On the other hand, through his Secretary he asked the Reserve Bank not to raise the Bank interest rate as it would hurt business ! Food inflation, his experts argued, was not demand driven but caused by supply restraint. The responsibility for supply restraint was cast on to 'drought' for which the government was not responsible. So none was in charge and the common people had to suffer meekly while the affluent classes like business people, builders, the actors and actresses of the Bollywood, wallowed in luxury of the five star life style with whom top politicians and administrators too appeared to have joined hands.

It was only when Mamta Banerjee, smarting under the steadfast refusal of the Prime Minister and other Congress leaders to respond to her demand for the dismissal of the left front Government in West Bengal, kicked up a row in Cabinet complaining against the intolerable rise in the prices of essential commodities with *dal* reaching Rs. 100/- or more per kg. and sugar Rs. 50, that the Prime Minister and his senior colleagues woke up and announced an eleven point programme to combat food inflation. These points are as follows :-

(I) Increase in Supply

1. Release of 2 to 3 million tons of wheat and rice from the stocks in government godown.
2. Import of sugar
3. Import of *dal*
4. Ten rupee subsidy on imported *dal* by State Government.

(II) Public Distribution

5. Distribution of 5 lakh tonnes of wheat and 2 lakh tonnes of rice through the agency of NAFED.

(III) Fiscal Measures

6. No VAT or other tax on sugar.
7. Liberalisation of rules regarding processing of raw sugar

by mill owners in U.P. by allowing processing outside U.P.

8. Continuation of subsidy for edible oil till Oct 31.

(IV) Regulatory Measures

9. Strict action against holding of food stocks.

10. Strict action against smuggling of sugar and sugar cane.

(V) 11. Meeting of State Chief Ministers to be convened by Prime Minister on Jan 27

There is nothing extraordinary about these measures and could have been taken long back to assuage, to some extent, the acute suffering of the common people. The fact was that after regaining power, those in Government had become insenstitive to the suffering of the common people. They stuck on to their neo-liberal policy of free market economy, minimal government and reduced state intervention and liberal concessions to big business and multinationals on whom the government depended for boosting investment and the rate of growth. Whether such growth would create adequate employment or bring about equitable distribution of income and wealth was none of their concern !

The government shirked their responsibility by attributing the so called supply constraint of essential commodities to natural factors like drought and untimely rain. They are a part of our climatology. The government has to evolve and implement a series of policy measures and programmes over years to counter drought, like increase in water availability through increasing irrigation potential, catchment area planning, water management particulary in drought prone areas and developing drought resistant crops. But government has simply neglected to provide needed investment resources. On the top of it, the whole cooperative system with an integrated programme of supply of credit, supply of inputs, storage and marketing has been allowed to go to dogs with government relying more and more on private seeds and fertilizers through supply agencies who are solely governed by short term profit considerations, passing on expensive but faulty seeds and insecticides. Marketing of agricultural commodities is allowed to be captured by private agencies of big business who have indulged in building stocks and profiteering in complete disregard for the interest of producers and consumers alike. Indeed all, this is part of the lopsided government policy adopted since 1991 to give priority to secondary and tertiary sectors giving short shrift to the primary sector which produces essential commodities. No matter it is this which generated demand but led to the so called supply constraint. Indeed the bias against agriculture has gone to such an extent that the Agricultural Minister Sharad Pawar himself has started echoing the view of the businessmen that agriculture including small and marginal farmers who constitute 80 per cent of the farming community is unviable and agriculture should be 'privatized', that is taken over by big businessman through 'corporate farming' and 'contract farming'. The Agricultural Minister has been openly asking members of farming community to leave agriculture and join other sectors. Also priority should be given not to the production of essential food supply but for using food grains to produce ' wine' which is 'profitable' and for which to make it profitable hefty subsidy should be given which will be cornered by the sons of influential politicians.

With the tilt in favour of market economy, government has, over the years allowed the various public systems including the public distribution system to go into disrepair and making it non functional. It has become incapable of reaching essential commodities at fair prices to the common people.

The general administrative machinery itself has started contracting out its functions to NGO's and private agencies, abdicating its responsibility to be a 'friend, philosopher and guide, to the common people as is expected in a 'Welfare State'. But the concept of a welfare state has become outmoded in a neo-liberal state and the public is left to face the vicissitudes of the market forces. Prices are bound to rise when there is supply constraint. This is the logic of a free market economy and the government cannot be held responsible for the suffering of the common people. Market is capable of making the necessary corrections in an efficient manner and not Government. Government must abdicate its responsibility in economic matters. This is the new philosophy of neo-liberalization. The frequent announcements by the Agricultural Minister regarding shortages of essential commodities only added fuel to the fire of inflation of food prices.

The Minister and his colleagues often claim that it is not necessary to be self-sufficient in respect of food grains, pulses, oil seeds and other essential commodities since they can always be imported. We have seen what this dependence on imports means dal is mainly grown in the Indian subcontinent and not consumed or grown elsewhere. Dal imported from Korea and supplied through ration shops was found uneatable and consumers stopped lifting it. The import from Mynmar was held up because of procedural problems. Despite adequacy of wheat stocks, rotten food was imported from Australia and had to be thrown away. Despite expected scarcity of sugar in coming years sugar was exported, that too at low prices and when actual shortage developed within the country it was imported at high prices! All these transactions of a suspicious nature showed utter lack of planning for ensuring supply of essential commodities at fair prices to the common people which is the primary responsibility of the Union Department of Consumer affairs. However the Minister Shri. Pawar has passed on the buck to the state governments as through the Centre and the States are not expected to work together in a cooperative federal system.

Then there is the continuing impact of 'globalization' on the price level. Globalisation leads to globalisation of income in sectors like IT and big business. For those who enjoy income at global levels, globalization of prices of food items is no big deal. It is those who are left out of the globalised part of the economy who have to suffer hardships because of globalization of prices (The so called 'safety net' provides no safety at all. So much for the 'inclusive growth' about which Prime Minister frequently talks.

13

ETHICS IN PUBLIC LIFE IN THE CONTEXT OF LIBERALISATION

Liberalization and globalization adopted as the hallmark of our recent economic reforms provide a new context to the subject of values and morality in our public life. Liberalisation means lesser role for the state in the management of economic affairs. The role of the public sector would progressively shrink in the total size of the national economic activity. The concept of the public sector gaining the commanding heights of the economy has been given up. On the other hand, it has come to mean 'less government in business and more business in government'. We seem to have accepted the American philosophy of government viz. 'the business of government is business'. Apart from the abandonment of the role of the state in the direct management of economic activity, the new policy also means less State regulation of private economic activity. The elaborate structure of laws, rules and regulations, the structure of command and control by the state, which came to be known as the 'license permit raj' is being dismantled. Market forces of demand and supply would now have a free sway. Market signals based on the calculus of profit and loss would now have a decisive impact on decision making not only in private enterprise but also in public administration and government. Even traditional public sector activities like education, health, power generation and distribution, construction of roads, highways and bridges, transport and railway services would enter into the realm of private enterprise. And in all these areas, consideration of profit would enter in construction, operation and management. Profit would no longer be a dirty word. Profits are good ethics.

Globalisation would mean that India would be a part of the

global economy. All the tariff and custom barriers would be progressively dismantled so that the country would move from a closed to an open economy. Investment from multinationals would be encouraged. Indeed India will aggressively seek billions of dollars of foreign investment as is taking place in the South East Asian countries and China. The new world economic order ushered in by the World Trade Organisation established at the beginning of the year 1995 is stipulated on the assumption of 'free economy' within a country and without. If this favours the multinationals in the developed countries, so be it. It is not necessary to dismiss it as the new economic imperialism. If India wants to have a dynamic and vibrant economy, if it wants capital and modern technology, it should go out of the way to invite and entice the multinationals. This may even need State guarantee to the returns of the multinationals as in the Enron Power Project case though how this is consistent with the concept of a free economy is not clear! In world design and strategy of the USA, as Noam Chomsky has pointed out in his book '*Deterring Democracy*', the multinationals would gain for USA a global acceptance of its economic values of free enterprise.

Liberalisation and globalisation are expected to lead to better ethical values in public life. Has not the Welfare State in India degenerated into a venal and rapacious state? 'License Permit Raj' has only bred corruption in the name of planning. It has put power in the hands of public authority and we have seen the operation of the law – 'power corrupts and absolute power corrupts absolutely'. It has been alleged that in adopting economic policies, in giving tax exemptions, in allowing imports and exports of commodities, in imposing and removal of controls, in awarding contracts, the policy makers have been governed by consideration of amassing unaccountable gains to themselves.

In running public enterprises people in power have, it is alleged, done back-seat driving again with the same venal considerations – whether in matters of recruitment of staff not needed or in awarding contracts or accepting tenders or appointment of persons to key positions. No wonder, the grabbing and acquisitive mentality has filtered down to the people holding positions at the lowest rungs of public ladder. The 'inspector raj' has proliferated at the field level and even minor functionaries must have their own pound of flesh from even small and tiny enterprises.

Private enterprise required to function in such a state governed economic environment has been used to habitual indulgence in the manipulation of the machinery of the state rather than in real managerial and technological achievement. When concessions by the State machinery can give windfall gains, why bother about productivity and professional management standards? Thus, came into being the tribe of P.R. men, lobbyists and liaison officers sneaking into corridors of public offices to corner concessions and favours. The work of liaison officer became more valuable than that of hard working managers. This gave an altogether wrong signal to economic and social life. Values of honesty and hard work were at a discount; the values of easy gains through manipulation at a premium.

If the above analysis is correct, liberalization may be expected to bring in a wind of change sweeping aside corruption, venality and manipulation and replace it by new values of enterprise and real performance and accomplishment. But has this happened?

A Survey of Morality in Public Life as a Sequel to Liberalization

China

China embarked on the course of liberalization in 1978. It has brought in its wake economic growth but it has destroyed the stern and spartan values of Marxist communism. China is said to be in the grip of rampant corruption. It has entered even in the last bastion of stern communist values i.e. the army. The New China News Agency, the official government controlled medium, has taken a swipe at the policy of liberalization and its progenitor Deng Ziaoping. It has highlighted the negative effects of Deng's open door policies saying that they had resulted in 'western ills such as fall in moral standards and traditional values'. This is, indeed, an agonizing reappraisal of Deng's policy of liberalization in China. Official corruption was one of the main catalysts behind the pro-democracy uprising that led to Tiananmen square massacre in June 1989. The crackdown against corruption has already taken a considerable toll. Beijing's Deputy Mayor, Wang Baosen committed suicide rather than face public disgrace. Beijing party chief Chen Xitong was forced to resign and now Mr. Deng's 79 year old wife Zhuò Lin had to suffer humiliation when her youngest son Deng Zhitang was summoned from Hongkong where he is a Director of Hongkong Subsidiary of China's mammoth state owned Steel enterprise, to answer corruption allegations. Mr. Deng's niece, Ding Peng is also being investigated by stock market regulators for allegedly embezzling more than 7.7 million pound sterling.

Russia

In Russia too, in the wake of the collapse of communism and disintegration of the erstwhile Soviet Union in 1991 there was such an increase in crime, violence, murder, gang rule, contract killing of prominent businessmen, thieving and racketeering that Moscow came to be known as the crime capital of the world. These crimes are now levelling off but new economic crimes like bank frauds and official corruption have gone up. Officials are often suspected of complicity in covering up major crimes.

Britain

Deng led China and Gorbachev led Russia and other erstwhile state of Sovietn Union in giving a go by to Socialism. Thatcher ushered in her own radical revolution in dismantling nationalization introduced by the first Labour Government led by Clemant Attlee after the Second World War. But though widely praised abroad, privatization has becoma a political albatross round the neck of the conservative government. Excessive salaries paid to the executives and excessive prices charged by the denationalized enterprises have come under attack. The 'regulators' appointed to control prices charged by privatized utilities are panicking and are forced to consider tougher price limits. Opinion polls in Britain do not consider privatization of water, gas and electricity utilities as a good thing. They favour re-nationalisation. No wonder John Major's conservative government has dropped plans to sell the post office.

Even more serious than overpaying the executives and overcharging the customers is the decline in public morality engendered by the Thatcher's revolution to roll back the Labourite legacy and to make pecuniary performance the sole criterion of achievement and excellence. British public life was rocked by controversies about MPs accepting cash for asking questions on the floor of the Parliament. One conservative MP was suspended after the privilege committee found that the cash for question allegation was true. A series of other allegations of sleaze among the MPs and Ministers also figured in the House of Commons. The Prime Minster John Major responded to the need for cleaning up public life by appointing a ten member committee headed by Lord Noan a senior appelate Judge. The report, according to Mr. Jack Straw, the Shadow Home Affairs Minister and spokesman of the Labour Party, was a thorough condemnation of Government and the way it contributed to the decline of the standard of public life over the last 16 years. It showed an undesirable nexus between the conservative party and business. The Committee observed that there was no precedent in this country for so many allegations of wrong doing. It underlined the need to take remedial action to allay public fears. The remedial action suggested by the Committee included the following – (1) MPs must accept a code of conduct to be able to put themselves about all accusations of sleaze and wrong doing. (2) The conduct of the MPs must be scrutinized by an independent commissioner because self regulation was found to be wanting. (3) The code of conduct would include the following : (a) MPs will be banned from taking paid work for the lobbyists. (b) there will be full disclosure by MPs of their earnings and contracts for providing parliamentary services, (c) Ministers should be subjected to the same restrictions as senior level servants on taking private sector jobs when they leave Government. They should have to seek permission for new jobs within two years of leaving office with a three month automatic waiting period for cabinet ministers, (d) MPs should be free to have paid outside interests and employment, provided it was unrelated to their Parliamentary duties. But no payment should be accepted for making representations or intervening in Parliament on behalf of interest groups or doing consultancy work for private firms. At present such 'consultancy payment' to MPs exceeds of 3 million a year. (4) A public appointment commissioner should be appointed to ensure that there was no political bias when candidates were chosen for semi-official or other bodies. (5) MPs should have seven guiding virtues viz. selflessness, integrity, objectivity, accountability, openness, honesty and leadership. The British Government has accepted the broad thrust of the report despite some murmurs amongst the conservative MPs that the recommendations wére draconian.

Italy

For long it had been known that powerful members of Italian politics were closely linked with the mafia. As the slain anti mafia Judge Giovanni Falcone assassinated on the orders of the mafia in May 1992 observed in an interview before his death – 'The mafia needs the protections of the politicians to survive and to flourish. The mafia does not just live off prostitution and drugs. It moves huge sums of money across continents and has now penetrated the heart of the Italian state itself through state run industries and public work contracts. There is relationship of inter-dependence between politicians and the mafia. Mafiosi are no longer the stereotype gun-toting guys with shiny suits and slicked black hair. They now sit in wall street offices and move millions of narco-dollars. This mafia has widened its frontiers and has become multi-national. If there was such a long standing collusion between the mafia and the politicians, the public too was responsible by their conspiracy of silence. One reason for the silence was their fear that the Italian Communist Party under Euerico Berlinguer would come into power if the corruption by the politicians of the Christian democratic party were to be exposed. Once Communism crumbled, there was no reason to prop up the old corrupt parties. The corruption trial in Milan led by Judges Antonio de Peerto and Francesco Saverio Borrelli exposed the ramification of corruption in Italian politics, government and public life. The crusades of these judges are a reflection of the public disgust and frustration with having to put up with corrupt politicians for so long. The trial of former Prime Minister Giulco Andreotti for collusion with mafia is the culminating point of this crusade. He was long considered the heart and soul of Italy's Christian Democratic Party.

Nothing moved without his consent. He was 31 times Minister and 7 times Prime Minister. Today this powerful politician is charged with having ordered the assassination of an over curious journalist and coluded with Mafia chiefs, even sending birthday and marriage presents to members of their families.

Japan

Recent exposures of politicians in Japan has shown that Japan can compete with Italy in venality and corruption in public life. Since World War II, the liberal party had an uninterrupted sway in political life of Japan. That monopoly has now ended and a socialist politician Muryama has now become the Prime Minister. The fall of the Liberal Party is entirely because of scandals of corruption and raising huge amounts illegally for conducting elections. A most powerful politician Watanabe had to undergo jail sentence on proved charges of corruption.

India

In India too liberalization period of the last four years has been marked by thousands of crores of security scam right under the nose of the Reserve Bank of India. The multinational banks were deeply involved in this scandal. The parliamentary Committee headed by Shri. Ram Niwas Mirdha exposed the ramifications of the scandal. The Parliament was not satisfied by the Action Taken Report nor has the public distrust assuaged. This had only added to the cynicism about the sanctity of public life. The manner in which assets of Public Sector enterprises were disinvested has also attracted adverse comments of the CAG. The imports of sugar created a scandal still shrouded in mystery. In a leading state, open allegations were made regarding that nexus between the builders, criminals and the leading politicians. Quite a large number of MLAs in several states are said to be criminals or having serious criminals cases against them. The Chief Election Commissioner who curbed the use of money and muscle power and misuse of the machinery of Government became a hero of the public.

Liberalisation has created a climate of consumerism in the country. The new rising urban middle class and the prosperous section of the rural society has become a solid consumer class of some 300 million people providing a market larger than that of several European countries. The revolution of rising expectations has been thrilled by attractive advertisements of novel consumer goods. This consumerism co-exists with stark poverty and malnutrition amongst disadvantaged sections of the society. and unconcern for this sections of the society has become the mindset of the people in privileged positions characteristic of the scale of values of the era of liberalization. The values of hedonism and consumerism have spread amongst the younger people of the country.

According to Marg survey of school and college going youth across the country, money matters most; other values like honesty, hard work, self respect and courage are considered important only by a few. 'Money is the most important thing in my career. If I also get job satisfaction well and good – otherwise forget it.' The private sector outranks all career choices for all categories of respondents. A new 'grab-for-more' culture has gripped the young minds. This does not bode well for the future of our society.

Ethics and Economics

The survey of the situation in different countries shows that liberalization is not synonymous with up-gradation of values in public life. It is necessary to ponder over this.

The basic question is whether pecuniary motivation and hedonistic values should characterize all sectors and aspects of our public life. Pursuit of self interest rebounding to optimization may be the theory of the market adumbrated by economists from Adam Smith to the World Bank and IMF economists today. But this cannot be applied to all aspects of national life. If people in Parliament, Government, Public administration, educational institutions and NGO's start concentrating only on promotion of their self interest, their bahaviour will be entirely inconsistent with two basic tenets of public work viz. (1) the work is entirely directed towards the fulfillment of a public purpose and (2) public position will never be used for aggrandisation of self interest. If these two principles ware given a go by, it will cause havoc to national life as has already happened. All concepts of idealism and higher values would vanish from national life. A nation cannot be run by purely pecuniary considerations. On the other hand, the seven guiding virtues pinpointed by the Nolan Committee in Britain ought to be the basis of public life in the country.

We in India started as an independent country with very high traditions of public life laid down by great people like Mahadev Govind Ranade, Dadabhai Naroji, Gopal Krishna Gokhale, Lokmanya Tilak, Rabindranath Tagore, Mahatma Gandhil, Jawaharlal Nehru, Sardar Patel and Subhash Chandra Bose. It is sad to find that all these values and traditions seem to have all been lost. There is no manner of doubt that without the eternal values enshrined in their lives and work, India would lose a sense of direction and purpose and the quality of national life would go down. Even the goal of economic progress cannot be accomplished.

As Bertrand Russell has said in his Autobiography – 'Love of country, public spirit were laudable motives; love of money, love of power, vanity were bad motives'. In another place he writes – "I judge pleasure and pain to be of small importance compared to knowledge, the appreciation and contemplation of beauty and a certain excellence of mind which apart from its practical effects appears to me to deserve the name of virtues".

We should not allow ourselves to be swayed by the winds of liberalization and abandon those ethical values which give strength to a nation. We should act on all the laudable recommendations of the Nolan Committee Report, but in addition we should ourselves undertake a comprehensive examination of the basis and purpose of our national life in the era of liberalization and globalisation – of the relationship between ethics and economics.

14

SATYAM EPISODE AND INDIAN CORPORATE IMAGE

The Satyam scandal has shaken not only the corporate world but the entire governmental system at the state and the central level. The Prime Minister was himself deeply worried. He described the scandal as a blot on the corporate image of India and expressed his determination to go at the root of the scandal. He should have rather realized that the scandal was a scar on the neo-liberal policy which he initiated in 1991 and time has come to get at the root of the policy and the government and the economic system which has come into existence as a consequence of that policy.

Satyam has been India's Enron. Satyam was preceded by several other scandals like the securities scandal and the financial adventures of desperadoes like Harshad Mehta, Ketan Parekh and Bhansali who played ducks and drakes with the Stock Market with the use of bank money. Enron in US was followed by many other scandals like the world.com and since September last, the collapse of one major financial institution after another like the Lehman Brothers, Fannie Mac and Freddi Mack, AIG, Merril Lynch, Goldman Sachs, Stanley Morgan Investment and Washington Mutual Bank. These are not fortuitous events. There is a clear link between the policy of neo-liberalism, unbridled capitalism and financial scandals. There should be a searching analysis and exposure of these and re-appraisal of the policy of neo-liberalism, however agonizing it may be.

Philosophy of Neo-liberalism

Policy of neo-liberalism is a modern incarnation of the nineteenth century policy of laisez faire which laid down that "that government is the best which governs the least" Modern policy of Neo-liberalism goes much beyond this and is based on the stipulations that "there should be more business in government and less government in business" and indeed "the business of government is business". This was based on a number of "mythologies" created in the name of sound economics propounded by the Chicago School led by Milton Friedman and zealously adopted by conservative radical leaders like Ronald Reagan in US and Margaret Thatcher in Britain. The first was that the free market economy (a non ideological term for unbridled capitalism) alone can lead to economic efficiency based on rational allocation of resources and distribution of income in proportion to "productivity". Second, free market economy is a self correcting system. If any problem like inflation or unemployment arises, the system would automatically bring into operation its corrective mechanism and cure the problem in due course. Thirdly any government intervention to solve the problem could only lead to aggravation of the situation. Indeed there should be complete deregulation, minimal government, vacation of traditional state sector in favour of private enterprise, reduced public expenditure and minimum taxation. Government has no business to claim a large chunk of tax payer's money as it could only lead to extravagance and waste at the hands of public agencies. The role of government agencies is only to promote private agencies and enterprise. There is no such thing as "public purpose" which government has to promote. Public purpose can only be the result of private enterprise governed by the signals of profit and loss in the market.

Nor should the heavy hand of public agencies control and regulate private enterprise. The "command and control economy" known in India as "license permit Raj" must be dismantled. Laws and rules thereunder, to control private business (like Industrial Development and Regulation Act, Monopoly and Restricted Pracices Act, Export-Import Control Rules, Foreign Exchange Regulation etc.) should best be abolished or at least drastically modified in the direction of liberalization.

In framing budgets and economic policies it become *de-rigueur* for the Government to take advice on management of private business. It become obligatory for the Heads of

Government to address annual conferences of Chambers of Commerce and Industry and Confederation of Indian Industries. Ministers of Finance and Industries started attending shows of private newspapers and T.V. Channels started distributing awards and even Ministers started accepting them. US set up a tradition of looking at executives of big business corporations and financial world for appointment as Treasury Secretary. Big business delegations started accompanying heads of government in their visits to important developed countries. Government and business delegations together started attending World Economic Summit at Davos.

Changing climate of public administration

The transformation of government in favour of big business inevitably influenced the climate in government agencies especially the economic ministries. The higher civil servants became "business friendly". Their mindset changed or had to change since instead of being controllers or regulators as in the bad old days of "socialism" they started playing second fiddle to the business magnates. They developed with them bonhomie as members of prestigious social clubs and started attending lavish business parties or even accepting hospitality. A theory was propounded that Civil servants should spend sometime in careers in business to gain useful managerial experience and wash away the obstructive bureaucratic tendencies of the past. Civil servants should, therefore be given permission liberally to move to private business for a tenure or even on long term appointment to be eventually absorbed permanently. The friendly civil servants could confidently look forward to lucrative assignments in private business on retirement. on the other hand, executivers from private business could be invited to hold crucial positions in government agencies on a tenure basis. The "conflict of interest" that may inevitably arise with this free to way traffic between government and business was conveniently overlooked.

The corporate world with high earnings became more prestigious than government departments with low salaries. The prestige was calculated on the basis of pecuniary affluence rather than "public service". The business executives started lecturing the public servants on efficient performance. "Corporate Governance" become the role model for governance in Government. Construction and management of Airports, Electricity and water supply projects, highways and metros, were assigned to private agencies, since public agencies were no good. Special economic zones were carved out where there would be no civil agency of government. They would be managed by the private business contractors and builders to whom they were assigned. They became "foreign territory" where normal rules of taxation, labour etc, would not apply. Lands for the SEZ could be acquired under the emergency clauses of the Land Acquisition Act. Lest the land acquisition should be delayed by the lethargic revenue administrative agencies, the agents of private business started sitting in government offices and directing acquisition proceedings.

Economics of Innocent Fraud

But to what extent were the encomiums showered on the capitalistic economic system and the corporate world justified? Did they correspond with reality? In his "*Economics of Innocent Fraud*", the late Prof. Galbraith exposed. The reality hiding behind the myths of capitalism and the corporate world. The myth is that the business world caters to the consumers because in the market "consumer sovereignty" prevails. In reality the big corporations and business interests manipulate consumer demand through misleading salesmanship and advertisement on TV channels for which they incur heavy expenditure ultimately borne by the consumer. The myth is that corporations are governed by the decisions of shareholders and representative Board of Directors. The reality is that corporators are managed by a small coterie of promoters and executives who award munificent compensations to themselves at the cost of the shareholders and investors. The myth is that high standards of corporate finance are ensured by professional accountants and auditors. The reality is that they themselves are a party to corporate scandals. The myth is that corporate scandals can be avoided by appropriate regulations. The reality is that corporate influence extends to regulators and public officials in the regulatory agencies can be unduly compliant. The myth is that with the dismantling of government controls over business, the scope for corruption by ministers and high official will be substantially reduced. The reality is that corruption takes a new form, more sophisticated and of greater dimension. Ministers and civil servants join hands with corporate management in appropriating for themselves huge gains by loot of public resources.

Satyam Scam

It is in the context of the above analysis of the capitalist economic system and corporate business that the huge Satyam scandal can be understood. The scandal of the order of more than Rs. 7000 crores would not have come to light but for the confession by the Chief Promoter Shri. Ramalinga Raju. The scandal was in the form of larger scale defrauding of accounts. False profits and cash resources were exhibited in the Financial Statements to create an illusion of a highly profitable business which duped gullible small investors. The Financial manipulation had been going on for seven long years but neither the so called "independent directors" nor the professional auditors discovered it. The independent directors were acknowledged management experts. They collected huge fees without discharging their duty to safeguard investors' interest because they were puppets in the hands of the promoter Raju. What the accounting firm Arthur Anderson did in Enron case falsifying accounts Price Water house Copper, the celebrated auditor firm did by failing to uncover fraud in "Satyam accounts".

This showed how hallow is the grandiose concept which goes by the name of "corporate governance", Raju was showered awards after awards for corporate leadership by prestigious award conferring Institutions in India and abroad on the "sound advice" of acknowledged experts and consultants. Now they are pleading that they did not know! Another example of innocent fraud".

Over seven years what is disturbing is that the businessman who systematically committed fraud was supported by politicians in power in Andhra Pradesh Government – former Chief Miniser Chandrababu Naidu and later his successor Y.R.S. Reddy. Association with the top leaders meant that Raju got huge chunks of prime land at throwaway prices for technology park and other purposes and many other facilities which enabled Satyam to expand and grow rapidly. Banks and financial institutions allowed Raju to open thousands of accounts without questioning. They provided statements about company's finance as Raju requested. Raju was allowed inside knowledge of government policies, development plans and projects even before the blue prints were prepared. This enabled him and his consortium Maytas Infra to bid for projects on favourable terms. The whole governmental system was harnessed to subserve Raju's interests. Now the bubble has burst and it is obvious how rotten to the core the whole system has become. The new President of US, Barrack Obama has vowed to end "greed and irresponsibility" on the Wall Street which led the prestigious financial institutions of US to collapse, one after another, like nine pins. He has taken to task the greedy business executives who appropriated bonuses of the order of $ 18 billion while the companies they were managing were facing financial ruin. Our government should also take a leaf out of Obama's book and break the racket of business government collaboration which has slowly developed after the policy of neo-liberalism was initiated in the year 1991. That should be the main issue of the forthcoming general elections.

15
FIGHTING THE CANCER OF CORRUPTION

Spate of Corruption Cases

In recent months a spate of corruption cases at very senior levels in administration have come to light. Two senior officers of the Ministry of Home Affairs, considered to be the *sanctum sanctorum* of Union Government, were involved in the alleged scam in the purchase of bullet proof jackets and excise evasion racket in the Union Territory of Daman. In the latter case, O Ravi, 1983 batch IAS officer of Gujarat cadre working as Joint Secretary in the Ministry was arrested by CBI for accepting a bribe of Rs. 25 lakhs to get the Administrator of Daman and Diu transferred. In the former case R. S. Sharma, a 1984 batch office of the Indian Railway Service of Mechanical Engineers on deputation to the Home Ministry was accused of taking a bribe of Rs. 10 lakhs from the owners of a security equipment company M/S. ATL to help them to get the contract for the supply of 59,000 bullet proof jackets.

Recently CBI raided the office and residence of a senior IAS Officer B.V. Selvaraj of Union Territory cadre currently serving as Secretary in the Union Ministry of Urban Development in connection with a graft case registered against several officials in Lakshadweep. Selvaraj had allegedly taken bribe from a private contractor promising him government contracts. (I.E. July 3)

A female officer Sumitra Banerjee serving as Additional Commissioner, Income Tax was arrested on graft charges by officers of the Anti Corruption Bureau of the CBI. She and her Assistant Commisioner, Anjali Banhole were accused of demanding

Rs. 2 Cr. from a builder of Thane for not conducting a search following a survey which disclosed a tax liability of around Rs. 25 Cr. her husband who went to pick up the bribe from the builder was also nabbed. Yet another case was that of the Chief Post Master General of Maharashtra and Goa Shri. Manjit Bali a 1978 batch officer of the Indian Postal Service. CBI caught him red handed while accepting the first installment of a bribe of Rs. 2 Cr. for issuing a no objection certificate for development of a plot reserved for post office in Thane district. He was the biggest ever catch of CBI. Bali's treasure trove consisted of the following – Rs. 34 lakhs in Indian currency, foreign currency consisting of $ 10722, £ 2050, Euro 3470, immoveable assets at Faridabad, Panchkula, New Delhi, Bhopal and Gurgaon totally valued at over Rs. 1 crore. 22 Bank accounts/ PPF accounts with a balance of 26 lakhs, 7 high end laptops valued at Rs. 5 lakhs, two cars and 45 imported liquor bottles. A superintendent of excise and customs office notorious for extorting bribe was arrested by CBI while accepting of Rs. 1.09 cr. from a businessman (*Indian Express*, Jan 10, 2011). Fourteen Custom officers were arrested by CBI for accepting bribes from Custom House agents. (*Loksatta Jan* 11, 2011)

All these cases of corruption are related to officers of various All Indian and Central Services – the top services of the country who held positions at senior echelons of administration. They were expected to set an example of high integrity to their subordinators but they betrayed the trust reposed in them by the government and people of the country.

Many other cases of corruption occurred in the state and local administration as well. Officers of the IAS serve the Central Government as well as the States to whose 'cadres' they are allotted. A shocking example of corruption was provided by the IAS couple Arvind and Tina Joshi both serving in the high position of Secretaries to government of Madhya Pradesh. The bribe they took was in crores or so. According to income tax department their accumulated assets are of the order of 266 crores. The IPS is also an All India Service. An officer of the IPS serving as S.P. Belgaum was raided by the investigating officer of the Lok Ayukta,

Karnataka. He was found in possession of assets disproportionate to his salary.

Corruption was not confined to the administrative services only. Raids by the Income Tax department and Lokayukta organisation on the palatial bungalow of Director of Public, Health and Family Welfare Dept. of MP, Yograj Sharma of Public Health led to the recovery of disproportionate amount of cash stashed in beds and cupboards, gold jewelery, investments and properties. (IE, March 2). As many as 85 bank accounts in the name of Dr. Yogiraj Sharma and his family members were found with a total of Rs. 30 Cr. Government funds were siphoned off into Companies of Gaurav Sharma and Shashi Sharma, son and wife respectively of Dr. Yogiraj Sharma. Sharma drew his power by flaunting his proximity to former Chief Minister Digvijay Singh. He could even dictate terms to his seniors because of his political connections. The Government compulsorily retired him but the High Court asked the government to restore him on some technical grounds!

Yet another case of involvement of a medical professional came to light – this time not an employee of government but an office bearer of the apex regulatory authority of the medical educational institutions in India viz. President of the Medical Council of India, Dr. Ketan Desai. The case assumed proportions of a major scam. Dr. Desai is facing charges under Prevention of Corruption Act for taking a bribe of Rs. 2 Cr. for giving recognition to the Patiala based Gyan Sagar Medical College. Dr. Desai was taken into custody by the CBI. Dr. Desai denied the charges. But after CBI raids, it came to light that Dr. Desai has amassed wealth and properties running into thousands of crores of rupees at places like Andheri in Mumbai where he owns a big shopping complex at a prominent place and an opulent office, five expensive cars like Honda City, Hyundai Sonata and Toyota Karmi. He has a bank account in Dubai. Gold and diamond jewelery worth Rs. 38/- lakhs was found in his lockers. The Chairman and Secretary of Apex organisation viz. All India Institute of Technical Education (AIITE) were found in indulging in massive corruption. They had to be suspended for giving recognition to technical institutes of higher education of doubtful credibility.

Jharkhand headed by the Chief Minister notorious for corruption had rampant corruption at high places. After the Shibu Soren Government went out of power in June 1 and President's rule was imposed, Governor M.O.H. Farook took action against a dozen tainted Government officers of the IAS and State Administration, including Managing Director of Jharkhand Minineral Development Corporation and Additional Secretary of the Dept. of Institutional Finance (IE, June 10). What is more striking is that the Vigilance Bureau has lodged FIR against Chairman and three other members of Jharkhand Public Service Commission. How can recruitment process be objective if the members of the Commission themselves are corrupt? Unfortunately such cases are taking place frequently. Some years ago, Chairman and officers of Public Service Commission of Maharashtra were accused of corruption. The Chairman had to spend long time in jail but subsequently on some technical grounds, the court exonerated the Chairman. Corruption has entered even in the army recruitment process. A Major was caught red handed while accepting a bribe to issue a medical certificate required for every candidate.

Latest case of this category is the suspension of the Chairman of the Railway Recruitment Board for Mumbai in connection with recruitment scandal involving alleged leak of examination papers for money. Those arrested by CBI in the case included chairmans' son Vivek Bharadwaj, Former Additional Divisional Railway Manager A.K. Jagannathan, Raipur and his son Srujan and some middlemen. Copies of the question paper were sold for Rs. 3.5 lakhs per candidate.

Local bodies are supposed to be nearer people and under constant public scrutiny. But here too corruption is rampant. The Jt. Director City Planning Sunil Joshi of Kalyan Dombivali Corporation was caught taking a bribe of Rs. 5 lakhs from Dilip Amrutlal Gutkha. Investigations revealed that this officer working comparatively at junior level had property worth Rs. 1.25 cr. including diamonds, platinum pen worth Rs. 14 lakhs, 154 sealed bottles of foreign wine and liquor and six lakhs in cash (IE & Loksatta June 19)

A corruption case at the highest level in the Army made disturbing reading. Court marshall proceedings were started against a General serving as the Principal officer of the Army Chief and a couple of Major Generals at the level of Corps Commanders for giving no objection certificate to a private businessman for construction of some school buildings on a site close to the Army establishment against the rules in Siliguri area in West Bengal. Though no corruption has been mentioned it appeared to be a case of nepotism and misuse of authority.

Corruption in Judiciary

Judiciary is required to be above corruption, if the people have to have implicit trust in it. But several cases of corruption have come to light at the highest level in the judiciary as well. The latest case is that of Justice Dinakaran, Chief Justice of Karnataka High Court who was being considered for elevation to the post of judge of the Supreme Court. He is alleged to have grabbed Government land by illegal means. Impeachment proceedings have been initiated against him. A judge of Delhi High Court was removed for fraudulently acquiring a piece of land while another judge of the Calcutta High Court was indicted for putting money deposited in the High Court by a litigant into his own private account. Recently the CBI filed a charge sheet against six district judges of Ghaziabad, three of whom later retired as Judges of Allahabad High Court and 71 others in a multi-crore Provident Fund Scam. One Ashutosh Asthana (he was found dead last year in Dasna jail under mysterious circumstances while the CBI probe was on) a Bill Clerk and Central Nazir, District Court entered into a criminal conspiracy with the six District judges to cheat the District Court, Ghaziabad. Asthana used to spend Provident Fund money for household expenditure of these judges. When such serious lapses can take place at the highest levels in judiciary, it should be no surprise that numerous cases of corruption have occurred at lower levels and some judges had to be removed from service.

Corruption Among Politicians

Civil Servants are accountable to the Ministers in a system of Parliamentary Democracy. But how can they curb corruption in civil service, when Ministers themselves are found to be corrupt. A notorious case was that of Sukharam, who was Union Minister of Telecommunications. Bundles of notes valued at crores of rupees were found stashed under the bed and in the toilet of his bungalow. He was proceeded against but he managed to continue to be active in politics and even win elections!

The more recent case is that of Madhu Koda who become Chief Minister of Jharkhand, after toppling the incumbent BJP Chief Minister Arjun Munda with Congress support. He used his power by illegally awarding mining leases (Jharkhand is rich in mineral resources) for which he took bribes running into crores of Rupess (some Rs. 600 cr.) Director of Revenue Intelligence detected the crime. The Income Tax Dept. raided some 60-70 persons involved. But the officer Ujjwal Choudhari in charge of the operations was summarily removed under pressure from 'some big people in Delhi'. (Feb. 19, Loksatta). Shibu Soren's private secretary Paul was found to be in possession of property worth Rs. 65 Cr. which he could not account for.

The latest case is that of A. Raja, the incumbent Union Minister in charge of Telecommunications. It is alleged that he sanctioned sale of G2 Spectrum in 2008 at 2001 prices leading to a huge loss estimated anywhere between 60,000 to 100,0000 crores of rupees. This was corroborated by the huge proceeds of the recent sale of G3 Spectrum. The opposition parties are clamouring for his immediate removal. But the 87 years old Chief Minister of Tamilnadu who nominated Raja in Union Cabinet, come all the way to Delhi to tell the Prime Minister that the allegations have been made against him because he is a *Dalit* and he should not be touched. In his press conference to observe the completion of his first year of office in the second term, the Prime Minister simply said that Raja had told him that he acted as per the rules then prevalent and if anybody is found guilty, then law will take its own course ! The office of Raja was raided but Raja did not think it necessary to resign ! Later such was the outcry that he had to be arrested. Now the case is before the Supreme Court.

The corruption has taken place even in the precincts of Parliament as well. The minority Government of P.V. Narasimha

Rao survived with the support of MP of Jharkhand Mukti Morcha, who bribed to vote for the minority Government. When the issue went to Supreme Court, it refused to intervene on the grounds that what takes place in Parliament, is according to the Constitution, outside the purview of judiciary.

UPA-I Government won a vote of confidence even after losing the support of the leftist parties and it was alleged that some of the MP's of the opposition parties crossed the floor because they were bribed. There was the unseemly scene of bundles of notes stacked on the table in front of the speaker. It was alleged that it was part of the huge amount of money used to secure the confidence vote. The Parliamentary Committee which looked into this unwholesome event did not establish the allegations of bribery by the ruling alliance. The clouds of suspicion however, remained and have become darker after the Wikileaks.

It is widely believed that politics in India is ridden with corruption. The polititicians before independence and in the early years after independence lived for politics (for a public purpose) while politicians now live off politics and make a good fortune for themselves, their families and kith and kins. There is tremendous use of money power during elections at all levels – national, state and even local as well as in institutions like co-operatives. Even after the Election Commission imposed a code of conduct, the expenses incurred by candidates far exceed the ceiling laid down by the code.

Recently Rs. 7 crore were found in the car of industrialist Haribabu in Andhra Pradesh Congress. It was alleged that the money belonged to Telugu Desam Party leader Chandrababu Naidu and was meant to be used during the forthcoming by-elections in 12 Assembly constituencies of Telangana. (IE, June 19, 2010)

No wonder it is believed that the money is recovered after the candidate gets elected by resorting to corruption. It has been noticed that successful politicians have quickly amassed wealth after they won the elections and assumed positions of power. Candidates of poor means have become affluent and most of the candidates now standing for elections have become *'Karodpatis'*.

It has been suggested that to eliminate corruption needed to recover the expenses incurred on election by the candidate, there should be provisioning out of public exchequare. Apart from the huge burden it will impose on public resources, it is a doubtful proposition whether this by itself would eleminate political corruption.

A disturbing political trend in recent years is the 'criminalisation of politics'. Politicians called into service criminals to use muscle power and gather voters. Now criminals themselves have become politicians. A recent list of MP's and MLA's show that a large number of them have a criminal background. A case of an unholy alliance between criminals, politicians and police is the notorious Abdul Karim Telgi case. "He was a former peanut vendor who had printed 320 billion rupees worth of forged revenue stamps, one of the biggest corruption scandals in the nation's history. He got away with the forgeries by bribing Bombay's politicians and cops wholesale." (Maximum City by Suketu Mehta, p. 584)

It is apparent that the cancer of corruption has spread throughout the body politics and body economics of the country. For a country which through centuries has upheld the values of Aparigriha and Asteya this is indeed a great moral fall. The Upanishadic prayer enjoins on all of us "Maa gridhah kasyachit dhanam" do not take anybody else's possessions, seem to have been all but forgotten.

The second half of the year saw some shameful scams of corruption at the higher level – The Commonwealth Games, the 2G Spectrum licensing (A. Raja Minister in charge had to resign), the Adarsh Housing Society Scam, LIC Housing Loans, Lavasa Hill Station Project, the Neera Radia tapes and the diversion subsidized grain for BPL families from U.P. Never before so many scams of such magnitude hit the headlines. (Subhash Kashyap, South Asia Politics, January 2011)

Corruption in politics has had a corrosive effect on India's public life and economic progress It has been stated that a lot of money meant for development is siphoned through corruption, thus adversely affecting the progress of the country. But even more significant is the fact that corruption makes people lose faith in government and democracy itself. They tends to believe that everybody is corrupt and nothing can be got done without greasing the palm of somebody in authority.

Opportunities for Corruption

If corruption in politics is attributed to expensive elections, corruption in administration is attributed to a variety of opportunities for corruption that exist in administration. Administrative corruption started way back during the days of World War II when essential commodities were in short supply and had to be rationed – whether food articles or commodities like steel and cement. The shortage in the economy persisted after independence and Essential Commodities Act and other restrictive measures continued. In fact they were tightened. In the name of planning, a command and control economy and 'license permit raj' soon came into existence. Permits for foreign exchange, license for opening industrial and commercial establishments and control on capital issues meant that no business could be done without going to 'controller'. A thriving class of agents and middlemen came into existence who took their margin for getting the permit or license or supply of the precious commodities in short supply through the black market. The entrepreneurial skill was identified with manipulating the machinery of administration rather than creative management. Manipulation became the principal qualification for business advancement. No wonder the economy was atrophied and frozen and lost dynamism. The country remained economically backward compared to the other economies like Singapore, Hong Kong and Taiwan which gave free scope for business India remained backward technologically and productivity low and the economy became insular and non-competitive.

The philosophy of liberalization and privatization led to the concept of public private partnership which was interpreted as availment of public resources for private profit. Allotment of land, mineral and other resources, telecommunications spectrum rights could be given away below market cost to big business and multinationals at a price in the form of bribes to politicians. Instead of playing the role of regulators of private enterprises, the administrative authorities were asked to work as facilitators. This led to mutually helpful relationship between business tycoons and politicians and civil servants in authority. Madhu Koda and A. Raja cases mentioned above are the outstanding products of the new philosophy. For SEZ, the Government machinery was at the disposal of business for compulsory acquisition of huge chunks of land by using coercive force of the state against the protesting land owners. 'Helpful' civil servants could look forward to well paid jobs in private companies after retirement or could even leave government jobs for the newly opened lucrative opportunity. This is a new face of liberalization in which public interest is at a discount and private interest of big business is at a premium.

Growing public expenditure in the name of development and defence provided big opportunities for corruption. With the advent of the policy of liberalization initiated in 1991, the command and control economy was largely dismantled and it was expected that corruption attendant to license *permit raj* will also end. But this did not happen. As Ramchandra Guha has pointed out, liberalization and privatization has opened up new and much vaster avenues of corruption. ('India after Gandhi'- p. 713).

The most notorious case of corruption in post reform India concerns a power plant that the American firm Enron wished to setup in Maharashtra. In June 1992 the State Government then controlled by Congress signed the deal with Enron which guaranteed the company a staggering 16% annual return on its investment.

The contract proved controversial. When the controversy was at its height, the head of Enron in India revealed that $ 20 million were spent on 'education' widely seen as a euphemism for corruption.

Public sector enterprises have also become partners in their unholy alliance with American firms. Officials of Indian PSU's like BHEL, NPT, Bhilai Electric and State Electricity Boards of Maharashtra and Haryana were beneficiaries of bribes doled out by California based Control Corporation Inc. On June 30, 2009.

The firm pleaded guilty in a US Court for having committed bribery in 36 countries from 2002 to 2007. (I.E. July 8, 2010)

In the wake of external threats from the neighbouring countries China and Pakistan, India launched upon ever expending modernization programme involving huge public expenditure on purchases of technologically advanced aircrafts, missiles weapons and equipments. The contracts with supplying firms in foreign countries involved negotiations which gave scope for corruption in a big way.

Bofors became the notorious example of such corruption related to 'defence' purchases. Purchase of submarines, bullet proof jackets were other examples. Government has repeatedly talked about the exclusion of agents and middlemen from Defence purchases but they seem to have their presence, visible or invisible, all the time.

A shocking example of involvement of a senior functionary in a corruption scandal is that of Chairman of the ordinance factories board Shri. Sudipta Ghosh. He and several of his associates received bribes from Indian and foreign defence firms. The scandal came to light in 2009 July. CBI has recommended black listing of these firms (IE, June 24).

Similar cases are related to the award of contract of huge mega projects in the infrastructure sector. Satyendra Dube a young engineer tried to be a whistle blower for corrupt practices in the construction of highways. This led him to lose his life. His killers were prosecuted and punished but there is a lurking feeling that the big business which hired the killers have gone scot-free.

Big projects apart, in the implementation of development schemes which are to be executed through small projects spread all over the country like Narega (rural works programme) or *Sarva Shiksha Abhiyaan*. There are constant exposures of corruption. Recently a Marathi newspaper *Sakaal* brought out a series of expose relating to *Sarva Shiksha Abhiyan* programme. Money meant for building of schools, improvement of facilities for students in schools, and midday meal programmes, was misused by educational officers,, local Panchayat officers and even teachers.

Controlling Corruption

The problem of corruption in Indian administration and how to control it if not to eradicate it altogether has received attention even since independence. One of the first reports on administrative reforms, the Gorwala one man committee report attributed corruption to delay and redtape and recommended streamlining administrative procedures to expedite disposal of cases. Along with speed in disposal of cases, several later administrative reforms commissions, recommended measures to make administration open and transparent. The computer revolution had opened up new opportunities for speeding and streamlining administration. The recent and probably the most important measure in this direction is passing of the Right to Information Act claimed by UPA-I Government as one of its most important achievements. Information Commissioners have been appointed both at the Central and State levels to enable citizens to obtain information on administration procedures and relating to actual disposal of cases. It needs to be assessed as to what extent this right of the citizens had led to making administration more responsive to the citizens, more open and transparent and to elimination of corruption. The fact remains that a large number of original cases and appellate cases are pending. The same delay in disposal that exists in government offices exists in the office of information officers as well. No wonder people feel frustrated.

Another important recommendation to curb corruption was made by the Santhnam Committee appointed by Nehru government after the issue was raised in Parliament. The Committee recommended appointment of Vigilance Commissioners at the Central and State level and in every Ministry and organisation. It is after that recommendation that the office of the Chief Vigilance Commissioner came into existence at the central level. To strengthen the machinery for investigation into corruption cases, the Supreme Court ordered that the CBI, the principal investigating agency at the central level should act under the supervision of the Chief Vigilance Commissioner, so as to make it independent and free from influence of government. Even after this recommendation came into effect, it is widely believed that the

CBI does not function in an independent and impartial manner and is under the thumb of the Central Govt. and works as its agency.

The first comprehensive reforms commission headed first by Morarji Desai and later by K. Hanumanthiah (1969) recommended the creation of the post of Lok Pal at the Central level and Lok Ayukta at the state level to bring under its purview Ministers of Government in adition to senior administrative officers. Lok Ayuktas have been appointed in several states but the office of the Lok Pal who has to function at the Central level has yet to come into existence. A bill to create this office came several times before Parliament (1968, 71, 75, 86, 89, 96, 98, 2001) but lapsed on every occasion. These seems to be political reluctance if not resistance to this Bill. Lok Ayuktas have been appointed in several states. How far have Lok Ayuktas been effective? The recent case of Justice Santosh Hegde, Lok Ayukta in Karnataka is most eloquent. He exposed many corruption cases relating to high level functionaries in government. But after battling corruption in Government for nearly four years, Justice Hegde resigned in frustration at the apathy shown by BJP Government headed by Chief Minister B.S., Yeduerappa towards corruption in allowing illegal mining of iron ore in the state. The Reddy brothers, the notorious mines owners of Bellary are themselves Ministers and so powerful than they almost brought down Yediurappa Government) The final straw was the mysterious disapperance of nearly five lakh tones of iron ore valued at nearly Rs. 200 cr. and seized by forest authorities at the state run Balekeri Port after it was revealed that the ore was illegally mined and transported from Bellary without permit. Rather than supporting the officer who exposed this illegal mining, under the pressure of a Minister, he was suspended on frivolous grounds of failure to attend a meeting Hegde alleged that Karnataka Government was targeting officers helping Lok Ayukta in the battle against corruption. On the other hand, corrupt officers indicted by Lok Ayukta are being reinstated despite assurance to the contrary given by the Chief Minister. Delay by Government in appointing Up Ayukta has led to a huge pendency of cases. In utter frustration, Hegde resigned saying, "I feel helpless, I feel useless. People in positions are not bothered about corruption." If this is the helplessness of an ex-judge of the

Supreme Court vigorously pursuing corruption cases as Lok Ayukta, the position of others can only be imagined. Governor H.R. Bharadwaj to whom Hegde submitted his resignation letter and Union Home Minister Chidambaram requested Hegde to withdraw his resignation but he refused. Ultimately after request from Lal krishna Advani, Hegde announced on July 13 that he had decided to withdraw his resignation. "The respect I have for Advani", said Hegde "has forced me to withdraw my resignation. Advani has assured me that the party and the State Government will co-operate with him."

The Constitution created an independent office of Controller and Auditor General (CAS) and under him the State Account General to audit public expenditure incurred by all Ministries and Departments and organizations functioning under the auspices of the Ministers and Departments. The CAG and AG's prepare annual reports which are placed before the Public Accounts Committees of Parliament and Legislative Assemblies respectively. The Committee considers the reports and calls before it the officers of Government concerned to seek explanation and clarifications and thereby hold government to account. These reports have over years exposed many cases of waste and embezzlement of public fund. Bofors case is one such case. The recent spectrum case is another.

Values in Public Administration

While all these measures to control corruption are important – viz. audit by CAG, Vigilance machinery in government offices, appointment of Information Officers, streamlining administrative procedures and computerization, more important than all those is the mindset of people who work in Government and the values they hold. Max Weber described bureaucracy as a rational legal institution which strictly works according to prescribed procedures, which does not own any office and has to work not in self interest but in public interest. The principle of public interest is all important. Self interest has no place in the work of a public functionary, whether political or administrative. Self interest, according to Adam Smith, the founder of science of economics, may be the motivating force in the market but it has no place in public administration. The touchstone for the act of a public functionary is public interest alone. In pursuit of public interest, the functionary has to be scrupulously honest and impartial. He gets his salary and other perquisites according to rules but beyond this he cannot have an eye on public funds. He has to follow strict canons of financial propriety. Every *paisa* of public expenditure should be accounted for and used in a most efficient manner to sub serve public purpose.

It is often said that the salaries of public servants are low as compared to the compensations in the private sectors and salaries of public servants in a country like Singapore which is free from corruption. Hence the panacea for eliminating corruption is to raise salaries of civil servants to the highest level. How far is this argument valid? The salaries of public servants in India have been raised from time to time on the basis of recommendations of successive Pay Commissions. The salaries can not be compared with those in the private sector. In a country of widespread poverty, salaries of public servants cannot be disproportionately high compared to the average standard of living of the people. It is time that salaries in the private sector which have gone through the roof, after ceilings on income imposed earlier, have been eliminated in the name of liberalization, are pruned. It is a doubtful proposition that higher salaries of public servants would automatically lead to elimination of corruption which is not just a function of level of compensation but more of values of public service.

Unfortunately the concept of public purpose seems to have been given a go by in the wake of liberalization. The philosophy of aggrandizement of self interest and pursuit of money and wealth seems to have infiltrated into and infested the domain of public administration and Government This has had a disastrous effect on the values of public service which have all but disappeared. An insatiable greed and uncontrollable impulse to acquire money and property by fair and foul means seems to have taken hold of in the minds of many public servants. Instead of maintaining the dignity and honour of a public servant and pursuing the high values of the profession of public service, they seem to have surrendered to the lures of hedonism which dominate the capitalist market economy. Instead of keeping a distance from businessmen, public servants seem to be hand in gloves with them, joining hands with them in exploiting public resources for private profit and in return getting their share. Public servants and ministers seem to have been addicted to five star style of living. Simplicity and dignity of a public professional service seems to have gone to the wall. Public administration has surrendered to business and works for them rather than for the common people for whom it exists.

If this analysis is valid then what is crucial for eliminating corruption – more important than machinery of audit, vigilance and information officers and streamlining and computerization of administrative procedures, is the need to restore the values of public interest and idealism of public service. This is more easily said than done. The social norms themselves have to change. Respect should go not just for money and wealth but values of public service and social good. For a country which has long up held moral values, this should be a moral code of conduct. We should all remember seven social sins as told by Mahatma Gandhi and shun them in our public life. They are –

1. Politics without principles
2. Wealth without work
3. Pleasure without conscience
4. Knowledge without character
5. Commerce without morality
6. Science without humanity
7. Worship without sacrifice

16

DEMOCRACY, ECONOMIC PROFLIGACY AND FISCAL CRISIS

Speaking recently at the World Conference on Democracy held at New Delhi. Dr. Amartya Sen, the Nobel laureate is reported to have observed that, "democracy keeps you out of trouble during fiscal crisis". He has obviously in mind the 'crony capitalism' in Indonesia which, thanks to its dictatorial regime under Gen. Suharto, could prevent the public from questioning the blatant misuse of banking resources initially acquired out of dollar borrowing from abroad, for providing loanable funds to financially doubtful enterprises owned by members of ruling family and their associates.

And when as a consequence, the Indonesian economy was caught in a financial crisis characterized by hyper-inflation and collapse of the Indonesian Rupiah, there were riots in the streets and the dictator had to resign. Prof. Sen probably implies that in a watchful democracy with an alert public opinion, such misuse of resources would not have gone unchecked and an orderly solution would have been found out through democratic process.

But if he were to analyse the Indian situation, he would have clearly seen that democracy far from countering the fiscal crisis could be the cause of it. Several bank scams exposed in recent years have clearly shown that it is with the blessings of the politicians in power that they took place. In the urea scam in which the State Bank of India, India's premier bank was involved, the people closely connected with the then Prime Minister were alleged to have pressurised the bank officials to provide funds for urea which had yet to reach the Indian shores.

In the Indian Bank case, the managing director, who was given several extensions at the behest of powerful politicians was alleged to have overlooked the sanction of loans for non-viable purposes and in the case of the biggest scam, viz. the security scandal, the joint committee of the parliament far from fixing responsibility tried only to white wash the whole affair leaving the main culprit to go scot-free and come back with a bang in the stock market to indulge in speculative transactions.

The government has been unable to contain the fiscal deficit for the last several years. And as a result inflationary pressure has been let loose in the economy. One of the main reasons is the wasteful public expenditure which has gone on unchecked year after year. Indian democracy has given rise to jumbo cabinets in almost every state. UP taking the lead.

The proliferation of the ministries with their accompanying staff and innumerable perks like a palatial housing, extravagant furnishing, travel expenses specially on foreign tours which hardly serve any purpose has put tremendous burden on the public exchequer. The VIP security has reached scandalous proportions. Ruling politicians are representatives of the people and should not need to be protected with a security barrier all the time. Such a situation which is totally inconsistent with democratic governance goes on with impunity. Ministers are now addicted to five stare culture and avail, at public expense of medical treatment abroad when common people who vote the government in power in democracy go without any basic services.

Instead of providing funds for sound schemes, projects which bring adequate returns, democratic leaders everywhere have wasted public money on populist schemes named after political leaders. They have proliferated but they have not led the poor to cross the poverty line or make substantial dent on poverty. Prime Minister Rajiv Gandhi himself once said that only 15 paise out of a rupee spent on anti-poverty schemes reach the people. But he did not abolish the schemes and they continued. It is frequently alleged that muster roles at works programme carry fictitious names. No solid work is done and no assets created. Loans under IRDP are taken only to avail of the subsidies attached to them. The loanee does not use the funds to acquire an asset and to engaged in a productive enterprise. After the nationalization of banks, loan melas were arranged to impress the rural people but they set a bad tradition of indiscriminate lending resulting in large overdues turning the banks sick. The remedy adopted was to write-off loans in a wholesale manner. Far from tightening the system, Prime Minister Narasimha Rao thought it fit to allot a fund of Rs. 2 crore to every MP to use it in any manner he likes. In the 2011-12 budget Finance Minister Mukerjee has raised the limit to five crores. The constitutional propriety to allow the legislators to operate on public funds had been questioned. The CAG evaluation has shown that funds entrusted to MPs have not been properly used.

The sanction of projects without any regard for availability of funds has been rampant in our democracy. Recently Mamata Banerjee, Railway Minister, sanctioned railway project in West Bengal when already there is such a huge accumulation of railway projects that funds for them will not be available for years to come. Every railway minister has thought it fit to sanction new railway lines in his area and to open new zonal offices requiring commitment of huge funds. Similarly Civil Aviation ministers force the Indian Airlines to operate flights which landed them in huge losses. Irrigation projects are sanctioned by ministers in several states without availability of funds. They go on languishing for years without getting completed, inevitably resulting in scheduled slippage and cost overruns.

The projects and services provided at huge public costs ought to bring adequate returns to public exchequer over a period of time so that a rotating development fund evolves which keeps on getting continuously replenished through returns. But our politicians in power go on making wild promises of free water and electricity. No wonder most of the state electricity boards have become bankrupt.

The fiscal crisis in India is the direct result of the economic profligacy of our demoncratic rulers. Our voters have continuously fallen a prey to wild promises of populist schemes and subsidies. The mood of the people and our democratic politicians was displayed through a chorus of opposition to the recent decision to raise the prices of commodities distributed through PDS. It is our democracy which has created an addition to subsidies of all kinds, open or hidden. It has also given rise to extravagant expenditure and even financial scandals and corruption. Prof. Sen has often praised democracy as a system which rebounds to the economic welfare of the common people. He has pointed out that, while mass starvation and death took place in China during famine in which millions of people died, place in this no such phenomenon took post-independent India. This was because of absence of democracy in China and its presence in India. However, if now thinks that democracy in India can save it from fiscal crisis, one cannot help feeling that even a Nobel laureate in economics can be a victim of naiveté.

Democracy, it is said, is a self correcting form of government. If mistakes take place, the correcting mechanism is set into motion through the democratic processes. But Indian experience has shown that this does not always take place. Mistakes are repeated and even exacerbated. Parties and leaders indulge in competitive populism and fiscal discipline is compromised more and more blatantly. Gresham's law prevails, bad politicians driving out the good ones. Politics gets criminalized and as in the fodder scandal case in Bihar public funds are looted from the public treasury by unscrupulous politicians in connivance with corrupt bureaucrats. In such a situation, how can one agree with Prof. Sen's statement that 'democracy keeps you out of trouble of fiscal crisis ?"

17

SHOULD WE DUMP SWADESHI ?

Cancellation of the highly inequitable Enron contract, attack on Kentucky Fried Chicken and breaking Pepsi bottles seems to have so upset the crusaders for liberalization that they have found fit to attack Mahatma Gandhi himself and dismissing his Swadeshi ideology as hogwash – an ideology which inspired the nation to fight for liberation from foreign rule. Even Finance Minister Dr. Manmohan Singh has thought fit to denounce Swadeshi at the recent conference of economic editors.

It is a pity that Swadeshi ideology – the ideology of our struggle for freedom – should be denounced in the cavalier manner on the 125th anniversary of Mahatma Gandhi and less than fifty years of freedom ! The entitics of Swadeshi seem to have neither a sense of national pride nor a sense of integrity. They seem to be deliberately distorting the concept of Swadeshi propounded not only by Mahatma Gandhi but also by his illustrarious predecessors like Lokmanya Tilak and Dadabhai Nauroji. The Mahatma said that he would like the windows of his house to be wide open and the breeze in the world to blow freely but refused to be swept off by it. The attackers of Swadeshi are indeed swept off by the philosophy of multinationals.

One part of the philosophy of multinations a is that national identity has become out of date in the post – modern era of globalisation. In our tradition, the concept of globalization is that the whole world is one family – '*Vasudhaiv Kutumbakam*'. But that does not mean that we should give up our sense of national identity in a world in which mighty nations are ceaselessly and strenuously pursuing their national interest. The French President is prepared to defy the whole world and conduct atomic tests which he considers necessary in his nation's self-interest. USA is prepared to pressurize Japan to promote American automobile industry. It does not at that time remember the principles of free trade which it preaches to India and other countries of the world. Recently. President Obama of USA has openly come out against outsourcing the work relating to information technology to India. He wants Buffalo to replace Bangalore.

The philosophy of Swadeshi was formulated by our national leaders during colonial times. They believed that the colonial masters looked at their colonies as a base of raw material and a market for finished products so that they got all the benefit of 'value added' while the people of colonies were exploited and were reduced to "hewers of wood and drawers of water". Before the advent of colonialism India had flourishing handicrafts and village industry. But under the onslaught of modern industry based on modern technology of the imperial countries, these traditional industries went down, creating a lopsided economy and chronic conditions of stagnation, poverty and unemployment. It is in this context that the economics and philosophy of Swadeshi was vigorously advocated by our leaders.

After Independence it became the duty of the Govt. of free India to abolish stagnation, poverty and unemployment. These still continue to be our overriding concerns. The meaning 'Swadeshi' today has to be dynamically interpreted in this new context. We have realised that Swadeshi is not synonymous with a closed economy or Autarky. It does not mean mere self-sufficiency. We do not have to erect tariff walls and deprive us of foreign capital, technology or management. Swadeshi rather means that these should be harnessed to realize our goals and objectives in the era of globalisation. We should bear this in mind in welcoming the multinationals and making contractual arrangements with them. It is only after the Enron fiasco that the Finance Minister made a public pronouncement that in future the contracts would be on the basis of international competitive bidding. If this had been done in the case of Dabhol power project, the nation would not have had to face the discomfiture of realizing that wholly one sided contract was entered into with Enron saddling it with a high capital cost, high tariff, project. Swadeshi means that we enter into international contracts in national interest and not in the interest of multinationals.

Swadeshi means that we do not give up our economic sovereignty. It means that adverse effects on the entry of multinationals on health and way of life of our people are not overlooked. It means that our national strength is enhanced – not weakened so that we can survive and succeed in an international competitive environment. It means that interdependence does not degenerate into dependence on dominant countries. If that happens our national interest would be sacrificed at the alter of globalisation.

A part of increasing our national strength is to make our enterprises more competitive. They are quite justified in asking for a level playing field. They cannot be handicapped by imposing taxes and other conditions to which multinationals are not subject. Nor should public enterprises be reduced from the position of favourite children to outcastes. Swadeshi means self-reliance and self-reliance means increasing our national strength.

Swadeshi means that the State does not give up its responsibility to give a sense of direction even in the era of globalisation nor should it abandon its responsibility for building up infrastructure including a fine system of education. Swadeshi means building national self-confidence. That is what make Gandhiji's Swadeshi relevant even today.

18

CO-EXISTENCE OF MARKET ECONOMY AND PLANNING

Central planning and market economy, on the face of it, are conflicting but they can co-exist and should. The market economy implies that decisions as to What to produce to How much to produce? For whom to produce, How much to produce, Where to produce and when to produce? Would not be decided by the Planning Commission, but by the economic forces of demand and supply in the market which would be governed by the signals of cost, price and profit. No longer would the targets of production of various commodities or of saving and investment be fixed by the Planning Commission; rather they would be the result of transactions in the market economy.

If we accept this, where is the scope for planning and the Planning Commission? Should they not stand abolished – unless of course it is possible to redefine the role and method of planning in such a manner that they become compatible with the market? In this respect we have much to learn from the concepts and methods of planning in France and Japan, both market economies, and adapt them to our own circumstances. Even if this means an agonizing reappraisal of our planning as carried out over the Eight Five year plans, we should not hesitate to undertake it.

The new economic policy prefers market to planning because of the belief that it is the market which can ensure efficient allocation of resources. It is the Supper-Session of the market mechanism by planning which had led in the past to an inefficient, stagnant and high cost economy and sub-optimal and even wasteful, allocation of resources. If market is to be the guide of all economic decisions and if growth has to be accomplished through the market, then planning should reinforce the market mechanism rather than supersede it.

The market cannot bring about an efficient allocation of resources unless it is perfect. If the information available in the market is inadequate and if there are rigidities and immobilities, the market cannot perform. The role of planning would then be to make available information and economic intelligence regarding the macro-parameters of the economy to the market at all levels. The Planninc Commission can be the fountain of information, which it should widely disseminate to various players in the market economy. The information should be not only about the current situation of the economy but also about future trends. Macro economic forecasting can be an aid to the market mechanism. The statistical and evaluation organizations of the Planning Commission can perform this task. This has been a strong point of planning in Japan and can with advantage, be assimilated in our planning system.

The Indian economy is full of rigidities and immobility's of all sorts. Through years of planning, in order to ensure allocation of resources to priority areas, we have introduced a mass of controls and regulations, which in fact resulted in reduced overall availability of resources. For example, legislation regarding ceiling on urban land has led to a sky rocketing of the price of housing accommodation in cities. Though it is for the various ministries to remove hindrances to economic development, the Planning Commission can play a dynamic role in identifying these hindrances and bringing about their speedy removal through changes in law and administrative procedures.

Though the new economic policy provides a central role to the market in bringing about economic development and provision of gainful opportunities, there will still be a large number of people below the poverty line especially in rural areas who cannot participate in the market. It would be for the plan to provide for such persons whom the market cannot take care of.

The market also cannot bring about economic development without the support of infrastructure viz. roads, transport, communication, and above all power. Infrastructure has emerged as the most severe constraint on the scope and pace of development in the country. Various attempts to involve private sector in this task have not been successful and it would, therefore, be a necessity to make a substantial provision in the Five Year Plan for infrastructural development through projects in the public sector.

The public sector, like planning has also come under criticism. The public sector enterprises once described in as the commanding heights of economy are now looked upon as a drag on economic development, though such criticism is not always justified. In any case, wholesale privatization of public enterprice has been opposed by some of the constituents of the UPA Government. However, there should be unanimity on the point that just because some enterprises are in the public sector, they cannot be allowed to work inefficiently with impunity. The public enterprises should be required to work efficiently in the market economy without support from the state exchequer. They should be given necessary autonomy.

The Nineth Plan, therefore, would have to clearly be divided into two parts – one dealing with the public sector such as infrastructural development and social sector programmes, the anti poverty programme and rural and agricultural development programmes. Here, there should be imperative planning with strict insistence on time schedules and expenditure control without giving rise to time and cost slippages. In respect of the public and private sector enterprises, there should be full scope for corporate planning without insistence on rigid target. Corporate plans will have to be produced by the individual enterprises in relation to market conditions. In respect of corporate planning, the nineth. Plan can only be of an indicative nature.

Planning has to be multilevel and not over centralized. With the amendment of the Constitution, Panchayati Raj Institutions and municipalities have now become constitutional entities. The States and local bodies, therefore, should play a more active role in the planning process.

A decentralized process of planning may be expected to improve the process of implementation of the plan. Our delivery system is not only weak but also corrupt, leading to a leakage of resources. Suspicious of the states. Rajiv Gandhi decided to release resources directly to the local bodies. This was resented by state governments. Actually, the machinery of administration at both at the local and stae level will have to be more efficient in the implementation of plan programmes. Unfortunately, the politicization of civil service has weakened their role as instruments of plan implementation. Administrative reforms, therefore, have to go hand in hand with economic reforms and reforms in planning.

PART - II
GLOBALISATION

19

MANAGING IN A GLOBAL ENVIRONMENT

Globalisation has become the keynote of human existence as humanity stands at the threshold of a new century and a new millennium.

Not that globalization was never known to humanity. As a philosophical concept it was the ideal of Indian Civilization from the ancient times pithily conveyed by our motto of *'Vasudhaiv Kutumbakam'* - the whole world is our family.

But today's globalization is not so much a philosophical concept or an attitude of mind as a concrete economic reality :

Historical Background

To understand today's reality of globalised world, we must go over the tremendous transformation that has taken place over the twentieth century.

At the beginning of the twentieth century also, there was a global system formed by the imperial powers. England, France and Holland and to a lesser extent Portugal and Spain, the original imperial powers, had carved out their empires all over the world. In the heydey of British imperialism at the beginning of the twentieth century it used to be said that the 'Sun never set on the British Empire'. While Canada, Australia and New Zealand were British colonies formed by migration of people from the so called 'Mother Country'. India, the jewel in the crown of the British empire, Burma, Ceylon, Malaya, Singapore, Hongkong, Nigeria, Tanganyika, Zanzibar, Ghana and several Caribbean and Pacific islands were countries of the coloured and black people which were conquered by the British in search of trade and later on ruled as a 'White man's burden' as a civilizing mission. French who were beaten by the British in the struggle to conquer India, had never the less had a far flung empire in Asia and Africa. The Dutch defeated the British to rule over Java and Sumatra now known as Indonesia. The colonies were exploited for the prosperity of the ruling powers.

The two new European nations Germany and Italy missed the 'imperial banquet' because of their late arrival. The two world wars of the twentieth century were fought between the established imperial powers and ambitious Germany who along with the axis powers – Japan and Italy during World War II challenged their hegemony. Behind these wars, was the desire to establish economic dominance. USA stood behind Britain and France. The decisive defeat of Germany and their axis powers finally fulfilled imperial ambitions.

The end of the World War-II marked the end of the era of imperialism. It began with the liberation of India on Aug. 15, 1947 and ended when fifty years later the British left Hongkong.

The newly liberated countries became masters of their own destiny. They could be expected to use political freedom as the instrument of economic development and social changes for improving levels of living of masses of its poor people. They came to be known as 'Developing Countries'. They expected the First and Second World to lend a helping hand with economic and technological existence to support their development plans, programmes and projects.

The end of World War –II also saw the emergence of global Institutions – The UNO and its affiliate bodies like FAO, WHO, ILO, UNESCO and UNICEF and the two specialized institutions – The IBRD (World Bank) and the IMF. The third world expected their help for development.

However these world institutions did not work for 'One World'. Rather, there were the so called three worlds – the First World consisting of the USA, Canada, the European Countries, Australia and New Zealand; the Second World of socialistic countries headed by erstwhile Soviet Union and comprising Eastern European power, China, Vietnam and North Korea; and the Third World of the countries of Asia and Africa which had newly attained freedom.

The latter half of the twentieth century was marked by a prolonged cold war between the two powerblocks headed by the two superpowers – USA and USSR. They represented two alternative economic systems – the capitalist and the socialist. Kruschev, head of Soviet Russia, vowed to 'bury capitalism' in course of his address to UN while President Reagan of USA was determined to 'end the evil empire'. Finally, the struggle ended in a decisive victory for capitalism – with the collapse of socialism and disintegration of Soviet Union.

As the only surviving superpowers, USA is now engaged in shaping the world according to its own design and promoting its own interests. It acts as the 'Supreme', brooking no challenge to its dominance. It is using international institutions to promote its own policies to shape the whole world – its economy, values and culture – in its own image.

The 'Second World' has ceased to exist while the 'Third World' is unable to speak with one voice. The NAM has weakened. Many of its members have come under the American influence. USA has changed its attitude towards China; USA seeks to 'engage' it rather than 'contain' it.

The global scene has become unpolar. And yet, some intellectuals talk of 'multi-polar' of 'Polycentric' world with European Union, Russia, China, Japan and India apart from USA shaping the global scene.

Global Institutions

The 'global environment' today is created by a number of Institutions and policies.

The United Nations Organisation (UNO) and its various affiliate Institutions have been part of the process of globalisation from their inception. For the past five decades the UN has been at the forefront of international effort to creat a new world – defining needs, outlining policies, sharing experience, talking and supporting action to reduce poverty, eradicate disease, promote food security, raise nutritional standards, abolish illiteracy and ignorance, create employment opportunities, promote universal immunization, address to the needs of women and children, contribute to family planning and balanced population growth, protect environment and promote sustainable human development.

Towards Liberalisation

But the new era of globalisation has also seen a marked departure of macro-economic policy from the 'statism' to liberalization – at both national and international levels. The collapse of the socialistic economy in the erstwhile USSR was followed by a desperate attempt in Russia and the Eastern European countries, to dismantle the elaborate structure of state planning and state ownership of means of production and introduce market economy and private enterprises in which they have not yet been successful. The crisis of transition has assumed an acute form especially in Russia. China did better. From 1978 onwards, under the reformist leadership of Deng Ziao Ping, China while retaining the political stranglehold of the Communist party, has introduced series of reforms towards capitalistic market economy. The Third World countries especially India, Sri Lanka and several Latin American Countries had taken to the path of industrialization through import substitution or Autarky and public or para-statal enterprises. The approach did not succeed in bringing about rapid economic growth. Instead it led to economic stagnation, low productivity and non-competitive economy. In the eighties, the Latin American countries beginning with Mexico were caught in a deb trap. The economy had to be salvaged through massive support from the IMF and the World Bank. But the support was conditional. The countries had to undergo a structural adjustment programme (SAP). The key elements of SAP were – fiscal discipline (i.e. reduction of fiscal deficit and public expenditure), privatization of para statal enterprises, removal of subsidies, deregulation, opening up of the economy by removing or reducing custom barriers and exchange controls. Several economies in Africa had also sought IMF assistance, which was conditional on SAP. In

1991 India too faced a crisis of balance of paymens and was compelled to seek assistance from IMF which was forthcoming on acceptance of similar SAP, IMF medicine was the same-irrespective of differences in the economic circumstances and consequences of SAP. SAP clearly reflected the economic philosophy of USA and other Western European countries. The people of the countries on which SAP was forced had to undergo privation in the shape of reduced welfare following cut in subsidies and austerity measures, closure of domestic enterprises and consequent unemployment, growing inequality and inflation. In Russia, capitalism has even led to widespread economic crisis. And yet there seems to be no going back from the liberalization of the economy.

Modern Era of Globalisation

The aim of the liberalization of natural economics is to enable them to participate in an 'interdependent world economy' towards which USA has moved relentlessly by influencing several world fora. National economics are getting increasingly integrated with the world economy. The process of integration has the following major elements –

(i) *Globalisation of Trade*

Free flow of goods and services – An International system of free trade is the foundation of economic interdependence. Multilateral and regional agreements and groups have supported market expansion. Invigorated by buoyant trade, the global economy has grown rapidly. The WTO was established in January 1995 to administer multinational trade agreements negotiated by its member countries. The Uruguay Round multilateral trade negotiations led to significant reduction in both tariff and non-tariff barriers to trade in goods and services. In 1947 the average tariff on manufactured imports was 47%; with full implementaion of Uruguay round it would be 3%. Spurred by the fall of trade barriers, global trade grew 132 fold in the post war period. It is expected to grow 6% annually in the next 10 years. The WTO embodies principles, policies and rules to promote free flow of international trade. It requires its members to ensure that trade policies are largely non-discriminatory and their rules and procedures transparent. It provides legal mechanism and dispute settlement procedures for resolving conflicts regarding trade matters between the member states and can no longer block the establishment of arbitration panels or ignore their findings. There is provision for appeal but decision of the appellate body is final. Every stage in the process is subject to strict time limits and countries that fail to comply to this face authorized trade sanctions. Developing countries are availing WTO's dispute settlement process far more often then they did under GATT.

(ii) *Globalisation of Investment and Free Flow of Capital and Finances :*

The era of liberalization has witnessed tremendous increase in direct and portfolio investment. Countries are removing restrictions on cross-border movements of capital. The number of countries with liberal capital regimes has grown from nine to thirty in the past two decades. World war capital flows – private and official have expanded. Controlled exchange rate polices have given way to market determined flexible competitive exchange rates.

Recent years have seen dramatic increase in capital flows. Foreign direct investment increased six folds over the level for 1981-85. In reached $ 315 bilion in 1995. Even more dramatic is the increase in the daily turnover in world's foreign exchange market which increased from $ 1 b to $ 1.2 trillion, following per capital account convertibility of currencies.

(iii) *Globalisation of Entrepreneur and Management :*

Multinational corporations have become the dominant performers in the global economy. The 350 largest corporations now account for 40% of global trade and their turnover, wealth and economic power exceeds the GDP of many countries. The wave of mergers and acquisitions crossing natural boundaries has brought into existence mega-corporators.

The operations of global enterprises are worldwide. In the words of Aditya Birla, the first Indian entrepreneur to have faith in globalisation – 'We produce staple fibre in Thailand, for which we buy pulp in Canada. The fibre made in Thailand is sent to Indonesia for converting to yarn. The yarn is exported to Belgium where it is made into carpets which are exported to Canada'. Thus, modern managementlies in internatinal networking. For such worldwide operations, cross national managers are becoming increasingly important. They are expected to improve efficienty by integrating national operations into worldwide productive enterprise. An example of cross-national management is the Ford Motor Company which recently embarked on an integrated global strategy that tries to link the company's far-flung operations in America, Europe and Asia in a tightly knit web of product development, supply chain and sales and marketing activities.

(iv) *Globalisation of Technology*

Miraculous advances in computer and communication technology has enabled lightening speed in transactions. Countries and companies have to respond rapidly if they are not to be left behind. Communications have become much easier and cheaper. The internet, the take off point for the information's super highway, is now used by 50 million people with the number of subscribers doubling every year. The 'internet' has not only made communications easier and cheaper than before; it is changing the ways corporations are run and they market services and products. Internet is making it possible even for the smallest company to compete on a level playing field with large multinationals. Between 1940 and 1970 the cost of international telephones fell by 80% and between 1970-1990 by 90%. Telecommunications traffic is expanding by 20$ every year. Transport costs have also fallen. Between 1920 and 1990 maritime transport costs fell by more than two-thirds. Between 1960-90. operating cost of world airlines per mile fell by 60 Percent. Truly, the world is shrinking.

(v) *Globalisation of Culture :*

Today a global culture is emerging through many media – music, movies, books, TV, Videos. International ideas and values are being mixed up with and superimposed on national ideas and values leading to revolutionary developments in styles of living. The USA exports more than 120,000 hrs. of TV programmes a year. Global trade in programming is growing more than 15% a year. Popular culture exerts more powerful pressures than ever before. From Manila to Managua, Beirut to Bejing in the East, West, South and North, styles in dress (jeans, hairdos, T-shirts), sports, music, eating habits and social and cultural attitudes have become global trends.

(vi) *Globalistion – A New Era of Imperialism :*

Globalisation trends described above have not always worked in favour of the poorer countries. Richer countries are gainers and poorer countries are losers. The latter come under growing dominance of the rich and advanced countries. Some of the specific ways by which this has happened are noted below :

(a) *Expanding Trade Opportunities*

(i) Liberalisation has benfits as well as costs. The benefits are in the shape of increased global income resulting from trade expansion, and greater efficiency and return on capital. Despite this, the least developed countries stand to lose up to $ 600 million a year; sub Saharan Africa $ 1.2 billion. The least developed countries with 10% of world's people have 0.3% of World Trade half their share two decades ago.

(ii) Producers in these countries are now exposed to international competition are unable to adopt international standards of quality control and process efficiency.

(iii) The terms of trade have been moving adversely against the poorer countries. They have suffered a cumulative decline of 50% since 1970s. – amounting to $290 billion between 1980 and 1991. Real prices of commodities produced by poorer countries in 1990 were 45% lower than those in 1980.

(iv) The Uruguay round table left intact most of the protection for industry and agriculture in industrial countries while ignoring issues of vital concern to poorer countries. For goods with greater potential for poorer countries such as textiles, leather and agricultural commodities, tariffs remain high. Higher tariff on processed goods than raw material locks the countries in volatile primary commodity markets.

(v) Industrial countries have increasingly switched to non tariff barriers like quotas, anti-dumping measures, voluntary export restraints and insistence on labour are environmental standards, thus evading the spirit of Uruguay round table. Countries exporting textiles and clothing – like Bangladesh, Sri Lanka and Africa and Latin America– are subject to specific quotas.

(vi) Industrial countries have been heavily subsidizing their agricultural exports – roughly half the value of agricultural exports of these countries. This not only restricts the exports of agricultural commodities by the developing countries, it keeps world prices of agricultural commodities low which reduces incentives. Poorer food deficit countries are forced to spend half their foreign exchange on food imports.

(b) Flow of Capital

(a) Most of foreign direct investment goes to the 'industrial triad'– North America, Europe and Japan. Together with 8 Chinese coastal provinces and Beijing, these countries receive more than 90% of FDI leaving less than 10% for developing countries. The flows of FDI are skewed.

(b) Poorer countries suffer from unfavourable terms of finance with inferior credit ratings and expectations of national currency depreciation, they had to pay interest rates that were four times as high as those charged to rich countries. Subsaharan African countries transfer to Northern creditors they spend four times on the health of the people. Debt payments suck up 20% of exports earnings. The pressure on meagre foreign exchange resources of these countries diminishes ability to import and increases dependence on aid at a time when aid itself in under pressure.

(c) *Flow of Technology*

The Uruguay Round enforced the protection of patents and other intellectual property rights – increasing cost of technology transfer to developing countries. Industrial countries in their own early phases of development, expected free flow of ideas and technology. In the 19th century, the USA adopted and developed European technologies with little regard to patent rights. After World War II Japan did much the same with US technology. Now these same countries are enforcing policies that will impose steep licensing charges on developing countries for using foreign technology. In knowledge – intensive global economy, access to technology on reasonable terms is vital for taking advantage of globalisation.

(d) Flow of People

The poorer countries also suffer from unfavourable terms for the flow of people. Even countries founded on immigration like USA, Australia and Canada are becoming choosy regarding immigration from developing countries. They give permission to immigration of highly skilled people, causing brain drain from developing countries.

Globalisation is thus working largely for the benefit of the more dynamic and powerful countries in the North and the South. An era of new imperialism seems to be emerging at the beginning of the 21st Century.

20

DISENCHANTMENT WITH GLOBALISATION

As the new century and the new millennium dawned, globaliston appeared to be the key to the future of humankind ushering in an era of unprecedented progress and prosperity. Globalisation held the promise to give the entire humanity the blessing of breathtaking breakthrough of technology. Globalisation was to create a single borderless world in which national sovereignty would become an out of date concept and goods and services, industry and trade, capital and investment would flow freely across boundaries of nations without any hindrance, without any physical or fiscal barriers. The whole world would be one free market governed not by laws and regulations of each nation, but by fair rules laid down by international institutions like the IMF, the World Bank and the WTO. Deeply buried was the concept of the New International Economic Order (NIEO) of the seventies purporting to be the charter for the third world countries. The latter would now join the first world countries in the processes of globalisation based on the basic principles of free market. These processes of globalisation appeared to be unchallenged as they had the sanction of the so called 'Washington consensus' between the USA, the sole super power of the world (especially the treasury department) and its associates in the G-7 countries, the international financial and trade instutions, and the multi-nationals most of them located in the first world countries. The main purpose of the former two was to subserve the interests of the latter. The 'Washington consensus' came to be known as market fundamentalism which had been propounded for many years by economists like Fredrick Von Hayek and Milton Friedman and whose doctrines inspired the policies of the first world rulers like

Ronald Reagen and Margaret Thatcher who aggressively pursued those doctrines to the exclusion of any traces of socialism. The disintegration of the Soviet Union in 1989 made the road free for the untrammelled onward march of the doctrine of market fundamentalism. Some of the third world countries like India who had chosen to follow the path of planned economy were also compelled to adopt the doctrine of the free market in the name of economic reforms as advocated by international institutions which with characteristic arroganced imposed on the entire third world the policies to promote free economy. It was firmly believed that it was only by pushing these policies that the third world countries can develop the competitive capacity to survive and succeed in the era of globalisation and enjoy the fruits of economic prosperity as already enjoyed by the capitalist countries of the first world.

A decade after the process of globalisation started, it is being slowly realized by the third world countries that the promise has not been fulfilled and they are nowhere near the prosperity that was supposed to be in store for them. The manna has not fallen from the heaven of globalisation. On the other hand, they seem to have lost whatever they had gained through planned and deliberate process of economic development and social change. Jeremy Breche, Tim Costello and Brendan Smiths have succinctly summed up both the processes of globalisation as their impact on the fortunes of the third world countries. The main processes are as follows :

1. The spread of free market capitalism to all corners of the globe covering virtually every country of the world.
2. The emergence of multinational corporations viewing the entire world as a single market in which they buy and see goods, services and labour through new corporate forms– strategic alliances, trans national mergers, global outsourcing, captive suppliers and supplier chains. They have managed concentration of control with decentralization of production. They have pressed ino service the new technologies of computers, satellite commkunication and the internet and removed the barriers to economic integration of their world-wide operations. A

more recent development is the new trend in the operations amongst the successful corporations like Nike, Intel, Tommy Hillfigers, and Microsoft is not to produce goods but brand and contract out actual manufacturing to sweat shops in the under developed world where labour is exploited by making workers work long hours at abysmally low wages while the multinationals enjoy astronomical growth in their wealth. The global institutions, viz. The WTO, the World Bank and the IMF and similar institutions at regional level have developed greater power and have used it to accelerate the globalisation process.

3. International capital markets have globalised with more than $ 1.5 trillion daily flowing across international borders.
4. Globalisation has reduced the power of the nation states in the third world countries to serve the interest of their own people through policies to promote full employment or social protection or to regulate corporations. They are perforce required to pursue policies of fiscal discipline, deflationary austerity so as to curtail the welfare programmes and promote privatization, deregulation, and an open economy.
5. Globalisation has ushered in 'a destructive competition' which has forced the countries of the third world to introduce policies resulting in cut in wages, weakening labour organization, and offer of more and more incentives by way of reduction of social and environmental costs so as to attract capital investment.

The consequences of these processes of globalisation have been as follows :

1. *Growing Impoverishment :* According to 1999 Human Development report more than 80 countries have per capita income lower than they had a decade and more ago. Some 1.2 billion people now live in extreme poverty. Global unemployment is approaching one billion.

2. *Growing inequalities :* Globalisation had led to growing concentration of wealth. The assets of the three richest people were more than the combined GNP of the 48 least developed countries. Indigenous people in the third world countries have lost their economic resources to the global corporations. The downward pressure of globalisation has discriminated against the vulnerable groups including women and indigenous people. Within USA itself wages have stagnated at the low end level over more then two decades and the richest man in USA has wealth equal to that of the 40% American people.

3. *Instability :* This has especially been caused by financial deregulation and capital market liberalization which has reduced barriers to the international flow of capital and resulted in dangerous and disruptive financial volatility.

4. *Environmental destruction :* caused by overexploitation of natural resources by multinational corporations and promotion of untested technology such as pesticide and genetic engineering. The oil refineries, the chemical plants, steel mills and other factories of global corporations have been the main sources of green house gases, ozone depletion and the toxic pollution.

5. *Degradtion of Democracy :* Globalisation has greatly increased the power of the global corporations vis a vis the national, state and local government. Corporations are able to dictate policies to governments backed by the threats of delocation. The authority of government has also been undermined by international financial institutions and the one sideds agreement forced by them.

6. *Fall in the ethical standards* : The growing domination of the market and deregulation and liberalization have promoted virulent individualism and fall in ethical standards. The spate of business scandals in the USA (Enron, Andersen@world.com) and the growth of crony capitalism 'in the developing and newly industrialised countries are pointers in that direction. The chief executives have lost the concept of right and wrong

because it has no place in the market. The CEO's have started feeling 'I can take out as much out of the till as I can and treat my subordinates as I please'.

Response to Globalisation

The Governments of the third world countries though accountable to their own people have been slow to take steps to reduce the hardships of the people lest their policy initiative should attract the ire of the international financial institutions. The protest against globalisation has been initiated by a number of voluntary organizations active in different countries of the world both in the North and the South. From the protests in Seatile against WTO in 1999 to the protests in Genoa against the G-7 Summit in 2001 in which 21 year young worker Carlo Guilliani died, the popular protests have only gained momentum. People from the first and the third worlds worked side by side in Seattle in 1999 to oppose a new round of WTO. Major demonstations were held in Washington DC in April 2000 against the unjust policies of the World Bank and the IMF. The Trade Unions, the environmentalists and Human Rights Organisations protested against the plans for Free Trade Area of the Americans and proposed social and economic alternatives to FTA. At The Earth Summit in Rio De-Janeiro in 1992 the NGOs pushed for agreements to control green house gases. In 1994 at the time of World Bank's anniversary the NGOs launched a campaingn – "50 years is enough". In 1998 an adhoc coalition of consumer right activists and environmentalists joined together to sink the Multilateral Agreement on Investment (MAI). More than 500 organisations from more than 60 countries signed the turn around agenda – shrink or sink for the WTO. The World Social Forum at Porto Alegre 2002 – Feb. 1-5. was the latest of the NGO initiative which attracted 70,000 participants including 15000 delegates from 5000 organisations belonging to 150 countries. It eloquently demonstrated that the world wide movement against the globalisation is alive and growing.' They made a plea for a broader international participation in decision – making in WTO. World Bank and the IMF. There was a consensus against foreign debt payment by the poorest third world countries. Despite the agreements on many issues, different approaches were visible at the forum. The academic participants and the intellectuals wanted negotiations with the international financial institutions for humanizing globalisation through reforms of these institutions while the radicals wanted mass mobilization of popular power for transformation of property rights and social relations of production. They wanted globalisation from below to counter globalisation from above. They wanted representative grass root assemblies and action such as that of the Brazilians workers party which runs the Porto Alegre city and has made a success of its public budget assemblies in which the entire population participates. Some of the NGO's were anti-globalisation while others stood for an alternative pattern of globalisation. Both the approaches – reformist and radical hold promise that some of the abuses in the name of globalisation dominated by G-7 countries would be eliminated in not too distant a future.

Reformist Agenda – International Financial Institutions

A variety of international organizations came into existence after the World War II to end once and for all the catastrophes from which the world suffered during the first half of the twentieth century. The first objective was to ensure peace and security and to create a world without war, a world in which differences amongst nations would be resolved through negotiations and not through an armed conflict. That was provided by the forum of United Nations in which all the countries of the world are members. However, the executive of the United Nations viz. Security Council is dominated by the five countries who are permanent members and who exercise veto rights. In more recent years, the UNO appears to have marginalized by the sole super power USA who has increasingly resorted to unilateralism backed by its enormous military strength which is more than that of other countries put together. It is USA rather than UNO which has started talking on behalf of 'the international community'.

The other major objective was to promote economic prosperity and stability so that people of the world need not suffer from deprivation and enjoy a higher standard of living. It was with this goal in view that the twin institutions viz. International Monetary Fund (IMF) and the International Bank for

Reconstruction and Development (IBRI) popularly known as theWorld Bank were brought into existence at the UN Monetary and Financial Conference at Bretton Woods. New Hampshire, USA, July 1944. During the inter war period there was a great deal of economic instability with violent currency fluctuations and the Biritish Pound had to go off the gold standard. The burden of reparation led to hyper inflation in Germany. The protectionist trade policies which came to be known as 'begger may neighbour policy' led to competitive shrinkages of the economies in several countries. This ultimately led to the Great Depression of 1930 which enveloped the whole world and led to unprecedented increases in unemployment. It was against this background that the famous British economist J.M. Keynes formulated his general theory of employment. The practical policy prescription of the theory was maintenance of adequate aggregate demand. Keynes was an important participant at Bretton Woods Conference and his ideas were reflected in the design and role of the twin institutions. The IMF was to provide the liquidity to the nations so that they could cope with the temporary setbacks in balance of payment and protect their currencies. The World Bank was to provide investment funds for the reconstruction of the war shattered economies of the western world and the development of the newly emerging underdeveloped countries of the world. As it happened, the reconstruction of Europe was taken care of by the Marshall plan and the World Bank was left with the responsibility for the development of the underdeveloped countries. In the beginning the bank funded large infrastructural projects. Later under MacNamara it started helping programmes for direct assault on poverty so as to bring families in the third world countries above the poverty line. It brought into existence a subsidiary organization called International Development Alliance (IDA) in 1960 to make loans to the underdeveloped countries on highly concessional terms. Its other subsidiary viz. International Finance Corporation (IFC) was there to give commercial loans for economically viable projects. The IMF gave special drawing rights to its member countries to serve as reserves in times of needs arising out of external deficits. Both the institutions appeared to be sympathetic to the concept of NIEO as put forward by G-77 countries in the seventies.

All this however underwent a metamorphosis in the eighties. Both these institutions from their very inception were under the control of the US and its allies because the voting pattern was based largely on the economic power of the member countries. It has been an unbroken convention that the President of the World Bank would always be an American while the Managing Director of the IMF a European. It all depended as to how the heads of USA and other rich countries chose to exercise their power over these two institutions. With Ronald Reagen as the President of USA and Margaret. That cher as the Prime Minister of UK, a new era began. Both preached free market ideology and wanted the twin institutions to use their clout to propagate and spread the free market or neo-liberal ideology throughout the world. There was change of guard in the World Bank in 1988 when Clausen became the new President and Ann Krueger became the new Chief Economist. They firmly believed in free market fundamentalism. Only free market can provide solution to the problems of the developing countries and reduce poverty and not the government whose market intervention only created problems. The economists in the World Bank under the leadership of Chenery who had shown how markets failed in developing countries and could not be expected to lead to development were shown the door. Both the institutions in new dispensation high handedly enforced a uniform structural adjustment programme (SAP) on all the developing countries in Latin America, Africa and Asia as a condition of aid irrespective of their different situations and problems. The policy makers of these countries, irrespective of their reservations, meekly accepted the SAP programme because they were in desperate need of resources. The main element in SAP were fiscal austerity, reduction of public expenditure on subsidies and welfare programmes, rise in interest rates, deregulation of private enterprise accompanied by privatization of public enterprise, free entry to foreign investment and capital account convertibility of foreign exchange. The SAP often led to the constriction of the economy, closure of local enterprises, growing unemployment, deprivation especially amongst the poorer strata of people and fall in their already low standard of living. The unfortunate people of these countries had the misfortune of being at the receiving end of SAP.

However, the sufferings of the common people were put aside with the argument that the pain of suffering was a price that had to be paid for creating the free market economy which alone in the long run can lead to economic efficiency and productivity. Competition in the free market economy was the sole panacea for growth in the long run. Keynes had said that 'in the long run we are all dead. But the ruling economists in the two institutions had no regard for the Keynesian diagnosis and solution which according to them had become obsolete and irrelevant. They completely forgot that it was the Keynesean vision which had brought the two institutions into existence out of the conviction that interventions were necessary for correcting the imperfections of the market which cannot be relied upon to maintain stability or to promote economic growth. They could not see the irony of their whole hearted support to the private enterprise when they themselves were public institutions. The US treasury was happy that the two institutions meekly fell in line with its economic philosophy and outlook.

But not everybody was blind to the disastrous consequences of the SAP policies of the two institutions. There were prominent economists who could see that 'the king has no clothes', that the policies of the twin institutions could not be supported either by sound economic theory or the empirical evidence available. Amongst them the most leading economist is Joseph Stinglitz who in his latest book has come out with scathing criticism of the policies of the two institutions. The policies have utterly failed in country after country in improving the lot of the poor people, in promoting economic stability and protecting the environment. Coming as it does from a former chief economist of the World Bank, former chairman of the President Clinton's council of economic advisors and the winner of the Nobel prize in economics, Stiglitz's criticism has weight and authority. Speaking with insider's knowledge, Stiglitz's book provides incisive case studies of several countries to show on one side the follies of the policies of the IMF and the World Bank, and on the other hand, the comparative success of those countries which showed the courage to resist the dictates of these institutions and chartered their own course.

The most prominent examples of the failure of he IMF's policies was in dealing with East Asia crisis in 1997-98 which almost resulted in global meltdown. The crisis which began with the collapse of the Thai Bath on July 1997, rapidly spread to Malaysia, Indonesia and South Korea and threatened the Japanese economy which was already suffering from stagnation for many years the Latin American countries which had already undergone a crisis in eighties and Russia which was desperately trying to make the transition from socialism to capitalism. The countries which remained unscathed were China and India which had not yet fully followed the IMF advice of capital account convertibility and Malaysia which boldly rejected the IMF's prescription for dealing with the crisis. The IMF had failed to anticipate the Asian crisis and was in fact an admirer of the rapid economic progress made by the Asian economic tigers. But the moment they were engulfed in a crisis, the IMF disowned all responsibility and refused to recognize it. The premature capital account convertibility under its advice was the cause of the crisis in the first instance and threw the entire blame on 'crony capitalism' which had eroded the sound working of their banking and financial institutions. Stiglitz points out that East Asian countries had been successful in promoting growth despite the fact that they had not followed the dictates of Washington consensus. The governments in those countries had played a prominent role in promoting high savings and investing them in development. This lead to the 'Asian miracle' in the form of unprecedented increase in income and reduction of poverty. The whole region became an economic power house. They followed the strategy of export promoted growth and only after it was firmly established did they gradually liberalise their economies. This progress suffered a jolt when the Asian economic crisis struck. The hot money which came with liberalized market was suddenly withdrawn when the real estate market in Thailand crashed and this triggered the crisis. In dealing with this type of crisis concrete action should have been taken to impose capital controls. But the IMF would not allow this to be done. But Malaysia risked the wrath of the IMF and put a break on the rapid flow of the speculative money out of the country with the result Malaysia's downturn was shorter. The IMF and the World Bank came out with a big package for saving the Asian tiger economies in crisis. South Korea received $ 55 b. Indonesia $ 33b and Thailand $ 17 b. But this huge bail out package was as in the case of Latin American countries, used to repay the loans borrowed from the western bankers by the firms who had been engaged in overheated real estate business. This no doubt prevented further currency crisis and sustained the exchange rate temporarily. Rich people inside the country took the advantage of the opportunity to convert their money into dollars at a favourable exchange rate. For receiving the bail – out of this sort, these countries had to follow the IMF prescription of cut backs in spending and hike in interest rates. The programme failed because the medicine did not work. The IMF criticized the countries for failing to take necessary measures and this criticim exacerbated the stampede of capital out of those countries. GDP plummeted, unemployment soared, and poverty rapidly increased. The slow down in the region had global repercussions. Prices of natural commodities fell and countries from Russaia to Nigeria which depended on natural resources were in deep trouble. The IMF sponsored financial restructuring involved closure of weak banks. The shut down of a large number of banks in Indonesia and Thailand left business without access to credit. The effects on the Indonesian banking and economy were particulary disastrous. On the other hand, South Korea ignored the IMF advice and rather than closing down banks recapitalised its two largest banks and this helped in relatively quick recovery of the Korean economy. Thailand languished for a longer time and has not yet recovered. By following the advice of IMF to drastically cut food and fuel subsidies, Indonesia invited social and political turmoil in the shape of street riots which further shook business confidence and drove out capital. Stiglitz blames the IMF for mishandling the Asian economic crisis. Because of its wrong advice, the Asian crisis was more severe than it should have been. He specifically blames the IMF for reflecting the interests and the ideology of Western financial community rather than the well being of the people of those countries. According to Stiglitz the crisis could have been handled by a stand still on existing debt repayment and maintenance of the flow of finance. The IMF concentrated as in the case of Latin American countries on large bail out strategies which went to help the foreign creditors rather than maintain the level of economy and employment. A particularly nasty example of the ways of the IMF was the how it stifled the Japanese initiative in 1997 to offer $ 100 b to help create an Asian Monetary fund in order to stimulate activity in crisis ridden East Asian countries. The US treasuries and IMF, while standing for competitive economy could not countenance competition in their own domain. They interpreted the initiative as a challenge to the American leadership and control.

The Indonesia case is particularly striking. It shows how a resource rich country can become a victim of machinations of the super power and the IFI under its control. Under Sukarno, the founding President, Indonesia had had few debts. He had thrown out the World Bank, limited the powers of oil companies and publicly told the Americans 'to go to hell' with their loans. But the big powers managed to overthrow him and place General Suharto in his place. Soon with US help he became a dictatorial ruler underwritten by them. Soon the big corporate giants major oil companies and banks parceled out the Indonesian economy amongst themselves in the name of aiding the rebuilding of the nation. Indonesia became the worst example of 'crony capitalism' where while President's family amassed wealth soaring cost of food and fuel and of the staple food rice were soaring and boiling water for drinking made lives of the common people very hard.

The failure of Russia to make a successful transition from socialism to market capitalism has turned out to be the worst example of IMF – World Bank policy directions. Instead of efficient market economy what Russia got was Mafia gangsterist economy. Stiglitz while blaming the Russian rulers specially Boris Yeltsin, who could not exonerate 'Western Advisors especially from US and and IMF who marched in so quickly to preach the Russians the gospel of the market economy.' They did not realise or perhaps chose to ignore the fact that Russia simply had no market institutions to run the market economy. They had first to be created but instead of that, they hustled the Russian rulers to undertake the radical economic reforms despite the advice of the Russian scholars to the contrary. Communist Russia had neither market entrepreneurship, nor the process of prices being determined forces of demand and supply in the market. Prices were simply set by government fiat. Prices for energy and natural resources were kept artificially low. There was no legal and regulatory framework, to ensure that banks and security markets operate in fair manner. Despite the absence of market institutions and regulatory framework the US treasury and the IMF forced to 'shock therapy' of privatization of all enterprises without the availability of the entrepreneurs. As a consequence, privatization led not to wealth creation but assets stripping by unscrupulous oligarchy to corner assets worth billions by using political influence after paying only a pittance. The sudden freeing of prices in 1992 set in motion severe inflation that wiped out the savings of the middle class. Since the prices of natural resources were kept low while other prices were completely freed, unscrupulous elements bought oil and sold to the West making billions of dollars. Such so called radical reform strategy was doomed to fail. The GDP in post 1989 Russia fell year by year. The devastation caused by these reforms was greater than what Russia suffered during World War II. Russian industrial production fell by over 60% during the late decade of the last century. The common man felt that the economic life under capitalism was worse than what the non Communist leaders had predicted. The devaluation of Russian Rouble might have helped the revival of the economy by improving the competitiveness of Russian production, but the IMF resisted it fearing that it would lead to hyper inflation. It was impossible to maintain Rouble at an artificially high rate. The IMF therefore pushed Russia in borrowing in foreign currency which Russia was unable to repay. Eventually Russia suspended repayment of the debt. Stiglitz holds IMF partly responsible for this bankruptcy. Stiglitz and his associates have questioned lending to Russia which was naturally a resource rich country. What was required was for the Russian government to introduce meaningful reforms such as collecting taxes from the companies. But such was the hight of corruption in Russia that the funds instead of going to the state treasury were diverted to the families and associates of the corrupt officials. But IMF overlooked the corruption. After analyzing the Russian case Stiglitz concludes – 'seldom has the gap between expectations and reality been greater than in the case of the transition from the communism to the market.'. The transition has greatly increased the number of the poor but allowed the few at the top to prosper. The middle class was perhaps the hardest hit and felt that migration to the West was their best option. Russia today has a level of inequality compared to the worst in the world. It got the worst of all possible worlds – an enormous declining output and an enormous increase in inequality. The IMF officials who applied 'Washington consensus' policies failed to appreciate the social context of the transition economies. What Russia needed was not shock therapy but gradual reforms advocated by many thinking people in Russia and outside economists like Stiglitz.

In marked contrast to Russia's failure, was the striking success of another Communist country viz. China which grew at an average rate of over 10% in 1990s. as compared with Russian decline at an average annual rate 5.6%. The reform process in China was gradual. It began in agriculture. There was not complete privatization but only a partial one under the individual responsibility system under which the produce in excess of the quota could be sold in the free market. The communists the freed from the responsibility of managing agriculture, concentrated on creating millions of new enterprises in villages and towns. China also created an institutional infrastructure in the shape of an effective securities and exchange commission, bank regulation and safety nets. It re-structured old state owned enterprises and downsized bureaucracy. Such reforms made China an attractive place to invest and China became the largest receipient of foreign direct investment.

Stiglitz's book does not extensively deal with the case studies of Latin American countries but – Mexico, Brazil, Argentina and many other which were the first to be administered the IMF medicine of SAP. These countries ran into heavy external debts, running into billions of dollars because of the profligacy of their rulers – many of them military dictators. Stiglitz however makes several references to the situation in Argentina which was long held up by the IMF as the poster child of reform because of its success of holding down inflation despite a double digit unemployment for years. Contractionary monetary and fiscal policy in Argentina led to unrest and caused political and social turmoil. Currently Argentina is going through a crisis. The contractionary fiscal policies insisted upon by IMF has pushed the economy into an even deeper recession. The bail out of $ 21.6 b. extended by IMF to Argentina has not served the purpose. The IMF encouraged Argentina to peg its currency peso to the dollar but this artificial pegging has worsened the situation. In the last few months, the leaders of the G-7 and the IMF have been forcing the government that followed the overthrow of President de la Rua more than six months ago not only to allow unrestricted free trade and to reduce public expenditure, but also to change internal laws and take other measures to benefit some individual bankers and foreign companies. While America has increased subsidies to agricultural production it and the IMF are preaching free trade to Argentina. This has infuriated public opinion there. In the arrogant style of the IMF vis-a-vis the third world countries, John Thorton the head of the mission in Buenos Aires had the cheek to openly say that the Argentinean Central Bank must stop selling dollars to keep inflation to control for those dollars are the property of the IMF. IMF has in the past lent endless amount to Argentina's most repressive regimes – the bloody dictatorships between 1976 and 1983 and to the most corrupt Menem presidency which implemented the IMF prescribed neo-liberal measures and privatizations schemes. Now variety of progressive groups in Argentina are united against the repressive tide under President Duhalde who took office in January 2002. The brutal attacks of his regime have taken a toll of more than 30 lives since December 2001. President Duhalde has in the face of massive demonstration decided to anticipate the next election which will be held in March 2003 instead of September 2003 as scheduled.

Brazil used to have one of the fastest growing economies in the world. During 1960 to 1980 its per capita income grew by 1.1%. But in the two decades since 1980 it has hardly grown, at a total of about 5% for the whole period. These are the decades of the 'Washington consensus' an era of economic failure well known throughout Latin American and most of the developing world. Washington panacea of replacing various economic development strategies with the standard formula of opening trade and financial flows, privatization of state enterprises and high interest rates has failed to produce the promised rewards and instead has led economic stagnation in the Latin American countries.

While the IMF and the World Bank authorities are prepared to shower largesse on Latin American dictators, they stymie well meaning and well considered efforts of genuine leaders of some developing countries. Stiglitz gives the example of Ethiopia and its Prime Minister Meles who assumed power after leading a seventeen years guerrilla war against the bloody Marxist regime of Mengistu Haile Mariam and embarked upon the hard efforts of rebuilding of his country. Meles combines personal integrity with intellectual capacity and knowledge of economies. He showed that with right policies in place, even poor African countries could experience sustained economic growth. He had formulated a rural development strategy focusing on 80% of population living in the rural sector. But he had problems with IMF who wanted that in the interest of the sound budgetary position, the development expenditure should be limited to tax revenues and not met out of foreign assitance which it argued may dry up at any time. Stiglitz felt after his visit to Ethiopia that IMF's position was utterly absurd. The foreign donors had given money for constructing new schools and health clinics and for that the country was not beholden to IMF. The IMF also insisted on opening the up the banking system to foreign competition. Ethiopia resisted the IMF demand since this would have had a devastating effect on rural credit. But instead of understanding the situation IMF concluded that Ethiopia is not serious about reforms and suspended its programmes. Stiglitz persuaded the World Bank to triple its lending but it tok months before the IMF relented on its position though IMF according to Stiglitz was entirely wrong in insisting upon financial market liberalization. The IMF cast itself as the sole supplier of the sound advice and took 'one-size-fits-all' approach without understanding the local position. Another example that Stiglitz gives is that of Botswana. Here too the country was making steady progress under sound leadership but then a drought threatened the livelihood of many people and the recession took place. IMF did not come forward to finance deficits in resources. Kenya also suffered because of the IMF's insistence on high interest rates to curb inflation.

At the end of his case studies Stiglitz comes to the clear conclusion that it is high time that the twin institutions realize their mistaken approach of high handed imposition of market fundamentalism on the poor countries of the world on purely ideological grounds without understanding the problems of developments of those countries. They must go back to Keynesian vision and understanding which in the first instance had led to the creation of these institutions. From this point of view Stiglitz goes on to present his agenda for reforming the twin institutions.

1. International financial institutions should realize the danger of capital market liberalization and short term capital flows (hot money) and help the countries, in crisis to intervene effectively to deal with it.
2. Instead of huge financial bail outs to help the creditors, they must consider bankruptcy reforms and standstills.
3. Instead of financial sector deregulation they should aim at improving banking regulations to prevent unsound lending.
4. The IMF should pay greater attention to help the countries face the risk from the volatility of exchange rates.
5. They should help countries to improve safety net for the vulnerable sectors of the society.
6. The IMF should pay attention to the poverty and unemployment impact of their SAP.
7. IMF should tone down its conditionalities which have made it difficult for the developing countries to focus on their priorities. The IMF experts should give greater attention to the local experts who understand the local situation better rather than send its expert to make short visits to the capitals of the poor countries and pressurize the governments of those countries to agree to their preconceived reports.
8. IFIs should consider debt forgiveness in case of countries where the proportions of current export earnings for

repayment of loans to the developed countries is so high that they simply cannot grow.

Stiglitz believes that his agenda would help in reducing the discontent caused by the globalisation strategy of the IFI and would be a move towards globalisation with a more humane face.

Another kindred soul who like Stiglitz looks towards globalisation with a human face is the international financier George Soros. As a financier, he profited from his transactions in the global financial market, and made huge profits but is also the one who is the founder of global networks of foundations dedicated to the betterment of the poor and giving support to the establishment of the open society, specially in the third world and also addressing the ills of global capitalism caused by the movement of capital and the increasing domination of national economies by global financial markets and multinational corporations. He does not believe in market fundamentalism and does not approve of the encroachment of market values into areas to which they do not traditionally belong.

Soros identified several negative aspects of globalisation as it has progressed so far. First, the vulnerable sections of society in less developed countries have been hurt by globalisation in the absence of safety net. Second, globalisation has caused a misallocation of resources between private goods and public goods. As a result social needs have been ignored and environment hurt. Third, financial crisis has brought devastation to the developing economies. Soros, therefore, feels that reforms are needed in the working of the international finance and trade institutions. According to Soros the provision of public goods in poor countries needs to be greatly augmented. This requires adequate resources. But the resource transfer offered by the existing IFIs falls very much short of requirements. Thirty years ago Pearson Commission set the target of 0.7% of GDP by way of official development from the donor countries. Only five countries have met or exceeded the target by 20,000. The biggest culprit in the shortfall is USA whose contribution was only 0.1% To meet the shortfall, Soros has offered a novel solution. He proposes that the rich countries should donate their Special Drawin Rights (SDRs) for the purpose of providing international assistance to the developing countries. The amount so released could be used for a number of worthwhile projects for promotion of education and health services, fight against infectious disease and protection of environment. But for these resources to be properly useds there should be proper government free from corruption. These do not exist in many developing countries. The IFIs are obliged by their charters to go through government channels. Soros is in favour of Tobin tax to reduce volatility in currency market. Finally Soros is in favour of concessional loans and debt forgiveness for highly indebted poor countries. Joseph Stiglitz 'has commended the proposals made by Soros as 'a fair deal for the world'.

Reformist Agenda WTO

The WTO which came into existence in January 1995 has now joined the IFI in promoting globalisation on the lines of 'Washington Conscensus'. It is the commercial counterpart of the IFI. WTO did not come into existence immediately after World War II. What came into existence was GATT in 1947 which provided the framework for international trade. It took another 28 years for the WTO to be formed after protracted negotiations. First there was a Tokyo round from 1973-79 and then the Uruguay round from 1986-93 at Punta del Este on the Dunkel Draft. As many as eight round table conferences were held and the final draft was signed at Marakkesh in Morocco. As many as 117 countries then signed the draft. Their number has since gone to 134 and 30 more countries are engaged in the effort to join the WTO. China has recently become a member.

The experience of the inter war years made the Western countries realize the hazards of competitive protectionist policies which led to contractions in economies and consequent unemployment. The lesson was that individual nations should be prevented from pursuing such policies, by creating a world trade organization which should ensure that the gains of free international trade are made available to all the countries of the world. Free international trade, it was felt, would become, powerful instrument for the world economic prosperity. The benefits of technology and higher production would be available to the consumers around the world in the shape of better products and reduced cost of living.

Though the WTO is the successor to GATT, its scope is vastly expanded and covers agriculture, textile and services which were not in the ambit of GATT. Moreover it has taken up altogether new matters like trade related intellectual rights (TRIPS) and trade related investment measures (TRIM). The Singapore Conference introduced new subjects like competition and procurement by government. The developed countries have also been pressing for new round of negotiations.

The WTO was to introduce a multi-lateral trading system which would be free, competitive, fair, predictable and transparent Free trade meant that there would be no barriers like physical quotas, licenses or high custom barriers. A competitive trading system would require elimination of subsidies and dumping practices. A fair trading system would mean that the same rules would be applied to all and most favoured nation treatment be given to member countries. However, this would not mear elimination on the regional preferential agreements like NAFTA, EU or ASEAN. Also the interests of the poor countries and the need for special concessions to them would be taken into account. Predictable trading system would mean that there would be no; arbitrary changes and the transparent system would mean there would be written down rules.

Some of the basic principles of the rule based system of WTO were to be as follows :

1. Rules should be definite, there should be no vagueness about them.;
2. Legal sanctions for rigorous enforcement of rules so that they are applied in a non-discriminatory manner in all countries.
3. Ensuring that the trade policies of the nation are within the framework of rules laid down by WTO.
4. Despite settlement machinery in case of differences between nations.

The organization of WTO consists of :

1. *The Ministers council*: This consists of trade ministers from member countries. The council meets once in two years and takes unanimous decisions. The first conference was held in Singapore in 1996 which introduced new items like trade and investment, competition and government procurement. The second conference was held in Geneva where WTO headquarters are located. The conference considered the subject of e-commerce. The third was held in Seattle in 1999 which ended in a fiasco because of the massive demonstrations held against it by voluntary organisations. The fourth was held in Doha in 2001. It was expected to consider the issue of trade and development. To what extent the Doha conference satisfied the developing countries will be considered later in the article.

2. *General Council:* This consists of the Ambassadors of member countries based at Geneva, WTO headquarters. It is a policy reviewing body and also dispute settlement body.

Specialised Committees, working groups/ parties for discussion of specific agreements.

3. *Secretariat:* It consists of 500 experts and has the following duties to perform viz. (a) implementation of trade agreement (b) providing a forum for discussions between nations on trade issues (c) constitution of panels for the settlement of dispute. The number of disputes has gone up dramatically after the establishment of WTO. Throughout the GATT period from 1947-94 there were in all 300 disputes. In the short period since WTO was constituted the number has gone up to 200 (d) review of trade policies of member countries and (e) training and technical assistance. The Secretariat is not supposed to take policy decisions but in practice it has great influence behind the doors particularly its legal department.

Though member countries in the WTO have the same voting

rights unlike the IMF and the World Bank and therefore have a more democratic construction, in practice, there is a great imbalance. The rich countries with 85% of world trade have much greater influence on WTO activities than the underdeveloped countries with 80% membership. The secretariat is dominated by them and the experts on dispute settlement panel are those who toe the line of the rich countries. The WTO rules running into thousands of pages are extremely complicated and the developing countries find it difficult to muster the resources needed to build up skills in negotiations. The developed countries have taken full advantage of the weakness of developing countries to influence the WTO policies. Though in theory, the decisions are to be taken through a democratic process in which all have equal rights, in practice decisions are taken behind the doors by the rich countries in collusion with the secretariat and thrust upon the developing countries who are taken by surprise and are unable to present their considered views and are hustled to agree to the decision already taken by the rich countries. It is this method of decision making which has enabled the rich countries to put in clauses like green box and blue box, sanitary standards and intellectual property rights which have proved detrimental to the interests of the developing countries. The poor countries are too weak to resist the pressure and have lost the economic sovereignty to determine their own trade policies according to their requirements. Despite this, the poor countries cannot get out of the WTO system because they fear that the alternative may be worse and they may be left to deal with rich and powerful countries on their own.

Tariff Ceilings Restrictions

For introducing the free trade regime, the WTO wanted countries to remove physical quota restrictions. Tariff would be the only instrument of trade policy but that too within limits. Because of the delicate balance of payment situation in 1991, India was given time to remove the restrictions but USA and other countries complained to WTO that India's balance of payment situation has improved and India should be required to phase out the quota restrictions by 2001. India has accordingly removed quota restrictions for 1429 items by March 2001 of which 208 belong to the agricultural sector. This has already created difficulties for marketing the products of Indian agriculture and industry.

While tariffs do remain, there have to; be tariff cuts, of 40% in five years for developed countries and 30% in the five years in case of developing countries. WTO has also prescribed tariffs ceilings in the form of 'bound rates' 40% in case of finished products and 25% for intermediate products. In the case of agriculture sector the bound rate for India would be 100% for agriculture produce. 150% for processed products and 300% for edible oil. However, in case, the reduction in imports duties were to lead to the surge of imports or in the case of anti-dumping, import duties could be increased temporarily.

WTO Arrangements

WTO arrangements envisage 60 types of agreements – some of them general and others special. The agreement on agriculture came into effect from 1.1.1995. Fishery, forest products, rubber, jute, sisal and choir have been left out of the agreement. Under agreement the developed countries are required to reduce the import tariff by 36% in six years i.e. by year 2001 while the developing countries would have to reduce the same by 24% in ten years i.e. year 2005. The agreement also envisages that the developed countries will reduce the aggregate measure of support (AMS) by 36% in case of developed countries and 24% by the developing countries. However, the green box and blue box support is not included in the AMS. The green box support includes expenditure on research, infrastructure, disease control and protection of environment as well as income support. The blue box support refers to payment to farmers to limit their production. The exclusion of this payment gives undue advantage to agriculture business of the developed countries, but WTO justifies the exclusion on the ground that such expenditure would not affect trade. As a part of the effort to reduce AMS, subsidies would have to be reduced in the case of developed countries by 20% and developing countries by 13.3%. Finally market access has to be increased by 1995 by 5% in the case of developing countries and 3% in the case of developed countries. However, several countries have been able to get special treatment. For example, Japan, Korea, and Philippines have been able to wrest special concession for rice while Israel got special concession for whole milk powder, cheese and sheep meat. India has reduced to 0% import duties on milk powder, rice, wheat, millets and maize. But India has to see that Indian markets do not get flooded with imports which might give a permanent setback to Indian agricultural production.

Subsidies – The WTO arrangements envisage three types of subsidies viz. (1) Permissible non actionable subsidies. These include blue box and green box subsidies for basic research and other items which are used by developed countries to give advantage of agro-industries. Subsidies for the development of disadvantaged regions also come under this category. Subsidies by way of domestic support to promote diversification and investment also come in this category. (2) Permissible but actionable subsidies. These include subsidies specific to an enterprise to sector or location. (3) Prohibited subsidies. These include those which promote use of domestic inputs over imported inputs or those which are intended to promote export performance. The rationale is that such subsidies affect the natural flow of trade. However, these are likely to affect adversely the export promotion policies of developing countries. While developed countries under blue box and green box items can provide huge subsidies to their agriculture and agro-processing enterprise, the developing countries cannot avail of exprt subsidies. If blue box and green box subsidies are claimed by the developed countries, the developing countries should ask for 'food security subsidies and livelihood of farmer's subsidies'. India does not provide for production specific subsidies but only gives market price support for 22 crops. India's AMS is actually Rs. 2442 crores because the international prices of agricultural commodities are more than Indian prices. India does provide non-specific subsidies for seeds, fertilizers, electricity and agricultural product of the order of Rs. 4581 crores. India does not provide export subsidies. However, it exempts export profit from income tax. In addition for the export shipment of fruits, vegetable and floricultural products, cost of freight on export shipment is reimbursed.

Agreement on Textile and Clothing (ATC) - Under the multiple fibre agreement which came into force in 1974 developed countries can negotiate bilateral agreements to restrict the quantities of exports from developing countries. The restrictions are often defined in fine details. For example, USA defined 148 MFA categories in 1996 for purposes of restriction. These agreements have been detrimental to the developing countries. ATC envisages a phase out of MFAs between 1995-2005. Hopefully with this phase out, higher export targets for Indian textiles would be possible. World textile export may go up to $ 25 b and India with the share of 2.2% can export greater quantities of textile particularly of great cotton yarn in which India has a better comparative advantage.

Small Scale Industry – India's small scale enterprises will have to compete on their own under the WTO regime. They will find it difficult to survive with the removal of quota restriction because their product will have to compete with imported goods of high quality. Most of them are weak one man shows with low bargaining power. They must be given knowledge of WTO regime, they must be made aware of patents. They must be provided with strong data base. Their technology must be upgraded and their marketing strategy should be improved.

Agreement on Sanitary and Phytosanitary Measures – the agreement provides that all member countries must adopt international standards. WTO has held that in order to ensure that adoption of these standards would not act as a barrier to trade, developing countries would be provided reasonably long interval of time to establish these standards. However, this provision has already been used for blocking imports from India. India's tobacco exports are affected because they contain four points per million PPM DDT resedue whereas the USA and Japan insist on less than 1 PPM according to their national standards. USA has placed restrictions on export of shrimps from India, Pakistan, Thailand and Malaysia on the ground that they are not caught with turtle excluding devices (BS Chimney – legitimizing unilateral trade restrictions – EPW, Jan. 2, 2002). In this case the US has filed the dispute with WTO. The appellate body of WTO held that the member country may legitimately require as a conditional access of certain products to its market, that exporting countries commit themselves to regulatory programme comparable to its own. This would not violate the sovereign rights of exporting countries to determine their own sea turtle conservation policy. This is one of the example of how the northern states pressurize WTO's settlement bodies to interpret WTO provisions on such a manner as to allow unilateral action to bring in environment issues in trade to restrict exports from developing countries. WTO appellate bodies are bent to the political will of USA and Europe.

Trims – Under WTO rules five types of requirements are prohibited to be imposed as conditions for investment in developing countries i.e. (1) Local content requirement (2) restrictions on the use of import contents as a proportion to export. (3) restrictions on access to foreign exchange and relating it to foreign exchange earnings and (4) domestic sale requirement. Foreign direct investment is concentrated in a small number of multinational companies who use TRIMS to their advantage.

Trips – The Paris convention of 1967 provides twenty years as a patent period. Patenting all life forms including plants and micro-organism has become compulsory. Plant varieties are protected either by patents or by sui generis system. UPOV convention protects breeders rights. The patent law has to cover both processes and products. These provisions are meant to provide protection to fruits of R & D which leads to the creation of intellectual property through (1) patent (2) copyrights (3) trade marks (4) industrial designs and (5) lay out designs, India amended its patent act of 1970 in March 1999. And passed sui generis legislation to provide for farmer's traditional rights to save, use, exchange, share and sell his farm produce except where the sale is for reproduction under commercial conditions. The FDI agreements now incorporate huge royalty payment clauses relating to the use of patents. Vandana Shiva has opposed these patent legislations as nothing but an attempt to globalise American patent system and law to enable huge royalty payments to MNCs who are often the IPR holder companies. This drains resources of poor countries. Intellectual property exports of USA as a percentage of export has gone up from 10% in 1947 to 37% in 1986 and 50% in 1994. Patenting of life forms goes against the rights of plant breeders to exchange and biodiversity provided by UPOV. They invade our accumulated pool of indigenous knowledge developed and used for centuries. W.R. Grace and other such companies had tried to obtain patents for *neem, haldi, jamun, karela* and *amala* and hundreds of plants used for medicine. They have threatened through an intellectual piracy our rights over Basmati rice. Companies like Monsanto have by the introduction of termination seeds tried to end the natural chain. Genetically modified food has evoked resistance even in EU countries. Free flow of knowledge is blocked by the provisions providing intellectual property rights.

The 272 page study recently brought out by Oxfam under the title 'Rigged rule and double standards' is a comprehensive study of the way rich countries are rigging WTO rules to their advantage. Due to trade restrictions by rich countries on agriculture goods, between them, India and China are losing more than $2b. The report has formulated a double standard index which measures the gap between the free trade principle expounded by the rich countries and their actual protectionist policy. The worst offender in setting up unfair trade barriers is the Europeans Union which is followed closely by US, Canada and Japan. The total subsidies to domestic farmers in these countries is more than $ 1 b. a day. The overproduction and the resulting surpluses are dumped on world market with the help of more subsidies. Agriculture super powers are exporting at prices more than one third lower than the cost of production. The governments of the rich countries talk of their commitment to poverty reduction but use their trade policy to conduct what amounts to robbery against the world poor. Development countries exporting to rich country markets face barriers that are four times higher than those encountered by rich countries. The barriers cost the developing countries more than $ 100 b. a year – more than twice what they receive in aid. The study conclude that WTO's bias in favour of the self interest of the rich countries and big corporations raises the fundamental question about its legitimacy. By requiring countries receiving loans to reduce trade barriers, IMF and World Bank only strengthen the bias of the WTO. Oxfam is launching a campaign on the basis of its report on 144 countries. But it is for the poor countries themselves to counter the manipulation of the rich countries by fighting on the WTO forum against non-trade barriers like patent and investment conditions as imposed upon TRIPS and TRIMS. Non-tariff matters like sanitation, environment and labour raised in order to act as trade barriers and huge subsidies in the name of blue and green boxes. They have also to raise the fundamental issues of trade vs. development. Would the trade conditions have an adverse impact on development, employment and environment? The Doha Conference was the forum for the poorer countries to raise these issues. To what extent did they avail of this opportunity and with what success?

The fourth WTO ministerial conference was held in Doha, Qatar from Novemner 9-14, 2001. It was held against the backdrop of failure of the conference held two years earlier at Seattle, USA. Many commentators (Kamal Malhotra of UNDP, Barry Coastes and Dave Timms of World Development Movement and Chakravartay Raghvan of Third World Network) have felt that despite rhetoric to the country. Doha ministerial declaration does not adequately reflect the needs and aspirations of the developing countries. For agricultural and food exporting developing countries, the main negotiation objectives were to have the EU phase out all the export subsidies, Japan; the EU and the USA to dismantle trade – distorting support measures, tariff escalation and tariff peak and for wealthy countries to provide greater market access. The developed countries should have adopted a genuinely transparent approach to the negotiations. But this was lacking. The process responsible for forging the consensus left much to be desired. The developing country delegation had voiced numerous procedural concerns even before they arrived in Doha. These concerns turned out to be true. The draft ministerial text was presented as a clean, non-bracketed text by the Chairman of the WTO general council despite the fact that many developing countries had contested parts of it and had launched their strong protestations. The appointment of the so called 'Friends of the Chair' to aid in the negotiations compounded the fears of the developing countries since the friends selected were too sympathetic to the views of the Quad countries (USA, EU, Canada and Japan) and the WTO leadership. The friends used their discretion to decide whether the consultation process would be bi-lateral, pluri-lateral or open-ended. Delegations of many developing countries did not know when and where meetings of friends was taking place.

For developing countries heavily dependent on agriculture, food security was a crucial concern. They wanted a Development Box which would give the developing countries greater flexibility and autonomy in pursuing the agricultural policies serving their broader developing needs. The expected stronger support for special and differential treatment (S & DT) to the developing countries.

However, differing view on the draft agricultural text in Doha appeared to be insurmountable. The EU remained staunchly opposed to the phase of export subsidy and refused to budge until the last day of negotiations. The USA justified its own domestic income support to farmers. In the end EU agreed to 'reductions; with a view to phasing out all forms of subsidies but only in exchange for a stronger environment, investment, and competitions policy (the Singapore issues).

Another contentious issue was about TRIPS and its relationship to the public health. The developing countries emphasized the public health issue while the developed countries led by USA wanted to limit the public health provision only to pandemics such as HIV – AIDS, Tuberculosis and Malaria. The USA resisted the negotiated settlement until the end. The final separate statement gave some flexibility to developing countries and this was considered to be some victory for them.

The USA did not want any restrictions on the export of genetically modified (GM) food, while the EU was keen on food safety and hygiene concerns. The EU got a commitment to start negotiations on the relationship between WTO rules and trade obligations in multilateral environment agreement (MEA) and elimination of tariff and non-tariff barriers to environment goods and services.

The developing countries wanted that before agreeing to a new round, the outstanding implementation issues should be addressed to. This request was rejected by industrialist countries who insisted that all issues should be addressed to only in the context of new negotiations. Ultimately the developing countries registered a modest gain when it was agreed that all implementation issues must be resolved by the end of 2002. Enhanced textile access was one of the implementation issues. It was rejected and opposed by the USA, Canada and EU. Finally there was no real commitment on textile though it remained in the agreed ministerial implementation text.

The EU pressed for immediate negotiations on Singapore issues while about a hundred developing countries wanted to continue studying these issues till the next ministerial conference in 2003. Ultimately it was agreed to do so provided there were immediate negotiations on transparency in government procurement and trade facilitation. Many delegations from developing countries expressed their unhappiness with this. The EU used Singapore issues for horse trading in exchange for the language on agriculture export subsidy. India firmly resisted inclusion of the Singapore issues and finally as a compromise postponement of negotiations on all the four Singapore issues until after the next conference was agreed to, provided there was explicit consensus on them.

Quad countries wanted lower industrial tariffs from the developing countries. The least developed countries opposed it because this would adversely affect industrialization in those countries.

Japan, Korea and Brazil were against the use of anti dumping laws by USA for protectionist purposes. Latter was intransigent on this issue. Recently it has imposed the tariff upto 30% on a range of steel products. The former countries have filed cases against USA before the WTO's dispute settlement body.

The Doha agreement mandated that the new negotiations conclude in approximately in three years. It is hard to see how this will be achieved. The Uruguay round took eight years. Specially taking into account the fact that implementation concerns may not be adequately dealt with by the end of 2002. Three years would be too short a period.

Even though many developing countries held their ground with sophisticated arguments at the Doha conference it could not be called a development round. It was only a first step in what remains a long struggle to create a genuine trade and development agenda. Giving three years for the conclusion of new round of negotiations is reckless and dangerous from the point of view of developing countries. More than hundred reforms are needed in the existing agreements.

The preamble of the ministerial declaration provides an uncritical praise for trade liberalization. This does not acknowledge the deep problems the Uruguay round has caused for the poorer countries such as de-industrialization, adverse effect on farmers because of collapse of commodity prices and net reduction in GNP. WTO's advocacy of trade liberalization as an end in itself is based on ideology rather than on evidence. If WTO is to become a means of achieving development it must put development at its heart Mr. Reghvan has gone to the extent of describing Doha declaration as 'everything but development'. It was a case of Orwellian double speech. Though the Indian Commerce Minister Murasoli Maran was not happy with it, he allowed it to be adopted.

Conclusion : Globalisation from Below

The unchallenged sway of globalisation from above inspired by the so called 'Washington consensus' and condescendingly and even arrogantly thrust upon the developing countries by the three international institutions viz. IMF, World Bank and WTO had been called into quesation not only by the voluntary organizations working in various fields but also by an eminent academic economist like Stiglitz who have worked in crucial positions both in American establishment and the World Bank and a successful international financier like George Soros. They have shown that 'the King has no clothes', that their standard policy prescription have no validity either in economic theory or in empirical evidence. They have therefore to realize their mistakes and go back to the original objectives for which they were brought into existence. They have to change their mindset and their methods of working and should be much more appreciative of the varying conditions in different countries their special problems and the views and opinions of the local experts. Also these institutions have no function in more accountable and democratic manner. Michel Camdessus who retired as head of the IMF had to check to tell a reporter, in the manner of the old Bourbon King 'If anyone is the voice of the people, it is me. I am elected by 185 countries. I am the one who can claim legitimacy'. Such breath taking arrogance is no longer acceptable.

Policy makers and opinion makers in the developing countries should themselves muster courage from the writings such as those of Stiglitz and Soros and give up their subservient attitude of unquestioned obedience. They should realize that 'Washington Consensus' is not the last word for them and measures do not become reforms just because IMF, the World Bank and the WTO call them so.

Those measures have to be evaluated with reference to the ultimate objectives like increasing the growth rate, sustainable development, employment generation and environmental protection. And if they fail in this test, they should be refashioned or even given up and replaced by more appropriate measures. In the past those who questioned the IFI prescriptions were banished from the scene. Even though they are not called back, their voice must be heard and their opinions respected.

It is also a hopeful sign that voluntary organizations working in various fields like poverty eradication, sustainable development, environmental protection and human rights are coming together and supporting each other.

The synergic effect is having an impact on world scene which the power that be in rich countries can no longer ignore. The various causes for which the agencies stand are getting integrated in a meaningful manner leading to a comprehensive document on their programme of 'globalisation from below'. In the book 'Globalisation from below' cited above, the authors have presented a synthesized statement of the solutions that diverse constituencies have proposed. Their goal is to usher in 'a new economy based on fairness and justice, sound ecology, a healthy environment and the one that protects the human rights and freedom'.

The seven basic principles of such a comprehensive programme are as follows :

1. Level labour, environmental, social and human rights conditions upwards.
2. Democratize institutions at every level form local to global.
3. Make decisions as close as possible to those that are affected.
4. Equalise global wealth and power
5. Create prosperity by meeting human and environmental needs.
6. Provide stability by eliminating global booms and busts and
7. Make the global economy environmentally sustainable.

The forthcoming world summit on sustainable development or 'Rio 10' which will be held in Sandton in Johannesberg from Aug 26 to Sept 4. would be a meeting ground for voluntary organizations from all over the world.

Hopefully they would be able to carry further the agenda of 'globalisation' from below.

References

1. J. Breacher. T. Costello and B. Smith – *Globalisation from below : the power of solidarity,* Chapter I, Globalisation and its Spectre, South end press, Cambridge, Massachusetts 2000.
2. N Kline. 'No Space No Choice No Jobs No Logo', *Flamingo 2*— Chapter one New Branded World.
3. Michael Prowse – Why plastering over capitalism's cracks won't work – *Financial Times* July 13, 20002.

4. James Petras, *Monthly Review.*

5. J. Stiglitz, *Globalisation and its Discontents,* Penguin Press 2001.

6. G. Soros, *George Soros on Globalisation,* Public Affairs Ltd. Oxford, 2002.

7. J. Stiglitz – 'A fair deal for the world' – *New York Review of Books,* May 23, 2002.

21

PEOPLE'S MOVEMENT AGAINST GLOBAL CAPITALISM

The month of July 2000. saw Europe play host to two important conferences. The first was the Earth Climate Conference held in Bonn, Germany while the other was the G-7 summit of the heads of the rich industrial nations held in Genoa, Italy. Both these conferences were concerned with issues of momentous importance that marked a turning point in human history.

The Bonn Conference was attended by representatives of 178 countries. The conference had to address itself to the action to be taken to give effect to Kyoto protocol of 1997 which had recommended that in order to arrest the seriously growing process of atmosphere pollution caused by the emission of carbon dioxide and other toxic gases, nations must commit themselves to bring about a definite reduction in the rate of emission of the gases. A serious impediment to the smooth deliberations of the conference was caused by the fact that ahead of the conference the American president categorically rejected the Kyoto protocol because according to him it was not in the interest of the continued prosperity of the American people. On the other hand, he wanted the Bonn Conference to put pressure on the developing countries which according to him were the main culprits. Following the wrong example set by America, other countries like Japan, Canada and Russia also started raising objections. Japan wanted the reduction of the penalty if there was any shortfall in conforming to the emission reduction standards laid down by the Kyoto protocol. The question then before the Bonn Conference was how to get over these objections and arrive at a consensus if necessary by entering into compromises. At the very outset of the conference

Jan Pronk the Dutch Minster for environment, presiding over the conference categorically stated that the Kyoto protocol was in the interest of the world community and all the nations of the world must agree to take action to conform to the Kyoto protocol. But the main question remained as to how to bring round US? In order to put pressure on the US and make it see sense, thousands of peaceful demonstrators from all over Europe and the world congregated with banners "stop Bush, save the atmosphere". But this appeared to have little effect on the American position.

The Genoa G-7 summit carried much greater prestige because it was attended by heads of government of the richest countries of the world – US and its allies Britain, Canada, Germany, Italy and Japan all toeing American line and France sometimes taking an independent position. They were to be later joined by president Putin of Russia. The heads were all accommodated in opulent surrounding befitting their positions. President Bush stayed in a grand style ina luxurious boat 'European Vision'. It was announced that the summit would come out with $1.2 b. plan to save the poor people of underdeveloped world from the scourge of AIDS and malaria. The summit was also to take steps to increase international trade so as to be conducive to the economic prosperity of the world – not just for the rich countries alone but also help the poorer nations.

But not all seemed to have been convinced of the humanitarian concerns of these world leaders who arrogated to themselves the role of world saviours. Much before the arrival of these leaders in Genoa, thronged on the streets and squares of Genoa, 1,20,000 workers belonging to 750 voluntary organizations united the umbrella of 'Genoa Social Forum.'. They came at their own costs by trains and buses. Their view was "the G-7 was the rich man's club; they have no plan to write off the debt of the poorer nations which has become so burdensome that for payment of interest and amortization of the debt they have no resources. What they pay out to their creditors in much more than what they get through the inflow of fresh loans. The rich nations do not want to create a fund for adequately supporting programmes of health and education in the developing countries. They are only interested in promoting limitless pursuit of consumerism by affluent section of their society without any regard for the lot of the common people or the consequences of economic activity on environment. They are prepared to use the international organization to bludgeon the developing countries to fall in line." It is against these policies of the heads of the rich countries that they organized protest demonstrations.

Perturbed by the massive demonstrations, the host country mobilized 20,000 police to protect the G-7 summit from the demonstrators. They declared the summit venue as the 'red zone' area and cordoned it off with steel and cement walls.

To denigrate the moral stand of the demonstrators, Condaleeza Rice, the US national security advisor airily stated that while the leaders of the G-7 countries were all democratically elected leaders, the demonstrators had no such representative character. She apparently forgot that democracy was not confined only to elections; there was also such a thing as public opinion. And it was the duty of the elected leaders to listen to public opinion.

On the very first day of the summit the situation turned serious. The police used tear gas and water cannons to drive away demonstrators. But they did not withdraw and succeeded in making a breach in the iron cement wall and entered the red zone. Though voluntary organization wanted very peaceful demonstration, as does happens on such occasions, there were some violent incidents. Some cars were burnt and glass panes of windows of some hospitals and schools were damaged. This provoked the police to indulge in shooting. A bullet pierced through the head of a 21 years old young worker from Genoa named Carlo Guiliani. As he fell on the ground, a police vehicle moved on his dead body. Six hundred other workers were seriously injured. Carlo became a martyr and the spot where he fell became a place for worship where flowers were offered the next day. But this did not stop the police from attacking the media centers of the voluntary organization housed in a school, where they beat up workers and took away photo films and other material. Never before after second world war had Europe been a witness to such police brutality reminiscent of Mussolini's fascist police. The police brutalities were condemned everywhere as a serious violation of human rights. There was widespread demand in Italy and elsewhere for the resignation of the interior minister in the Berlusconi Government.

The police brutalities shown on the TV completely eclipsed the deliberations at the G-7 summit. Perturbed by the death of a volunteer, British prime minister Tony Blair talking again in a similar vein to Condoleeza Rice stated "while we the democratic leaders are trying to solve the problems of poverty, the demonstrators are coming in the way. But we will not stop our summit meeting" Blair forgot that the last British elections saw the lowest voting ever seen in British democracy and he was elected by only 25 per cent of the electorate. But the big leaders were apparently scared of the demonstrations. The next summit is being held in Canada and the Canadian prime minister stated that the summit would be held in a remote place in Rocky Mountain where no demonstrators could reach.

It was symbolic that while these conferences were being held in Europe, the volcano of Mount Etna in Sicily also erupted. The lava reached a height of 3 m. Almost similar to the lava of anger against the inequitable and unjust policies of the rich countries. If globalization of capitalism is only going to increase the power of MNC's and the disparity between nations, it is not acceptable to the millions of common people in developing as well as developed countries. But the leaders of the capitalist countries are not prepared to take note of the opinion of the common people. The host Italian prime minister Berlusconi in his summing up address observed that the world had no alternative to capitalism. But the demonstrations at Genoa and earlier at Gothenburg, Seattle and elsewhere show that the fight against global capitalism and in favour of bettering the lives of the poorer people and the protection of the life supporting system of nature is going to be the main theme of the 21st century.

Will India, which stood for these causes throughout the freedom struggle and in the early years after independence take the lead in this fight against global capitalism or will it go down, abandon its policy of self-reliance or Swadeshi, of non-alignment and its independence and capacity to take its own decision and meekly capitulate before the dictates of the rich countries, the world institutions like WB, IMF, WTO and the MNCs? This major challenge before India needs to be discussed by the intellectuals and no less also by common people at all levels in India.

I - WB, IMF and SAP

The two Bretton Woods institutions – the World Bank and the International Monetary Fund have been playing an active role in promoting market capitalism in the developing countries through the imposition of the structural adjustment programmes (SAP) as a precondition for their aid and assistance to countries of Asia, Africa and Latin America to get out of difficult economic situation. Walden Bello and his associates in their book 'Dark Victory – United States and Global Poverty' have explained at length the harmful effect of SAP on economics of developing countries. Bello considers that acceptance of SAP by India in 1991 was as significant an event as the collapse of the socialistic economy and the disintegration of Soviet Union. The foreign exchange crisis of 1991 forced India to approach the World Bank and IMF to get out of its predicament. India was the leader of the developing countries in their quest to be the architects of their own economic destiny through the policies of economic self-reliance, planned and state sponsored economic development, programmes of a welfare state, the growth of the public sector and the policy of non-alignment. With the acceptance of SAP, India abandoned all its policies followed in first 40 years after independence.

The World Bank was established to provide funds for development projects and programmes while the IMF was to provide funds for the short term purpose for bailing out economies whenever faced by the foreign exchange crisis. It was in the Reagan era that the orientation of both these institutions changed to focus on disbursal of funds for SAP in developing countries. The objective was to bring all developing countries under the dominance of the American economy and in the grip of the multinational corporations by opening the economies of the developing countries to their investment and operations. While this goal has been accomplished, it is doubtful whether it has benefited the developing countries. The SAP prescribed by the two institutions to all the developing countries was the same irrespective of their different economic situations. Common SAP included deregulation of private enterprise, privatization of public enterprises, reduced role of the state in the conduct of management of economic affairs, reduction of public expenditure, dismantling of economic planning and controls, and opening out of the economy by drastically reducing custom tariffs and doing away altogether with physical control and quotas relating to exports and imports. The medicine of SAP was supposed to cure ailing economies, stimulate economic growth, boost production and productivity and create employment opportunities. Bello points out how several developing countries availed of repeated SAP loans but the intended benefits did not accrue.

On the other hand the local enterprises went to the walls, the ability of the government to manage and stimulate the economy got attenuated, public expenditure for welfare activities like health and education got reduced, poverty and unemployment increased, prices of essential commodities sky rocketed and went out of the purchasing power of the poor leading to serious economic deprivation and all in all to loss of economic sovereignty and weakening of the economies of the developing countries. Bello has given case by case illustrations of several developing countries of Asia and Africa to show how this happened.

Today, after several SAPs, the per capital income of African countries is no better than what it was in the 1950s when these countries became independent. Similar is the position of Latin American countries who are no better off from what they were in the 1970s. The countries of east Asia like South Korea, Thailand, Malaysia and Indonesia were known as the Asian tigers and their economic performance was commended by the World Bank and IMF. But both these institutions had no inkling and did not warn against the crisis which hit these countries in July 1997. After that, instead of taking the blame for compelling these economies to agree to capital account convertibility of their currency they started finding fault with their crony capitalism and financial corruption. They agreed to bail out South Korea, Thailand and Indonesia through a huge package of $120 b. But insisted in return that they must open their economies to US and other western capitalist countries. Foreign capital had to be allowed up to 55 per cent and public expenditure had to be curbed. The consequence was that the recession deepened, unemployment increased with South Korea and Thailand having more than two million people unemployed. Ten years after the first generation and second generation reforms, the position in India is no better. Small enterprises are getting closed, and big enterprises are resorting to retrenchment. Despite reduction in rates of lending, the banks to not have enough takers. Fresh investment is not taking place adequately. Cuts in public expenditure mean, agricultural and social sectors have suffered.

The general consequence of SAP has been that the increase of population below poverty line from 130 million in 1980s to 180 million in 1990s. The agricultural and industrial development in the developing countries seen in the earlier years of independence has languished. Unemployment and economic insecurity has led to decline in the health standards, return of epidemics like cholera and malaraia, increase in crimes like murder and decoity and deterioration of the environment. The gap between the poor and the rich countries is increasing with the latter becoming more dependent. The picture is by no means encouraging.

II - WTO, TRIPS and TRIMS

The World Bank and IMF – two institutions reflecting the American world view on economic management, were reinforced by WTO established on the first day of 1995. The WTO arrangements were a culmination of prolonged round table discussions called the Uruguay round table based on the Dankel draft. The discussions were dominated by the US and its allies. In the beginning the underdeveloped countries tried to take a united stand but soon through pressure tactics, the US was able to break their unity. Branzil was brought round and India became isolated and had no alternative but to sign on the dotted line to signify approval to the Dankel proposal. What was regrettable was the fact that neither the then commerce minister Pranab Mukherji nor the government as a whole found it necessary to seek the approval of the parliament. At years passed the adverse effects of the WTO regime are becoming apparent.

The head of the organization and particularly its secretariat are under the dominance of the US and other advanced countries. They unreservedly follow the American policy of free market economy and its globalization though not free from the dominance of the multinationals. There is no place for different problems related to the development of the poorer countries. They assume that free trade and investment would automatically promote the development of the under developed countries. While the latter are still struggling to grapple with problems arising out of WTO arrangements – and they are quite complicated and couched in legal terminology which makes it very difficult for the underdeveloped countries with their limited resources to negotiate – they are now threatened with yet new proposals of the rich countries in the ensuing WTO conference at Doha scheduled in November. In making the new proposal the WTO secretariat did not consider it necessary to consult the governments of underdeveloped countries. It thinks that these are technical matters in which it is not possible to involve every country. They can be decided only through an informal discussions with US and few other developed countries. As a matter of fact WTO has a democratic constitution in which one country has one vote. However in actual practice this is conveniently forgotten and the rich countries take decisions after informal discussions among themselves to further their own interests. From the point of view of underdeveloped countries there is no transparency in the decision- making process of WTO.

If the underdeveloped countries have to save themselves from this unenviable position, they should (i) evolve a common strategy and (ii) develop negotiating skills for putting their point of view in a more effective manner. In fact the underdeveloped countries would have to go in the extent of bringing about basic changes in the arrangements of WTO regime which are titled in favour of the rich countries. Dot Keet of the Alternative Information and Development Centre Capewotn, South Africa has prepared a comprehensive discussion paper under the caption 'alternatives to the WTO regime – tactics and strategy' which makes a plea for a global movement for a different global system. In this paper the author has drown attention to the two major features of the WTO regime which are harmful to the future of the underdeveloped countries : (i) there are several provisions related to a world trade through which the WTO can compel the governments of underdeveloped countries to follow certain policies not only related to international trade but to macroeconomic policies generally and (ii) the arrangements cover a number of matters not strictly related to trade but to certain matters relating to intellectual property and investment which should hardly fall in the province of WTO. Evidently they are thrust in, taking advantage of the weakness of the underdeveloped countries in course of regotiations, to safeguard the economic scientific and technological advantage of the rich countries to the detriment of the interest of the poor countries of Asia, Africa and Latin America. The latter have to pay the price of the consequences of these arrangements.

The pre-Dunkel scope of GATT arrangements was limited to international trade in industrial commodities. Dunkel added products of agriculture and services as well. This has opened vast scope to multinationals to extend their operations worldwide in fields like banking and financial services, insurance, communication, transport, tourism, entertainment and energy production and distribution. In many of these fields the developing countries have established public enterprises with social objectives in view. Now these countries have been compelled to privatize them so as to bring them within the ambit of the MNCs. This change is bound to be disruptive and even painful. Very recently we have the example of the entry of Enron in Maharashtra on the basis of one-sided contract which put a financially strong state like Maharashtra and its state electricity board in dire straits. Enron wanted to charge tariff rates which the consumers could not simply bear. Now the MNCs even want to enter fields like education, health, housing and welfare services. If there the same Enron approaches follow, the plight of the large majority of common consumers can be well imagined.

While rich countries in the name of the free market economy and a structural adjustment programme want to poorer countries to abolish subsidies, they have mananged thus far in the WTO agreement to protect huge subsidies to their own agricultural producers who are also given several other supporting services.

It was not considered necessary to give due protection to small and marginal farmers in the developing countries or to their food security system.

The WTO arrangements provide for a machinery to settle disputes between countries. Disputes are referred to panels of experts. This is cited as an excellent example of WTO's rule based regime. But if it is closely examined how these panels are set up and how they work it would be apparent how the panel mechanism is used to impose decisions on the developing countries. It is the WTO secretariat which makes appointments to the panel. Only those experts are appointed whose names are cleared by the legal department of the secretariat; and the legal department clears only those who are totally committed to free market economy. No wonder the decisions of these panel clearly favour the rich countries. An outstanding example of this bias is the permission given by the WTO to retain clause 301 of its trade law under which US routinely threatens countries like India. Instead of putting pressure on the US to remove the clause, the WTO has allowed its retention on the basis of the American assurance that the clause will not be used in a manner which would be inconsistent with the WTO regime. It is evident that this self-serving assurance hardly means anything to the countries at the receiving end of American action under clause 301. How can this clause be retained in what WTO calls a multilateral regime?

The poorer countries find it extremely difficult to put their arguments before the panel. The experts of world standard are required to be appointed to put the case of the developing countries and they charge astronomical fees beyond the paying ability of the poorer countries. No wonder the decisions of the panel mostly go in favour of the rich countries. This is also bound to happen in the future.

The maters not directly connected with trade but are supposed to be indirectly llinked and therefore included in the WTO are the notorious 'trade related intellectual property rights' (TRIPS) and 'trade related investment measures and services' (TRIMS). The objective of the former is to give due returns to those who have patents to their credit and to prevent the entry of imitative or counterfeit products. But the MNCs have started taking undue advantage of the patent regime. They have started drawing patents on what have been the traditional community practices of the develping countries as also their biodiversity. The cases of 'neem' and 'haldi' patents are well known. Patent claims of the MNCs had to be fought at great expense and trouble before they were a nulled. But there is no doubt that in future MNCs will continue to file patents of such nature a to approviate to themselves the community lore and nature's product evolved over years in the developing countries. The patent regime is bound to create difficulties for developing countries. It was hitherto believed that the development of knowledge is a common heritage of humanity. A country like Japan could show spectacular industrial and economic advancement only by assimilating the technology of the developed contries. In future economic progress though diffusion of science and technology is likely to be halted. This would be a great setback to a developing country like India. Once a patent is obtained by an MNC, a developing country can avail of the technology of new products or processes only after paying hefty sums to the MNCs. This would be a great burden to poor countries.

The objective of TRIMS is to remove all hurdles to investment by MNCs and to give them a free scope all over the world. In the past, before allowing the entry of foreign capital, the developing countries would impose clauses relating to transfer of technology, use of local material, provision of employment to local people, availing of the services of the local contracor, entering into partnershp with local capita and entrepreeurship and a stipulated amount of exports so as to earn foreign exchange for the host country. Under TRIMS all these restrictive clauses have to be done away. The MNCs wo;uld have to be given the same scope as the local enterprises. No special concessions or facilities can be given to local enterprise because that will amount to discrimination against the MNCs which is not permitted by TRIMS. One the other hand, the MNCs will have full freedom to procure inputs from their own branches in other countries and market their products through their own branches thereby extending their monopoly network throughout the world. How can the small local enterprises have a chance of survival in competition with such mighty MNCs with worldwide network and backed up by advanced technology and ample rêsources? The decks are cleared for MNCs to establish their economic empire not only in manufacturing sector but also in the service sector without any regard to the wishes and policies of the governments of the developing countries. Indeed under TRIMS they have to come to term with the situation in which they have lost the economic sovereignty.

Obviously TRIPS and TRIMS would be very harmful to the economic progress of the developing countries for years to come. What should they do to get out of the vice like grip of the WTO and its arrangements? One approach is to make a united effort to eliminate the harmful clauses and arrangements. The other is to bring to an end the regime itself. The alternatives are 'shrink' or 'sink'. Which of these two approaches should be adopted in the ensuing WTO conference scheduled at Doha in the month of November?

If the first approach is adopted then the harmful clauses and aspects would have to be specifically identified. They are as follows:

(1) The scope of the WTO has been expanded far beyond what existed under the erstwhile GATT arrangements. A body concerned with trade has hardly any legitimacy to deal with exclusive rights on intellectual property under TRIPS and flow of investment under TRIMS. Now the developed countries want to bring in labour standard and environment under the ambit of the WTO disregarding the fact that there are specialized bodies to deal with the matter. The developed countries should not use these under the umbrella of the WTO to place hindrances on the exports from the developing countries.

(2) The scope of WTO should be confined to manufactures of commoditie. Agriculture and services should be left out as in the past.

(3) The approach of the WTO should be facilitative rather

than coercive. It should not abridge the economic sovereignty of the government of the developing countries.

(4) Matters which are concerned with a number of developing countries should be treated as general issues and not as a dispute between two countries.

(5) In dealing with disputes the WTO should not take a narrowly legalistic approach but take into account the impact of a decision on the economic fortunes of the under developed countries.

(6) The WTO secretariat and particularly its legal department has appropriated for itself powers which do not belong to it. The secretariat at present makes rules, implements them and takes action to settle disputes. In other words, legislative, executive and judicial powers are concentrated in a single body. Under the constitution the secretariat is answerable to the executive and the general body consisting of representatives of the member countries, but in actual practice accountability hardly exists. The accountability should be insisted upon.

(7) The dispute settlement machinery of panels is tilted in favour of the developed countries. This bias should be corrected. The WTO should provide legal assistance to poorer countries which do not have the necessary resources to put them before the panel. The WTO should collect information related to trade and the issues under dispute and make it available to underdeveloped countries.

(8) The WTO arrangements follow double standards. If the developed countries are unable to take any action under any rule, they are only asked to give an undertaking that whatever possible will be done to correct the deficiencies. On the other hand, the developing countries in a similar situation are simply penalised. This imbalance should be corrected.

(9) There is a need for a fundamental re-attunement of the attitude and outlook of WTO. The WTO must give

importance to the development of the underdeveloped countries in considering any trade matter and not assume that free trade would automatically help the underdeveloped countries. If the underdeveloped countries pass any law, formulate any policy or take any measures for their agricultural, industrial or general economic development, the WTO frowns on them as illegitimate interference with the free trade. If on the other hand, as a result of free trade and the removal or reduction of custom barriers, there is an adverse effect on agricultural production or industries close down, there is no way the developing countries can approach the WTO. This is a reversal of the approach adopted during the decades of development.

All in all, the World Bank, the IMF and the WTO are but instruments of the rich countries and their MNCs to tie the developing countries to the apron strings of the world economy dominated by the rich countries. Ever since the Reagan administration, US administration has systematically tried to reorient the working of these institutions so as to strengthen, in the name of free trade and democracy, the stranglehold of the monopoly capitalism of the MNCs in the rich countries on the world economy. This is nothing but a new economic imperialism. The old imperialism began in 1948 with Vasco de Gama setting his foot on the western coast of India and ended in 1998 with the departure of British from Hong Kong. But the new and the more powerful imperialism under US and other G-7 has already taken its place. The governments of the developing countries have lost their freedom to shape their own destiny. To a great extent mismanagement, maladministration and corruption by the leaders of the developing countries are themselves responsible for this loss of freedom.

Energy and Environment

This US with increasing assertiveness is demonstrating the claim of the former US secretary of state Madelaine Albright that it is the only indispensable country in the world. As a result it has a right to have its own way no matter what the other countries of the world decide. This tendency was witnessed at the world climate conference held in Bonn, Germany during July 20-24. The conference had to consider action to be taken to give effect to the Kyoto declaration of 1997. The president of the conference, the Dutch minister for environment Jan Pronk made an earnest appeal at the very beginning that the issue of environmental pollution due to the green house effect or the emission of toxic gases has become so serious that no time should be lost to take immediate worldwide action on the Kyoto declaration. All nations should reduce the toxic emission by 5.8 per cent which should be considered as the minimum. All the countries represented at the conference were agreeable to the proposal including the G-7 countries except US. George W. Bush soon after his election as US president categorically declared that America would not agree to Kyoto declaration because it ran contrary to the interests of its people. America cannot reduce the consumption of energy because it will adversely affect the pace of the economic progress. US cannot be a party to a decision which will in any way diminish the material prosperity of its people. On the other hand, with cynical brazenness Bush stated that it is the developing countries of the world Which were responsible for the growing pollution of the earth. Restrictions therefore must be imposed on the third world countries. In justification of this position, Bush asserted that America has enormous extent of area under forest which automatically served to control pollution. It was not necessary for the US to do anything more. Taking advantage of 135% obstructive stand, Canada, Russia and Japan started raising objections or asking for concessions. After night long deliberations, the conference succeeded in arriving at a consensus but not without compromising the Kyoto standard. This was a great victory for the cause of environment but even in the face of unanimity. The American representative had no compunction in reiterating the American position that it would never agree to the Kyoto declaration. This must be considered to be the darkest chapter of the American performance on the world stage. America took the position that the whole issue was being re-examined from a scientific point of view and it was only after the results are available that America would declare it policy. But the American representative did not even give a broad indication of what that policy would be.

A subsequent attempt was made at Marrakesh in November, to work out a compromise. But why did America under Bush take such an extreme position – a position quite contrary to that of his predecessor Bill Clinton and his electoral rival Al Gore who in fact had taken a lead in initiating the Kyoto protocol? The July issue of the New York review carries an article by Bill Mckibben under the caption 'some like it hot' gives the background of the summersault of the American position. It begins with the analysis of the third assessment report by the intergovernmental panel on climate change which has been presented in three fat volumes dealing with (a) the scientific reason behind the climatic changes that are taking place, (b) the harmful consequences of the changes and (c) the steps that need to be taken to deal with the consequences. The scientific advice of more than 1,500 experts on various aspects of climatic change was taken into account by the expert panels before their reports were finalized. Following are some of the important points contained in these reports.

As far back as 1980 the NASA scientist James Hanson showed with the help of a computer model that if oil and gas continue to be burnt for energy production at the existing level, then the emission into atmosphere of toxic gases like carbon dioxide, nitrous oxide and methane would increase significantly. Already during the last 20 years the emission has increased by 10 per cent. As a result of this blanket cover of these toxic gases the solar heat will be trapped and as a result of this green house effect there would be a significant increase in the temperature. There was terrible heat during the summer of 1998 in North America. This has been attributed to the green house effect. Orissa in India has been experiencing hot summer in recent years. This may also be a part of the phenomenon of warming of the earth. Experts have estimated that as a result of the emission of the gases the temperature on earth would increase by 3 to 11 degree F.

The consequences of earth warming would be as follows:

(i) While on one side the arid regions would face shortage of water, there would be floods on the other parts of the world. The phenomenal floods in Orissa this year as well as the heavy downpour in Islamabad in Pakistan unequalled during the last 100 years could be attributed to this phenomenon;

(ii) In the tropical regions crop productivity would fall. This may not happen for the time being in the temperate regions but over a period of time they would suffer the same fate;

(iii) the polar glaciers would start melting as also ice cover of mount Kilimanjaro would start melting by the year 2015. This would raise the sea level. Already the sea level has been raised by 2 meters. As a result Pacific islands like Kirbatti and large part of countries like Bangladesh would go under water;

(iv) the Gulf stream would slow down, increasing the cold in many European countries;

(v) effect of El Nino on monsoon will increase; and

(vi) there will be increase in breeding of mosquitoes leading to spread of malaria and dengue fever.

The worst affected would be the poorer countries of the world. America is likely to be less affected. The world would be saved from the harmful consequences only by reducing the number of energy projects emitting toxic gases on a large scale. The rationale of Kyoto protocol was to protect the people from these disastrous consequences of the green house effect.

Disregarding the recommendations of the panel of scientists, the energy committee appointed by Bush under the chairmanship of his vice president Dick Cheney and consisting of several Republican luminaries including the secretary of state, Colin Powell submitted their report on energy policy within 100 days of Bush regime underlining the fact that by 2020 America will face an energy shortage of 32 per cent and this can be made good only by producing more energy. The Cheney Committee recommended the setting up of 1,300 to 1,900 new coal based energy projects since America has enormous reserves of coal. That the coal based projects are most polluting was no concern for the Cheney Committee. American energy policy based on this recommendation is bound to increase the emission of toxic gases. The committee did not feel it necessary to take notice of the harmful effects of such emissions. The previous Clinton administration had given commitment that it will not allow increase the level of carbon diaoxide in the atmosphere. But the Clinton administration took no concrete steps and compared with the 1999 level it went up by 12 per cent by the year 2000. The new policy of Bush administration would further exacerbate the situation. The American population is 4 per cent of the world population but its share of green house emission is 25 per cent. America is the biggest consumer of energy but is least prepared to reduce the emission of harmful gases. Behind the Bush administration reneging from the Kyoto protocol is the fact that the administration is the voice of oil barons with whose help of 10 billion dollars Bush fought his election. America ought to reduce its emission of carbon dioxide by 60 per cent to 80 per cent. This goal is sacrificed at the alter of the new policy of Bush administration.

Mobilisation Against Globalisation

It is evident that the self-centred policy of the US in total disregard of the world opinion is getting more and more aggressive. Apart from the examples given above of such an approach, there are many more other examples in recent times. America has launched upon a new programme of defensive missile stating that the old ABM treaty with Russia agreed upon in 1972 is obsolete and invalid. In another world conference America has disagreed with the proposal on which all other countries had agreed for the end of the biological germ warfare. Nor has America agreed in another conference with the proposal for the restrictions on the use of small arms. Evidently America is determined to push forward its own agenda in complete disregard of the world opinion.

The psychology behind this approach seems to be that after the disintegration of Soviet Union and the collapse of the Soviet economy, US has become the sole guardian of the world. Its historic mission in the new century and new millennium is to establish all over the world democracy, human rights (as America sees them) free market economy and capitalism. The American thinker Francis Fukuyama has already provided the philosophical underpinning to such an approach. No country in the world today has the power to oppose the American position. Even president Putin of Russia, a strong protagonist of antiballistic missile treaty had to enter into negotiations with Bush even after latter's categorical declaration that America will embark upon a new missile programme. China after asserting that its views on human rights are different from those of US was compelled to release from jail America resident Chinese authors accused of espionage in Taiwan ahead of the visit of the American secretary of state with a view to mollify him. In such a situation a weaker country like India can hardly be expected to assert its voice or to take an independent stand.

However, what the leaders of the nation have been unable to do is now being done by the representatives of the voluntary organizations all over the world. The massive demonstrations at Genoa have been followed by demonstrations in several European capitals like Berlin, Paris and London against the brutality of the Italian police. President Clinton had to face these demonstrations in his home ground at Seattle while his successor president Bush had to face demonstrations at European summit held in Gothenburg in Sweden. It is only to be expected that the momentum generated by these protest movements will only increase in the years to come. Whatever be the claims of Bush or Blair that as democratically elected leaders they are entitled to shape the destiny of the world, it is obvious that there is a growing resistance against the American design of globalisation of capitalism. History has not ended as Fukuyama asserted. A new history has begun. Behind the protest movement is a new intellectual and philosophical perspective which is gaining a world wide dimension.

What is this world perspective? Though socialism has been defeated and capitalism has triumphed, it does not mean that issues of equality and social justice have ceased to exist or the market economy purely governed by the short term profit motive can ensure the welfare of humanity. If the SAP imposed by the World Bank and the IMF on the underdeveloped countries leads to their economic dependence, increases the gap between the rich and poor countries, worsens poverty and unemployment and leads to deprivation of the common people, if market economy and capitalism erodes natural resources and pollutes atmosphere, then surely it is necessary to find an alternative. In the name of free market economy there cannot be modification of everything – of human values, cultural diversities and free gifts of nature. In the name of competitive efficiency the basic impulses of cooperation between people cannot be eliminated. In the name of free economy MNCs cannot be allowed to run riot. The civil society and the local community must have the space to act and where necessary the state has to intervene. These are some of the ideas which the protest movements stand to bring together in a new consistent design of thought of wide application to social and economic aspects of human life. This is the meaning of the new slogan – 'mobilisation against globalisation' through which a more humane and equitable economic and social order will take shape.

References

Bnelo Walden (1994,1999) : 'Dark Victory – the United States and global Poverty'. Pluto Press with Food First Institute for Food and Development Policy California, US and Trance National Institute Paulus Patterstart, Amsterdam.

Keet. Dot (2000) : 'Alternative to the WTO Regime' : discussion paper, Alternative Information and Development Centre. Cape Town, South Africa, November.

Mckibben, Bill (2001) : 'Some Like It Hot', New York Review of Books, July 5.

Sayle, Murray (2001) : 'After George Bush, the Deluge'; London Review of Books, Volume 23, Number 12.

22

COLLAPSE OF THE FINANCIAL INSTITUTIONS OF AMERICAN CAPITALISM AND ITS WORLDWIDE IMPACT

The first two weeks of September 2008 saw the collapse of American giant financial institutions which fell, one after another, like nine pins. Actually earlier in March itself, the fall of Bear Sterns, the third or fourth large bank, itself was an indication of the shape of things to come. The bank was taken over by American Government but then itself it was feared that the salvage of the bank was not enough and the rot would not stop. Rumours started floating that yet another bank would follow suit and that turned out to be another big investment bank, the Lehman Brothers. This time the government chose to take a tough stand on the ground that the bank should bear the consequences of its wrong financial transactions. However, what was "sauce for the goose was not sauce for the gander". A few days earlier another two huge financial institutions – Fannie Mae and Fredric Mac – were taken over by the government. These two are actually not lending institutions but guarantors of mortgage loans. The government justified its action on the ground that if the guarantors failed, it would pose a threat to the entire mortgage loan business. Another big blow followed AIG (American Investment Group), the biggest insurance company with world wide network turned bankrupt. It was salvaged by the Federal Reserve Bank which undertook to lend up to 80% of its financial burden in return for government ownership of stocks of the company in the same proportion.

Next was the turn of other reputed investment banks – Merrill

Lynch, Goldman Sachs and Stanley Morgan Investment. The Merril Lynch was taken over by Bank of America while the two latter were converted into a holding company. Next on the chopping block was Washington Mutual, biggest bank taking deposits from and lending to ordinary clients. This too was nationalised.

The American government and the Federal Reserve soon realized that dealing with individual financial institutions as they collapsed was not the right way to stem the tide. The fall of these big institutions had created a panic situation in the entire financial world. The repercussions of the fall of the financial institutions were felt in the entire economy. There was loss of confidence. Banks would not lend to each other or enter into transactions. The entire credit system was under the threat of being frozen. There was fear of recession. The situation had to be tackled as a whole.

It was in such an emergency situation that the American Treasury Secretary, Henry Paulson in consultation with Birnanke the Governor of the Federal Reserve, came forward with big "bailout plan" of $ 700 billion. President Bush came out on the lawns of the White House to take the people and the press into confidence regarding the bailout plan. What America was faced with was an unprecedented situation which required an unprecedented solution to tackle it. The 'plan' provided the solution. He added that the Treasury Secretary would enter into discussion with the Congressional leaders of both the parties to pass the necessary legislation to sanction the plan. President Bush urged upon the leaders to pass the legislation on an urgent basis.

But the Congressional leaders were not in a mood to act immediately to the President's bidding. The Democrat members of the Congress squarely blamed the Republican Administration for following policies which led to the financial mess. They particularly blamed the Treasury Secretary Paulson for weak or non-existent regulation of the financial institutions. Being himself an erstwhile "Wall Street Mughal" – he was the Chief Executive of Goldmen Sachs before he became Treasury Secretary – he gave a free hand to the financial institutions and their CEO's. Now he cannot be trusted they argued, with $ 700 billion in the name of the "bailout plan". The public opinion was also very adverse. Why should the tax payer's money be used to pay for the cost of the blunders of the CEO's of the financial institutions who failed in the discharge of their duties? What is worse they not only failed to do their duties, some of them walked away with hefty terminal benefits running into millions of dollars. The common man lost his residence and came on the street if he failed to repay the loan installment on time but the CEO's go scot-free.

The Republicans were also reluctant to use the taxpayers' money for the bailout plan. They indeed had basic ideological objections. Since the days of Ronald Reagon, the Republican party had vehemently upheld the gospel of 'free market economy' with minimum state intervention. This was the gospel preached by the free market "guru" and leader of the Chicago School of Economics. Prof. Milton Friedman. According to this gospel, the market is always right and efficient too. If there were to be any problems, market itself would provide automatic solutions. Government cannot provide solutions since every government intervention was a problem not a solution. Under Miltons influence, the Republicans had banished all types of interventions which for then became an anathema.

The more radical thinkers like Naomi Klcin, characterized the plan of Bush Administration as an example of "socialism for the rich "while it preached capitalism for the poor" according to its concept of minimal state. The poor victims of storm Katrina who had lost their houses and belongings had fully experienced the misery caused to them by capitalism under which in the name of rehabilitation, they were exposed to the hired contractors to provide houses which were left half built after the contractors deserted them. There was no public agency to provide housing or education.

The leaders of the developing countries also looked askance at the behemoth bailout plan. When the Latin American and African countries were in dire straits and when there was the "Asian meltdown" in 1997, America and under its influence IMF and World Bank were vehemently opposed to any "bail out" plan. It was inconsistent with the gospel of a "free market economy" which was at the core of its uniform ally prescribed "structural adjustment programme". But when there was a meltdown in America a helping "bailout plan" came out !

Looking at the reception given to the bailout plan of his administration, President Bush came out thrice to persuade the reluctant Congressional leaders to support the plan. His "Bailout plan" now became a "rescue plan" not bailing out institutions but rescuing economy under siege. He said that the Wall Street crisis would engulf the whole economy unless checked on time. He also tried to muster the support of the American people by saying that their own fortune, their ability to get credit to support their life style would be atrophied if the crisis is not gotten over.

But Bush was in for yet another shock. When the Bill to support the plan came before the House of Representatives, it was decisively defeated. Not only 96 democrats but two-third of the Republicans voted against the Bill. This was a resounding slap. Bush expressed a grave disappointment and sat with his economic advisors to find a way out. He was able to get the Senate approval and again brought the bill before the House of Representatives. This time he succeeded in bringing to bear enough pressure to get the bill passed. But not before a number of clauses were added which turned a three page document submitted by Henry Paulson into a lengthy document running into 104 pages. It incorporated clauses to provide assurances to assuage the anxieties expressed. *First* there house committee mechanism to "supervise" the implementation of the plan. They did not want Henry Paulson to be left to himself *Second*, they wanted to limit the CEO's remunerations and their benefits which had gone hay wire at the cost of ordinary investors. *Third*, they wanted provisions to compensate the taxpayer for his sacrifices, as and when the economy improved. The implementation of the plan and bringing it to a successful conclusion would not be easy. Paulson has entrusted it to one of his young assistants, Mr. Neil Kashkari, a person of Indian (Kashmiri) origin.

In the meanwhile, the ramifications of the American crisis spread to Europe as well. In Britain with its big Bank, Bradford and Bingly, failing, the government took it over as it did last year when Northern Rock failed. This was followed by financial crisis in Bank of Scotland, HBOS, Lloyds, TSB Barclays to which British government extended a support of £ 50 billion. Fortis a big Bank in Belgium started falling despite sound business and had to be taken over by the combined support of Government of Belgium and Netherland. A Scandinavian country, Iceland saw a complete meltdown of its banking system. Its President had a heart attack and its Prime Minister asked his people to go back to fishing. German government gave a support of $ 50 billion to its banking system. The European Bank serving the centre European Union also came out with its plan.

But despite the approval of the mega plan, the confidence in the stock market was not restored since the plan was considered inadequate to salvage the situation. Dow Jones plunged, so did the European and Asian stock markets.

American now decided to muster the help of all the world to support its tottering financial system. Treasury Secretary met with Finance Minister of G7 countries and came out with a five point plan. He also sought the support of G20 countries including India.

President Bush and Henry Paulson were candid in admitting that despite the plan, the recovery would be slow and recession could not be averted easily. The gravity of the situation was widely recognized. Warren Buffet, one of the top American billionaires, described the calamity as America's financial Pearl Harbour, Many called this the greatest calamity after 1929 depression, from the position that everything was OK with the triumphant American capitalism, the American policy makers had to come down to the position that there were "systemic defects" which had to be identified and removed. This, despite the realization of the gravity of the situation. The American policy makers have failed to do so, far. They have to make a candid analysis of what went wrong.

The proximate cause of the financial crisis in US was the phenomenon of sub-prime lending for housing by land mortgage credit institutions. Many of these loans turned into "toxic" because of the failure to repay the loan installments. As the failure to repay became spread wide, it was noticed that the institutions resorted to reckless lending without insisting on down payment and proper examination of the repaying capacity of the borrower. The lending banks were confident that the loans were secure because the values of the real estate for whose purchases loans were given were continuously rising. When the real estate values started falling, the assets turned "illiquid".

The recklessness of the lender was stimulated by the recklessness of the borrower. Every American was carried away by the "American dream" of a huge luxurious house in the suburb even though it required commuting over a long distance to reach the place of work involving additional expense of transport which started mounting with rising petrol prices. Americans craved for luxurious living beyond their means and this addiction to high consumption was facilitated by credit institutions ever willing to lend at low rates and the ubiquitous credit cards which encouraged spending sprees at the supermarkets. A century ago Thorstein Veblen had drawn attention to "ostentatious living" by the leisure class. Now it tended to be a universal feature of the American society.

Cheap lending in turn was facilitated by the low interest policy assiduously promoted by the Chairman of the US Federal Reserve Allen Greanspon over his long tenure.

The country itself was living beyond its means. It ran huge budget deficit and external deficit which was bridged by vigorously exporting country like China whose export earnings were parked in dollars in the American financial system. US debt has risen to 2 ½ times nations GDP, and approaching $ 44 trillion of the entire world.

The illiquidity of the real estate lending sector extended far beyond it and enveloped the entire financial sector because of "Securitisation" of the mortgages, trading in derivatives and operations of the Ledge fund, which encouraged financial speculations on a large scale. This huge superstructure of financial system with worldwide operations was facilitated by the new computer technology and instant internet communications. The financial superstructure started operating on its own steam unrelated to the "real economy". This was rightly characterized by noted economists Henry Magdof and Paul Sweezy as "financial capitalism" covering the whole gamut of investment banks, hedge funds and stock markets.

The CEO's of these financial institutions were the new "nawabs" Whose ins satiable greed led to reckless financial operations. The goal was maximization of profit" in the short run and not sound long term development concept like honesty, loyalty to an institution and sound business which became old fashioned and disdainfully discarded. The greed of the CEO's soon turned into personal acquisition in an unscrupules fashion. They awarded to themselves hefty compensations in various forms including salaries, perks, bonuses and stock options. The CEO's deserted the investors they were serving at the first opportunity after making a fast buck. They did not hesitate to indulge in trends in which they were joined by the reputed accounting firms as was brought and by the Enron case whose fabulous boss Kenneth Lay,. a favourite of President Bush, had to end his last days in jail undergoing a sentence after the scam came into open and the firm collapsed. As a result of the greed of the CEO's of the American corporations, the gap between the top and bottom of society in financial wealth and income has reached astronomical proportions.

Financialisation of American capitalism began in 1960 and became prominent by 1970. The main characteristic of the change was the increasing role of finance in the operations of capitalism. Economist James Tobein, a Nobel Prize winner in 1981 drew attention to the "Casino aspects" of financial markets. Financial activities, remote from production of goods and services, generate high private rewards disproportionate to their social productivity. Thanks to the computer power, the paper economy of financial exchange ballooned in quantity and variety. As a result "speculative bubbles" and stock market crisis have become a recurrent and growing problem.

How and when American capitalism and its European counterpart would be able to overcome the current financial crisis is yet to be seen. The vigorous implementation of the bailout plan and the coordinated, worldwide efforts may succeed eventually. But one thing is clear American capitalism and its ideology have received a big blow. No longer would the arrogant claim of Francis

Fukuyom that American capitalism marks the "end of history" would carry conviction. Capitalism is not perfect. It has no magic qualities to correct itseif and state intervention is not a taboo. Indeed capitalism is per force required to take the help of the state to survive. The logic of free market capitalism that pursuit of profit invariably led to the good of the society turned out to be "Adam's fallacy" reference to Adam Smith's "invisible hand". Unabridged capitalism is not the last word. Capitalism may not have ended but surely it has to be mended.

What does a country like India learn from the experience? The Indian Prime Minister and Finance Minister, both keen "reformers" were anxious to insulate the Indian economy from the American and international crisis. The tumbling stock market and severe liquidity crunch forced the government to take suitable measures to provide liquidity. Already CRR which was raised to curb inflation has been brought down to increase liquidity of Rs. 60,000/ year. But even this appears to be inadequate and more cut is to expected. But what happens to inflation? And would India continue to maintain a high growth rate alone of seven per cent? The export and service sector may get adversely hit after the growth rate.

The impact on the Indian economy would have been much more severe if the Indian financial system had been more exposed to the international system. This would have happened if the so called "reforms" of the Banking and Insurance sectors, with greater privatization and foreign equity investment and pension fund investment in stock markets, which were dear to the Finance Minister were allowed to take place. This could not happen thank to the resistance of the Left on to "financial reform". But for their obstruction, the crisis in India would have become more severe but Finance Minister is not prepared to acknowledge it. The capital account convertibility and more deregulation of the financial system might have proved dangerous.

This is the lesson that the Indian economic reforms should learn from the current crisis. Hereafter blindly following the reform process and structural adjustments declared by the IMF, World Bank and American treasury would be a sure recipe for disaster.

India should pay greater attention to the real reforms – the rejuvenation of the agricultural and rural economy, improving the infrastructure, more active role of the state through improved machinery of administration (rather than outsourcing everything) and checking growing inequalities and disproportionate earnings in the luxury and speculative (non productive) sectors.

23

RECESSION – DIAGNOSIS AND REMEDIES

The New Face of Financial Capitalism

Business cycles i.e. upswings and downswings in the economy, booms and busts, have been a characteristic of the capitalist economy. Many economists have analysed the phenomenon and have come out with empirical findings as well as theories regarding causes and nature of these occurences and remedies either for moderating the impact, or for preventing their occurrence. Gottfeied Haberler's classic treatise "Prosperity and Depression' brought together several theories regarding business cycles – monetary, structural and even those related to psychological waves of optimistic and pessimistic expectations in the business world. In the heyday of neoclassical economies and policies of *laissez* failre, it was believed that the equilibrating forces of demand and supply in the market, and the balancing of costs and prices would automatically provide the remedy. Thus, during the downswings and recessions, demand and prices fall and the producer will perforce be required to reduce costs. Wages and returns to other factors of production will fall. Reduced costs will reduce prices and demand will consequently pickup. However, it was found that this only exacerbated the situation, converting recession into deep depression. It was in the aftermath of depression in 1929-30, the worst setback to the capitalistic economy, that it was realized that there was something wrong in assuming that there would be an automatic cure through the equilibrating mechanism. It was at this time that Keynes came out with his theory of macro economies. Briefly, it stated that the level of the economy depends on the aggregate demand.

consumption and investment are the two main components of the aggregate demand. In times of depression when both fall, it is the state which should take initiative in boosting both these components through public investment and welfare programmes. The validity of this approach of public intervention to supplement the market was demonstrated by the New Deal Programme of President Roosvelt. Keynesian Theory brought back the formulations of pre-classical and pre-neo classical economists regarding under consumption and under production.

The current recession which is so severe in nature as to bring back the memories of the great depression of 1929-30, is however, the aftermath of "over consumption' rather than under consumption'; hence it requires different kind of analysis and theory. However, economists have not come out with it so far.

For the last several years, the successful working of the market (capitalistic) economy was taken for granted. This created a sense of complacency. Keynesian economies itself was thrown aside and superseded by the Chicago School under the leadership of Milton Friedman and his associates which celebrated the triumph and infallibility of the capitalist market economy.

This despite the fact that there were clear signs of new systemic defects creeping into the capitalistic economy of the affluent countries especially the USA. First was the tendency to live beyond means – both at the individual and national level. The families in USA Government became used to living on credit for fulfilling their extravagant life styles. The credit card revolution supported such a life style. Every family would boast of possessing several credit cards which would be operated without discrimination. Also, the sustained policy of low interest rate promoted by former head of the Federal Reserve, Allen Greensparn, encouraged financial institutions to lend extravagantly at low interest rates. The leading example was 'sub-prime lending' by the mortgage banks – they lent without insisting on down payment and proof of ability to repay the loan, simply depending on the assumption that the loan was covered by an appreciating asset like a house. Securitisation of these loans provided the basis for further rounds of 'financial products' floated by the investment banks and hedge funds. Soon this gave rise to tremendous facade of 'financial capatalism' in which financial products and their transactions themselves became the core business of investment banks and financial institutions like hedge funds without any regard to 'real' transactions. Finance ceased to be the support for the production in the real economy but became a product in itself.

The same tendency seeped in the world of 'real production'. Chief Executives of companies in the production business started aiming at increasing share values in the stock market rather than attending the technological upgradation, human resource development, organizational improvement, and rationalization of production process to raise productivity. Soon this degenerated into corporate scams in the forms of falsification of balance sheets just to improve the image of the company in the stock market in order to attract investors. This had disastrous consequences as illustrated by the Enron scandal in USA and Satyam scandal in India.

The CEO's of corporations started transforming Adam Smith's concept of 'pursuit of self interest' into unscrupulous, greed using their positions to appropriate for themselves disproportionate salaries, bonuses, and corporate facilities like aeroplanes, helicopters and holiday resorts. Neither the accountants and auditors, nor the Board members could stop this naked pursuit of self interest.

This philosophy of insatiable greed became characteristic of the ruling classes and the policy makers as well. After all it was money power which placed them positions of political power. Their policies made America the largest debtor country in the world with internal and external deficit running into trillions of dollars. Yet the dollar could maintain its value because countries like China with higher balance of payment surplus, chose to keep their surpluses in US Treasury bills.'

Recession – Causes and Strategies

This is the background of the US capitalistic economy against which the present recession which had it origin in USA can be understood. The reckless (sub-prime) lending by mortgage banks led to their inevitable bankruptcy. The banking and financial institutions like Fanny Mac and Fredic Mac, Lehman Brothers, AIG, Merill Lynch, Goldman Sachs, Stanley Morgan, Washington Bank etc, which had their financial empires built by securitarisation and leveraging of these loans collapsed like a pack of cards. The disastrous failure of banking institutions, led to collapse of confidence in the market choking the credit system. What started as a Wall Street crisis soon became a Main Street crisis.

The financial crisis rapidly spread to Europe with similar pattern of collapse of financial institutions followed by collapse of business confidence, both leading to the outset of recession. There was not only fall in growth but also contraction of the G.N.P. and rising unemployment.

President Bush had to face the crisis in the sunset years of his administration. His treasury Secretary Henry Paulson and Federal Reserve Chairman Ben Bernanke worked out a $ 700 billion bail out plan to resurrect the financial institutions. The plan was quite out of tune with the economic philosophy of the Republican Party which for several years had forcefully advocated and pursued the policy of free market economy of the Chicago School. According to them, the state should keep away from meddling in the market economy. And now here was a huge plan to bail out big financial institutions on the Wall Street – all in the private sector – at the cost of the tax payer. No wonder the plan was severally criticized as 'Socialism for the rich' reserving capitalism for the poor !

However, Bush administration justified it by saying that the common people themselves would suffer if the credit line for consumption, education and housing would be clogged. The credit institutions had to be revived in the interest of the ordinary people. The road to Main Street was from the Wall Street.

Obama who followed Bush had however a different view. He severely chastised the Wall Street barons for their 'greed and irresponsibility' which led to the bankruptcy of the financial institutions. He instead had an alternate plan of $ 899- for surge in public expenditure on upgrading infrastructure, health and welfare measures. He however persisted with the bail out plan. The person whom he selected to succeed Henry Paulson for the post of Treasury Secretary, Timothy Geitmer was himself, a head of New York Federal Reserve Bank, closely connected with the business world and has become a leading architect of the bail out plans and justified them in the name of helping business and consumers and making credit flow again. Obama had however the discomfiture of seeing the bailout funds used for making hefty bonus payment to those very CEO's whose malfeasance had led the financial institutions to bankruptcy. The extravaganza of buying corporate jets and helicopters and holiday resorts did not stop. The Citi Bank at its annual meeting of shareholders did not serve coffee and doughnuts but spent high sums for hiring 50 security guards.

USA and Britain took initiative for convening G20 meeting at London on April 2. There was clear difference of approach in tackling recession. While the US plan was to boost public expenditure to stimulate the economy, the France-German approach was to tighten regulations since it was lax regulation which led to financial mismanagement and consequent collapse of financial institutions. Britain wanted severe action against 'tax havens' which drew away funds from productive investment in business. The meeting agreed to provide a booster dose of $ 1.1 trillion through IMF and other multilateral institutions particularly to the poorer countries.

While admitting that it was the financial mismanagement in USA which led to loss of confidence in the credit system and consequent onset of recession, US Treasury Secretary felt that US needs to be supported by other nations especially the emerging economies like China, India and Brazil in dealing with the recession and protecting the poorer economies from the impact of recession.

The reaction of Indian policy makers to recession was in the beginning, one of denial. Indian banking system, they argued, was strong, thanks to sound regulatory mechanism. Indian economy would be insulated from the recession that hit USA and Europe. India would stand 'decoupled'. However, as months passed, the impact of world recession was apparent. The stock market plunged. Export sector enterprises like Surat based Gem and

Jewellery industry, Kanpur based leather industry and textile industry in different parts of the country felt the impact of recession as cash rich markets of US and Europe dried up. Lakhs of skilled workers lost jobs. The flourishing IT Software industry too lost business as outsourcing by banking and other companies in US and Europe substantially went down. Consequently fresh recruitment was halted and compensations of existing staff were reduced in one way or another. Building industry too slowed down and real estate prices plunged. A further set back to the economy was withdrawal of $ 15 Billion by the foreign investors.

Government had to come out with a series of monetary measures to improve liquidity such as successive reduction of CRR by RBI and extension of credit line to Mutual Funds. This was supplemented by reduction in Repo and reverse Repo rates to facilitate cheap credit to industry by the banks. But the banks were reluctant to reduce interest and give loans liberally. The recession atrophied the repaying capacity of business establishments and banks feared rise in NPA's. Government supplemented monetary measures by fiscal stimulus. There was across the board cuts in excise duties to reduce costs and prices and stimulate demand. All these measures had only limited success. Prime Minister Manmohan Singh has promised fresh packages of measures for the voters to bring Congress back to power.

The recession does not seem to have been handled with a sure touch in USA, European Union and elsewhere. As the Economist has pointed out in a recent article, through the rate of decline is showing, glimmers of hope, this cannot be interpreted as the beginning of strong and sustained recovery. The worst global slump is far from over. Central banks have pumped in trillions of dollars, policy interest rates are approaching zero and government has provided fiscal stimulus, but the banks have not been purged off toxic assets', and European Banks face $ 1.1 trillion in losses. Budget deficit of the order of 9% of GDP have created serious dangers of inflationary spiral. World Economic Outlook expects global output to sink by 1.3% this year – first fall in 60 years. Big automobile companies like General Motors and Chrysler are facing bankruptcy. If they fold up, there would be cumulative fall in the economy.

Though several months have elapsed after the onset of recession, there is still no clarity of understanding amongst the policy makers and economic thinkers, as to how exactly it should be tackled and how long will it last. While some are already seeing signs of recovery, others fear that there will be further waves of recession. The confidence in the self correcting capacity of the free market has been severely shaken and the concept of minimalist state has already been abandoned in favour of the interventionist state. The brash and arrogant claims on behalf of unbridled capitalism have given way to grudging concessions in favour of mending the defects of capitalism. While the shortcomings of the capitalist system have been exposed, there is yet no clear formulation, no comprehensive theory such as that of Keynes after 1929-30 depression, which could provide an alternative reformed model of capitalism. Economists needs to do fresh thinking regarding economic theories and economic policies.

Alternative Models of Capitalism

A realization has dawned that government measures are at best palliatives and efforts have to be made to remove the systemic defects which have crept in the capitalist economic system in recent years. Shri. Narayan Murthy, the founder of Infosys who has become an icon, has came out with his concept of 'compassionate capitalism'. Obviously he has been disturbed by the ravages of 'rapacious capatalism' as exemplified by Enron and Satyam. A company like Infosys he said, will not, in the face of recession, resort to indiscriminate hiring and firing. Rather it will use the slow down as an opportunity to upgrade the skills of workers through extended programme of training. While Narayan Murthy's zeal to 'reform' capitalism is commendable, the limits of the concept of compassionate capitalism' are quite apparent. With all its best intentions, Infosys in the face of falling profits, has been compelled to stop fresh recruitment. Even Infosys, for all its success in the boom time, will not be able to ward off the consequences of recession.

What is required is an alternative model of the economic system and fresh set of policy measures to bring it into existence. The neo-liberal model followed since 1991 has created economic, legal and administrative systems which have favoured few 'billionaires' at the cost of ordinary urban workers and millions of farmers toiling on land in the country side. Inequalities of the order that exist in India and the world cannot lead to sustainable development. The massive earnings in the luxury sectors like Bollywood and Cricket and ostentatious style of living of a few cannot be allowed to co-exist with horrible conditions of slumdogs who have to live without minimum facilities like clean drinking water, sanitation and housing.

Inequalities in the field of education and health are also quite appalling. Private schools and colleges charging exorbitantly high fees co-exist with substandard municipal schools which even the poor families do not want their children to attend. Public hospitals are in an appalling state, while the luxury hospitals provide up-to-date medical treatment and facilities at a cost which only the rich can afford.

Recession is an opportunity to bring about a root and branch change in the economic policy and the economic system with an aim of not only eliminating systemic defects in capitalism and the evils of in-satiable greed and bubbles of prosperity which they gave rise to, but also by deliberately building public systems of education, health, transport, housing etc, free from corruption, entirely handled by professionals and free from interference by self-serving politicians and parties and devising policies to support agriculture and promote agro processing and village industries like handloom which provide employment to masses of people. 'Safety nets' attached to basically iniquitous economic system will not do. The system itself needs to be made more equitable. Unfortunately neither the Congress, nor the BJP nor the left parties have taken the opportunity of the General Elections to place before the people a comprehensive economic philosophy and policy measures and agenda of action to deal with the consequences of recession and other shortcomings of the present economic system.

24

GLOBALISATION OF KNOWLEDGE AND CULTURE

The tenth general conference of the International Association of Universities, took place at Vigyan Bhavan. New Delhi from 6 to 9 February 95. The theme of the conference was 'Global Civilization and Cultural Roots – bridging the gap through international cooperation'. For discussing such a multi-dimensional theme had gathered Vice-Chancellors incharge of higher education, from the seven continents of the world. They came from countries of diverse backgrounds of geography, history, culture, race, religion and academic traditions. Here therefore, was a truly global gathering to consider the theme of global significance.

Globalisation has become the watchword of our discourse today. It specially refers to globalisation of the economy. After the successful culmination of prolonged negotiations has come into existence at the beginning of the year, the World Trade Organization. Globalisation means free flow of goods, services and capital and hence reducing if not removing altogether the trade barriers.

However, more significant than globalisation of commerce is the globalisation of knowledge. Knowledge is universal and must be at the disposal of humanity. It, therefore, follows that universities all over the world must cooperate with each other in the production and dissemination of knowledge and its application to the myriad problems of humanity. Cross cultural cooperation is inherent in the concept of globalisation of knowledge. This cooperation has to be on the basis of equality and mutual interest.

Having said this however, the problems, tensions and frictions arising out of such cross-cultural cooperation cannot be overlooked. Though knowledge may be universal, it is also time and location specific. This is particularly true in the case of Social Sciences. Economic, political and social theories, formulated in the context of the developed countries may not necessarily be applicable to the developing countries. Each country has its own social and economic background and the mould and traditions of the people. Motivation of human behaviour may also be different in different countries. All this has to be taken into account in socio-economic formulations. Even in the field of natural sciences, the process of globalisation may well mean that scientific research related to the socio-economic conditions, factor endowments and environmental conditions in the developing countries may well be overlooked in the priorities of scientific research. This will lead to the concentration of attention on the relevance of higher education and research to those countries. It is indeed in this context that one has to take note of the phenomenon of brain drain which has now become widespread. For example, the products of the IITs, the top most institutions of higher education in India, tend to leave their own countries since they find better opportunities in the developed countries.

The globalisation of knowledge has also led to globalisation of language. The emergence of the English language as the medium of instruction in higher education and research has pushed native languages into the background specially in the field of higher education. If languages go down under the dominance of the English language, then people will themselves lose their diversity and cultural identity.

Moreover, the use of foreign language as the sole medium of higher education is bound to discourage the capacity for original thinking. Indians in the ancient past made original contributions in the field of astronomy, medicine, music and dance, but under the impact of the foreign language, this capacity for original thinking has almost come to an end.

This of course, does not mean that inter-university cooperation and the process of flow of teachers and students from the developing countries to the institutions of higher education in the developed word should come to a standstill. Rather, such a flow should be encouraged to make knowledge truly universal. In this context, an interesting development is the initiative taken by the European Economic Community in setting up the Erasmic Foundation which gives financial support to students of countries in the community to institutions of higher education in other countries. This is a splendid example of globalisation and similar initiatives should be taken by other regions and countries as well. However, the flow of teachers and students should not be a one-sided flow. It should be a two-way traffic. Students and teachers going from the developing countries must eventually return to their own country and give the benefit of their knowledge to their own people.

While on one side, the impulses of globalisation and integration are making their presence felt, there are at the same time tendencies towards fragmentation, disintegration, and marginalisation. The disintegration of USSR and Yugoslavia have been traumatic events, and the tragedies that followed in the wake of the disintegration are still not over. Minorities of various sorts are feeling marginalized and are in search of their identity. They are stridently articulating their rights to be recognized as distinct entities.

With the disintegration of USSR, socialism as an ideology has lost its appeal. Capitalism and its concomitant, the free market economy has remained supremely triumphant. It would appear as though there is no alternative to capitalism and the market economy. Fukuyama has described this development as 'the end of history'. But history will never end and will continue as long as human civilization exists. What he has described as end of history is in fact the end of an 'ideology' or rather of socialism as an alternative to capitalism.

However, if socialism stood for values of equality or equity or social justice, then the collapse of socialism does not make those values irrelevant. Nor can the incessant pursuit of material goods and services, do away with the human craving for spiritual satisfaction. There is a limit to the pleasure derived from material success, and human beings will continue to look for higher sources of satisfaction. They will continue to reflect on the purpose of life. They will continue to find solace in peace and contemplation, and proximity to nature. That is why humanity is seeking ardently for ways to preserve the environment.

Environmental preservation has emerged as a great cause of humanity today. The Universities have also joined the world wide concern for preservation of natural environment. The Stockholm World Conference in 1972, the Brundtland Committee report of 1987 and the Rio Earth Summit of 1992 called for sustainable development as the goal of human endeavour. In October 1990, 20 University Vice Chancellors from all regions of the world met at Talloires, France and expressed their concern about environmental degradation and came forth with the declaration asking for urgent action to reverse the trend of environmental degradation.

In December, 1991 at Halifax, Canada, the United Nations University and Association of Universities joined 20 universities presidents and expressed their dismay about unsustainable environment. In August 1993, the Commonwealth universities' fifteenth quinquennial Congress at Swansea with 400 Vice Chancellors from 47 countries gave a call to the Universities to deploy their unique common tradition to respond to the challenges of environmental degradation and for a balance between environment and development.

On 19th November, 1993, 90 international University leaders assembling at Ninth International Association of Universities (IAU) Round Table issued the Kyoto declaration on sustainable development and called for the Universities to utilize their resources to encourage better understanding of public at large of interrelated biological and social dangers facing the world and to recognize significant factors and international dimensions of sustainable development.

At the Delhi IAO Conference (February 6-10), Mr. Hector De Souza, Rector, United Nations University called upon the academic community to contribute to the national agenda 1991. The report of the advisory team appointed by the UNU called for eco-restructuring, understanding of the eco-capacity, and eco-governance for proper environmental management. More specifically, it has evolved Zero Emission Research Initiative (zeri) on manufacturing through waste and calling for major shifts in the present technological and social organizations.

The Delhi Conference called for inter-university collaboration through teaching and research and recommended setting upon intensive task force on the project of sustainable development. The Conference called for the Universities to join in a unique collaboration plan with the Earth Council chaired by Brenst Strong who led the Rio Earth Summit in 1992, and the international Institution for Sustainable Development established in 1990 with headquarters at Canada.

The age of enlightenment was the beginning of modern civilization based on rational thought and action, belief in progress and reliance on Knowledge for the development of humanity. However, these principles of enlightenment when carried by the imperial countries to the colonized countries became the carriers of racial superiority complex and contempt for civilization on the oppressed people. The phenomenon of globalization should not degenerate into domination of the affluent countries with command over modern science and technology. If the values of the vision of a humane society and world order are to survive, globalisation has to be reconciled with the preservation of cultural roots.

As P.N. Haksar, Chancellor of Jawaharlal Nehru University emphasized in course of his address, "For too long has the world been governed by people with a rigid mindset. Flexible and open minds are needed for reconciling globalization with cultural roots." The key note of the conference was 'think global and act local as' the motto.

'Only think globally and act locally' can provide the balance between forces of globalization and preservation of cultural roots.

PART -III

CRITIQUE OF THE THEORY OF NEO LIBERALISM

25
CRITIQUE OF NEO-CLASSICAL ECONOMICS

Like all academic disciplines, economics has also been continuously engaged in the examination of its definition, nature, scope and significance. This article seeks to give an overview of this from Classical Economics to modern times.

Classical Economics

The foundations of Economics, more appropriately known as political economy in those days, were laid by the "classical economists" in the wake of rise of industrial capitalism in Great Britain (1760-1820). Adam Smith's "Enquiry into the Wealth of Nations" 1776 is acknowledged as the first comprehensive treatise on the subject. He considered broadening of the market as the key to the Wealth of Nations. He brought out some of the basic forces and impulses governing the market economy - most important of which was the basic impulse of the economic agents participating in the market to pursue "self interest".

In a famous sentence he pointed out that the butcher, the baker and the brewer do not supply meat, bread and wine for satisfying the consumer but for serving their own self-interest viz. making a living for themselves; yet thanks to the invisible hand in the market, their self-serving activities rebound to public good.

He emphasized the importance of division of labour and specialization in increasing the productivity of the market economy. He identified demand and supply as the basic market forces. His successor, Ricardo (*Principles of Political Economy and Taxation*, 1817) extended the thinking to international trade and formulated the law of comparative advantage, which holds ground till this day. He formulated the law of diminishing returns especially in relation to land. J.S.Mill, the last amongst the classical economists synthesized thinking in his. Principles of Political Economy, 1848.

He made a distinction between production and distribution, the former being the sphere of the free market economy while the latter leaves scope for intervention.

Thomas Malthus (*Principle of Population,* 1798) brought out the long-term race between economic (agricultural) and population growth – while the former grows in arithmetic proportions the latter in geometric proportion thereby creating an imbalance, which can only be rectified by pestilence, disease and famine.

Karl Marx (*Das Capital*) was the deviant who predicted the collapse of capitalism because of its inner contradictions. Exploitation of the working classes (wages paid being less than the value of labour) would lead to under consumption, collapse of demand and fall in profits leading to economic crisis of capitalism.

Neo-classical Economics

1870's and later years saw the emergence of neo-classical economics which formulated precise "economic laws" regarding consumption, production and distribution based on the theory of optimisation through calculation of cost and benefit at the margin. Consumer optimises his purchasing power by equalising marginal utility of all commodities, purchased according to his scale of preference, derived from the last unit of money spent on them.

The producer optimises the use of the factors of production by equalising their marginal productivity to the amount paid (i.e. wage equals marginal productivity of labour, rate of interest equals the marginal efficiency of capital and rent to marginal productivity of land except as pointed out by Ricardo in the case of land of higher productivity which would receive higher returns called rent). A firm would produce up to the point where marginal cost equals marginal revenue.

There would be the tendency towards equilibrium in the market at which point demand and supply of goods, services and factors of production would be in balance through the operation of the price mechanism. If at any time demand exceeds supply there would be the tendency for the price to go up which would result in fall in demand and increase in supply, the latter because of increase in the profit margin. In the case of some commodities there would be equilibrium in the short-run, while in the case of others it would be in the long run depending on the elasticity of supply. Pareto equilibrium states the theoretical property of the competitive market to produce optimum results. The general implication of the competitive market equilibrium theory is that the role of the government should be as small as possible.

There was increasing sophistication and precision in the formulation of these laws. Alfred Marshall in England (Cambridge), J.B. Say in France, Knut Wicksell in Sweden, and Irving Fisher, and J.B. Clark in USA were some of the leading economists who gave shape to neo-classical economics.

Mathematical Economics

Two economists of the neo-classical school viz. William Stanley Jevons of Manchester University and Leon Walras, of Lausaune University felt that the economic laws being concerned with quantities lend themselves to mathematical formulations. They introduced mathematical systems of analysis. Walras pioneered the concept of "general equilibrium" based on simultaneous equations relating to all the transactions in the economy. The culmination of the mathematical approach to economics was P.A.Samuelson's, *Foundations of Economics* (1947) a 379 pages book of mathematical formulations. Econometrics evolved as a specialized branch of Economics but it had no empirical content.

Recent contribution of mathematicians to economics is the fascinating "Game Theory" which dates back to "The Theory of Games and Economic Behaviours" 1944 by John Van Newmann and Oskar Margenstern followed by John Nash, on whom the movie "A Beautiful Mind" has been prepared. One classic example of the games theory is the "prisoner's dilemma". There is a best strategy for each individual but if chosen it will make each individual worse off. Economists like Thomas Schelling, winner of 2005 Nobel Prize made game theory popular. But Game Theory does not give concrete examples with real data or observed facts. The techniques of complex theory also have had a big impact on Economics which worships mathematical techniques, pays little attention to behavioral and institutional forces in the real world, which is too messy to model with tidy equations. Alfred Marshall who did include some mathematics in his Principles had wisely observed, "Use mathematics as a short term language rather than as an engine of enquiry". Keynes originally trained in Mathematics decided that purely mathematical approach to Economics was not fruitful.

Though economic phenomena are often measurable, mathematical methods are hardly appropriate for the problems, which economics has to handle. Analogy between Physics and Economics is misleading.

The Classical Economists used the term "political economy"; after 1870s the term went out of fashion and was replaced by the term "Economics".

Economists started talking of their subject as science like Physics. This distinguished Economics from other Social Sciences and lent it a prestige, which the latter lacked because of their imprecise formulations.

Definition of Economics

The term "Political Economy" had wider connotation while the term "Economics" was narrowly focused. Adam Smith who wrote the treatise on Wealth of Nations had earlier published his *Theory of Moral Sentiments*. Though his theory of the market was based on the concept of self-interest, he considered moral values as important. He condemned the tendencies of business people to indulge in conspiracy against the interest of the common people. He recognized the role of the State in supporting the moral and legal framework in which market has to operate. Ricardo considered that the whole purpose of the subject of Economics was to improve human welfare.

Even Alfred Marshall, the fountain head of neo-classical economics, defined Economics in wider terms. On the first page of Principles (1890) he gave the following definition: "Political Economy or Economics is the study of mankind in the ordinary business of life, it examines that part of individual and social action which is most closely connected with the attainment and the use of material requisites of well being".

The break came in 1932 with the publication of the essay *Nature and Significance of Economics* by Prof. Lionel Robbins. It re-defined Economics as the science of individual choice concerned with the optimum use of "means" which are limited for the attainment of "ends" which are unlimited. Thus, economics became a technical subject, cutting its umbilical knot with the social phenomena and social sciences. Its focus became narrow and highly specialized.

Teaching of Economics

The narrow focus of Economics soon started getting reflected in teaching of Economics in the Universities and other academic institutions. The courses in economic history and history of economic thought which formed an integral part of syllabi for graduate and post-graduate courses started getting omitted and replaced by technically and mathematically oriented courses. Students started getting involved in curves and equations without any background of classical economics and historical evolution of the subject. Economics taught in abstract terms started getting divorced from economic reality and perspective of historical evolution.

The Birth of Keynesian Macro Economics

Inspite of its scientific pretensions the so called laws of Economics divorced from reality were found wanting in anticipating and providing sound policy prescriptions to tackle challenges with which capitalist economies got confronted. The greatest challenge was posed by the un-precedented severe and long lasting depression in the US economy from 1929 onwards. Laws of Neo-classical Economics required cut in wages to cut costs and create profits, which would stimulate business and raise the economy out of trough. But this did not happen. On the other hand, cut in wages reduced demand and deepened depression. Market did not provide an automatic correction and public intervention on a massive scale in the shape of President Roosevelt's 'New Deal Programme' became necessary. It is against this background that J.M. Keynes came out in 1936 with his "General Theory of Employment, Interest and Money". He presented a new theoretical construction. He moved from micro to macro and focused attention on Aggregate Demand and Aggregate Supply. Aggregate Demand and Aggregate Supply could be in equilibrium but at less than full employment level. For the economy to be lifted to equilibrium at full employment level, public authorities would have to stimulate aggregate demand by augmenting investment and consumption. Inducement to invest and propensity to consume are the dynamic elements in the economy, which have a multiplier effect. These new concepts and insights came like a breath of fresh air ushering in what came to be known as the "Keynesian Revolution". Books on new Economics known as Macro Economics soon appeared embodying and elaborating the Keynesian analysis. Papers on Macro Economics came to be included in the syllabi of academic courses. Whole statistical systems focusing on income, investment, consumption, money and interest were designed. Robert Engle and Clive Granger who won Nobel Prize in 2003, made statistical analysis of series such as, GDP, inflation, stock prices, etc.

But World War II intervened and the economic stimulus provided by war effort absorbed unemployment. On the other hand, demands for war supplies created scarcities and inflationary pressures, which continued even after World War II. Keynesian remedies i.e. fiscal policies in reverse were required to cut public expenditure and curb excessive investment and consumption. Instead, Keynesian economics was held responsible for inflation. The center of gravity shifted from fiscal to monetary remedies. Under the leadership of Milton Friedman, the Chicago School emerged which debunked the Keynesian economics and returned to the orthodox economics and its remedies and focused on inflation rather than employment. If inflation is curbed through a steady money supply, flexible labour market, cut in wages, control over demands and curtailment of social benefits of a welfare state, free market would take care of the economy. The sole function of the Central Bank of a country should be to keep a stable money supply and prevent emergence of inflationary pressures. If there is still some amount of unemployment, it should be treated as "natural unemployment", which was bound to exist in any economy. Thus, to the old concepts of "frictional unemployment" and "structural unemployment" was added "Natural Rate of Unemployment" (NRU). There is trade off between inflation and unemployment. When inflation accelerates, actual unemployment persists below NRU. The concept of natural unemployment was vague but it served the purpose of exempting Central Bank or the Government from any responsibility. The pain caused by "Natural Unemployment" was considered necessary to provide incentives to working classes to work harder on lower wages. The influence of this kind of thinking was reflected in the increase of more than 200 in the average working hours per year in USA.

Macro economics is also sought to be brought within the fold of Micro economics. Some economists of neo-classical type have envisaged that if "an auctioneer" would be placed in charge of the Macro economy, he will govern it according to optimizing rules of Micro economics. New macro economics books are full of analyses of prices, market, competition, etc. Ozgur Gun of the University of Remschampague Ardene considers that the whole effort is "absurd". There is no need to give "micro economics" foundations to "macro economics".

Development Economics

From about the middle of the twentieth century, several countries of Asia and Africa started emerging as independent countries free from the yoke of imperialism of the Western Countries. They felt that political independence should be used for rapid economic development so that their people can get out of the vicious circle of poverty and enjoy better conditions of living and reduce the gap between their own living standard and that of the Western countries. These countries came to be known as "developing" countries as compared with the "developed" countries of the West. "Development" had to include building infrastructure of transport, communication, education and health facilities, power generation, modernization of agriculture, industrialization and diversification of the economy. Countries like India felt that such comprehensive and balanced development could not be left to the vicissitudes of the market forces of demand and supply; development had to be deliberately designed and fostered by the State as was pointed out by Freidrich List at the time of German economic development. While economists like Raul Prebisch of Argentina advocated the strategy of import substitution, which was followed by a country like India, others like South Korea followed the strategy of export promotion. In both models, it was recognized that entrepreneurial activity needs judicious state support. Through a combination of visionary government and entrepreneurial society, Singapore has risen rapidly to a level higher than that of many European countries. But Government has to be efficient. Waste and inefficiency in public sector should have no place. Public sector in Singapore works like a company. Various alternative strategies like big push (Rosenstein Rodain, 1943), unbalanced growth (Alber Hirschman), take-off (Walter Rostow) were advocated. In all these different approaches, capital formation through investment emerged as the key factor though the importance of technology and human resource development was well-recognised. Ragnar Nurkse suggested capital formation through mobilization of manpower as in China. A lot of economic literature emerged, which came to be recognized as a distinct branch of Economics i.e.– "Economics of Development" for which academic courses were established as a part of the curriculum. A number of textbooks were written such as, W.A. Lewis's *Theory of Economic Growth*, or Kindleberger's "*Economic Development*". But orthodox economists like Peter Bauer rejected any special category of "Development Economics".

Neo-classical economics had paid little attention to answer the question – "What makes economies grow?" apart from dwelling on the theme of static equilibrium with optimum allocation of resources. But faced with the challenges before the underdeveloped countries, economists tried to provide a theoretical analysis to supplement record of empirical evidence the most comprehensive of which were studies published by Angus Maddison – *The World Economy: A Millennial Perspective* and *The World Economy: Historical Statistics*. Economists identified savings, investment, and accumulation of capital, innovations and technology as key factors in development. The first amongst the models of development was the "Harrod Domar Model" – investment rate divided by capital-output ratio determines the rate of growth. Robert Solow's 1956 article emphasized the role of technology for long-term growth. Papers by Robert Lucas (1988) and Paul Romer (1986-1990) focused on human capital (stock of knowledge) and technological innovation respectively. A paper by Arvind Dixit and Joseph Stiglitz (1976) drew attention to the role of differentiated products and increasing returns to scale. Paul Krueger emphasized the role of geographical clusters, education, research and innovation in boosting productivity and growth. In addition to traditional, physical capital of machines and buildings, investment in skills and abilities of work forces were emphasized.

Eradication of poverty has been the greatest challenge before the developing countries. It was expected that if economic growth takes place, the fruits will eventually percolate to the poor. However, microeconomics has not explained how the percolation theory works. In several LA and African countries, poverty has proved intractable. Most of the decline in poverty is in China and to some extent in India. On the whole, income level of poor countries has failed to cope up with the income level of rich countries.

In recent years, it is realized that per capita income figures are not adequate; they should be supplemented by human dèvelopment index, as developed by UN. The index includes items like availability of drinking water, sewage disposal system, and rates of infant mortality, life expectancy, etc. In affluent countries too GNP growth is supplemented by measures for economic welfare. Economic growth has allowed fewer working hours, for example, Sweden, a welfare state, has 1300 to 1400 hours in a year as against 1600 in Britain and USA and 2000 in Japan. But in these countries domestic labour with no help absorbs much of leisure time.

Development Economies however, suffered a set back when as a part of "Washington Consensus", World Bank and International Monetary Fund and later World Trade Organisation after it was set up in 1995, started insisting that countries approaching them for assistance should strictly follow the Structural Adjustment Programme (SAP) which envisaged marketisation of the economy as against planning; liberalization as against dirigism or state control and regulation and privatisation as against public sector; open economy as against autarky and fiscal discipline implying minimization of public expenditure and "minimal state". The programme was uniformly insisted upon irrespective of different socio-economic, geographical and historical backgrounds and different problems faced by different countries. The approach was "one size fits all". The result was hardly beneficial – several countries of Latin America and Africa suffered a set back after the SAP was imposed as brought out by economists like Jeffrey Sachs and Joseph Stiglitz.

When poster boys of development, the East Asian countries like Thailand, Malaysia, Indonesia and South Korea suddenly suffered an unanticipated economic crisis, in 1998, the remedy suggested was also on the lines of SAP which made for painful recovery. A country like Malaysia, which did not follow the advice, did better.

Under the leadership of Milton Friedman and the Chicago boys, a "shock therapy" was imposed by dictator Pinochle's regime in Chile. A similar strategy was imposed on Russia after the collapse of communism. In both countries it led to the emergence of oligarchies who looted the natural resources of these countries.

Shaky Foundations of Micro-economics

While market economy seems to have emerged triumphant in today's era of globalisation, there is a keener realization that neo-classical micro economics which is supposed to provide intellectual support to the free market economy, is itself based on questionable assumptions. Kenneth Arrow, a Nobel Prize winner, through his papers, made economists aware of stringent conditions required for competitive equilibrium.

First, the concept of "homo economies", the individual economic agent, whether consumer or producer, making choices or taking decisions is a faulty one. An individual does not exist in isolation. He or she is a member of a family and society and his or her choices and decisions are influenced by interpersonal relationships and community values. The economic activity is embedded in a web of social institutions. An individual should be placed in a social context, as observed by economist, Nobel Prize Winner Trygve Haavelmo, in his lecture "Economics and Welfare State" (1989).

Secondly, the stipulation that an individual makes "rational" choices and takes "rational decisions" in "self-interest" is not valid. The behaviour of the individual is influenced by many factors including moral and ethical considerations and is not purely "hedonist" in character. Impulse buying, spontaneous consumption decisions, adventure and desire for the unknown are not always rational. But they do characterize individual decisions.

Thirdly, the assumptions relating to a perfectly competitive market are inconsistent with the conditions in the real world. One of the assumptions is that there are innumerable buyers and sellers none of whom by themselves are able to influence the market. In actual world, there are conditions of monopoly, oligopoly and imperfect competition based on differentiated products. In the thirties, E S Chamberlain and Joan Robinson wrote books to modify the "laws" formulated to suit a perfectly competitive market. This was before the emergence of modern corporations. As J.K Galbraith has pointed out, corporations of today are so powerful that with the aid of advertisements and money power, they are able to reverse the proposition that supply is according to demand. Corporations manipulate demand to be in accordance with supply.

Nor is the assumption of "perfect knowledge" valid. Consumers are often ill informed about the products and services they buy. There is no "instantaneous omniscience".

Fourthly, firms in the real world do not take decisions regarding production by equating marginal cost with marginal revenue or by constantly substituting at the "margin" one factor of production for another with a view to optimization. These decisions are often influenced by compulsions of machinery and capital equipment and technology. There are no "constant coefficients of production", no perfect divisibility of goods or factors of production.

Fifthly, market as conceived in textbooks of micro economics bears no resemblance to the market in the real world. That is why syllabus relating to marketing in business courses deal with practical issues like "brand" and "goodwill" rather than the theorectical stipulations of a competitive market.

Sixthly, market equilibrium as envisaged by micro economics is in "stationary state". It does not deal with dynamics in the economy. Uncertainty is an integral part of economic life and yet will not be analysed in any rigorous way in the competitive model until early 1950, Kenneth Arrow introduced uncertainty in equilibrium analysis, although in a specific and restrictive way. Its input-output relationship is lineal whereas in the real world there are dynamic changes and non-lineal and even chaotic relationship is the rule rather than exception.

Seventh, micro economics completely overlooks the institutional set up in the context of which the market functions. The institutional set up includes legal framework, educational set up, cultural institutions etc.

Eight, micro economics confines its attention to economic activity in the "market", overlooking economic activity conducted in the fold of family, health and educational institutions and government to give a few examples. It has been estimated that the family activity in the Western economies accounts for 40% of the GNP.

Ninethly, record of micro economics in understanding and forecasting the economy at macro level is not impressive.

Economists in recent years, some of them Nobel Prize

winners, have tried to grapple with these uncomfortable questions for the votaries of Micro economics. Below is provided a succinct review of this literature.

Recent Works in Micro Economics

Rational Man – Though Adam Smith based his theory of market on "pursuit of self-interest", he was well aware of the influence of "moral sentiment" in organization of society. His colleague David Hume stated, "rational conclusions vanish like phantoms of the night". However, latter day neo-classical economics broke away from "the richer psychological tradition" of "soulful economics" and placed "rational economic man" at the center stage". But in recent years, economists have tried to explore the "psychological realm" leading to the emergence of behavioural economics. In 1977, Amartya Sen, a Nobel Prize winner described the selfish calculating agents of economic theory as "rational fools". George Akerlof, another Noble Prize winner and Janet Yellen presented "efficient wage" hypothesis on the basis of psychology of workers. Economists have started using results from psychological and neurological studies and laboratory experiments to explore the ways of real humans – sometimes non-rational – which differ, from those of "economic man". Nobel laureate, Herbert Simon introduced the concept of "bounded rationality", which aims at "satisficing" as against "optimizing". Vernon Smith and Daniel Kahneman created the field of "experimental economics". Neuro-economists use medical techniques to monitor peoples' brains as they take economic decisions. Experiments have demonstrated inertia and short-sightedness in financial decisions which people take. Decisions are often taken spontaneously and intuitively. Preferences are not purely self-interested; a strong sense of fairness also prevails. Loss aversion and reciprocal altruism influence utility functions. Utility functions are not stable. Immediate gratification gets the better of long-term calculations. Behavioural insights are important in labour economics, savings and insurance.

Information - By 1980 rich literature developed on Economics of Information. One of the active contributors to this literature is another Nobel Prize winner – Joseph Stiglitz. He explained why "share cropping" apparently an unjust system for the tenants is "rational" in the context of tenant's uncertainty about the future and a asymmetric information available to the landowner about the worker's skills and efforts. Another example of information gap is the modern corporation, where managers are paid high salaries to incentivise them to perform well without knowing how productive these managers actually are. Another Nobel Prize winner George Akerlof in his 1970 paper "The market for lemons" showes why in the absence of information, only cars in terrible shape (lemons) get sold in second hand car markets in the absence of "information". Michael Spence in his Ph.D. Thesis on "market signaling" (1976) shows how employers figure out which potential employees are more highly skilled than others. The concept of "asymmetrical information" has been found relevant in a number of areas like insurance, contracts, labour markets, industrial organization, corporate finance, development economics, public services, etc. In two and a half decades since the pioneering work on economics of imperfect information, a huge amount of research on specific application of these insights has emerged. The research has led to flourishing field of experimental economics concerned with how best to design markets; how to combine administered and market based policy. Trading schemes regarding environmental pollution, being widely adopted is another example. Information markets, it is suggested, can out perform experts in collecting, aggregating and sharing private information. The reach of markets should therefore be extended into areas, which have traditionally been reserved for social and governmental action.

Economics and Social Institutions

Just as Darwin discovered the law of evolution in organic nature, Marx discovered the law of evolution in human society.

Thorstein Veblen, in late nineteenth century was next in the line of social theorists of capitalism. He made a critical analysis of the idle rich and their conspicuous consumption.

In the twentieth century, Austrian economist Joseph Schumpeter was the one to present sociological critique of capitalism in his book *Capitalism, Socialism and Democracy.* He identified innovation as the dynamic element in the capitalist system leading to "creative destruction". In this he focused on the dynamic role of the entrepreneur. Despite disagreeing with Marx he also felt that capitalism was doomed. He saw the emergence of bureaucracy stifling entrepreneurial initiative. According to F A Hayek, modern capitalist economy was an interconnected system made possible by institutions and laws which replaced personal trust underpinning transactions in a traditional society.

Recent revival of evolutionary theorizing in Economics was pioneered by Richard Nelson and Sydney Winter, who published their papers on evolutionary growth models in late 1960s and 70s. Firms constantly innovate and allocate investment in profitable technologies. Many firms exist while few, increasingly large, survive as in car industry.

More recently economists have turned to sociology i.e. study of social networks, norms, culture and social institutional capital from which neo-classical economics had abstracted itself. Family is one such institution to which Gary Baker's work is related. He applied economic approach to social phenomena. Another approach was provided by 1991 Nobel Prize Winner Robert Coase. In his article on "The Nature of the Firm", (1937), he pointed out that big firms reduce transaction costs involved in using market, by "internalizing" the transactions.

Nobel Laureate, Douglas North gave rise to "New Institutional Economics" which showed how institutions throughout history have been built to create order and reduce uncertainty in exchange. Another economist was Oliver Williamson who analysed structure of organization – business corporations and trade unions.

All these economists came together in 1997 to set up International Society for New Institutional Economics.

Gvanovetter took Sociology to the heart of Economics through his research, which showed how both social obligations and self-interest play, some part in decisions, which make up economic and social life alike.

The study of "Social Capital" shows that participants in the economy are more than the sum of self-interested individuals. Social Capital enhances cooperation between individuals for mutual benefit. Social capital gives good economic results. It builds up trust, which is fundamental to economic development. According to Partha Dasgupta, social capital comprises of social network of the economy.

Social capital, social networks, cultural norms, in addition to markets and governments turn individual choices into collective action.

Extension of Principles of Micro economics to Politics and Government

Nobel Prize winner, James Buchanan extended the tools of micro economics to politics and government through his "public choice" approach (Calculus of Consent, 1962). It opened up debate on motivation of politicians and public officials. He argued that like business people in the market, elected representatives too are motivated by self interest rather than public interest or social concern. Politicians are vote maximisers rather than concerned with matters of people. He advocated his "Theory of Collective Choice" as analogous to the economic theory of markets. Following Buchanan, Mancur Olson in his "Logic of Collective Action", looked at politics as a competition between the private interest of specific groups advocated by "lobbies" rather than a process of delivering "public interest", Politicians engineer short term economic booms in the period before elections. This contradicted the idealistic view that government and public administrators are guardians of public interest. In any case, economic performance of government has marginal influence on election results. This gave a radical conservative like Margaret Thatcher to argue that government cannot set right social problems. "No government can do anything except through people; people must look after themselves. There are individuals and families. There is no such thing as society".

Economics and Ecology

Environmental Pollution and threat to natural resources have emerged as the grave danger to future of humanity. From early

1970s, studies relating to limits to growth imposed by ecological factors were taken up. Continuous emission of toxic gases from industrial enterprises and transport vehicles etc., have polluted air and water. Adverse impact of development in the form of pollution and waste, need huge defensive expenditure. Development has created "illth" not just wealth. Green house gases have led to the phenomenon of global warming which has upset the balance of nature. Different parts of the world have suffered from unexpected torrential rains and cyclones in some parts of the world and droughts and high temperature in others. This has upset the agricultural cycle and caused forest fires. The Intergovernmental panel on climate change have recommended the planned reduction of emission of toxic gases by 5.8% but the biggest polluter USA has refused to accept the target on the ground that it would put a constraint on its economic growth and its high living standard, which it is not prepared to accept. Emerging economies like China and India are also unwilling to accept limits to their growth. Economic processes create wastes, which negatively impact on human welfare. On the other hand, unrelented demands of the economy have created the possibility of exhaustion of finite and non-renewable resources. The super power is attempting to grab control over scarce hydro carbon resources through invasion and lets loose violence on other countries who are endowed by nature. At the same time, technology for development of alternative sources of energy like solar, wind and wave energy, as well as, biological energy has received less attention than it deserves.

Economy is embedded in ecology; it is a part of the ecosystem and cannot function without natural resources, which however, in neo-classical economics are taken for granted with no or little value attached to them. With its short-term perspective, it takes no notice of threat to natural resources in the long run. The cost-benefit analysis of projects does not account for cost in terms of depletion, denudation or degradation of natural resources nor in terms of ecological benefits, which some types of economic activities can confer. This leads to wrong assessment of projects. Running down the stock of natural resources reduces future capacity to produce and is unfair for future generation.

The idea of externalities was a step in the direction of recognizing social costs and social benefits as against private costs and private benefits. But this is hardly enough. A whole new subject environmental economics needs to be developed going far beyond, the narrow vision of mainstream Micro economics in order to come to grips with the issues relating to "sustainable development". Economy has to be ecologically sustainable.

Micro economics and Neo-liberalism

The basic weaknesses of Micro economic go far beyond those imposed by its unsound assumptions mentioned above. They arise from its preoccupation with the short-run rather than the long run, with static state than dynamic changes, with efficiency in terms of optimum allocation of resources rather than equity through deliberate redistribution of income, with money and wealth rather than welfare and well-being. That is what made Paul Ormerod talk of "the death of economies". Conventional economics (main stream of micro economics) gives a very misleading view of the way the world actually operates and that needs to be replaced. The preoccupation with theoretical and mathematical equations rather than great problems of the day has reduced economics to "esoteric irrelevance". Economics should reinvent itself and rather than arrogating to itself the exclusive status of being "scientific" as distinguished from other social sciences, it should join hands with them to understand reality and tackle problems of the real world. An interdisciplinary approach with inputs not only of Economics but also other Social Sciences like Political Science and Sociology, as well as, history, is likely to be more successful than theoretical models and mathematical equations. It is high time that economists go far beyond the narrow limits, which Micro economics has imposed, on itself.

Ideological Biases

With all its scientific pretensions, Micro economics claims to be a positive, value neutral discipline, but its ideological biases are quite apparent. It has provided in recent years intellectual support to a neo-liberal policy, initiated in 1982 by Ronald Reagan in USA and Margaret Thatcher in UK and imposed by the "Washington consensus" on all economies and the world economy.

Deregulation of the private sector and minimal government became the key words. This has created acute disparities between countries and people within countries. In neo-liberal Britain, managers of companies draw salaries thousand times more than the wages of its own employees on the ground of efficiency and productivity. The underpaid are asked to improve their own productivity before claiming a better deal. Farmers in India, who commit suicide are asked by the Chief Minister not to be lazy. In the home of neo-liberalism viz. the USA, when hurricane Katrina wiped out the homes of the poor, the local Republican Senator was cheerful that natural disaster has removed the blot which human agency could not have! The task of rehabilitation of the homeless was entrusted to a private company because public agency could not be trusted which not only made money but also made a hash of the job leaving the poor in a miserable state. The task of security in Baghdad was entrusted to a private agency which itself shot dead eleven Iraqis, an act which scandalized even the puppet government. The wreckless lending for sub-prime housing mortgages threatened the banking system not only in USA but also in Europe and there was a run for return of deposits on the North Rock Bank in England forcing Gordon Brown, the PM to assure the depositors that Government would guarantee the safety of their deposits and yet the run would not stop. Such is the rationality of the market. Some years back, deregulation of financial markets in USA led to savings and loan scandal. With her fetish for privatization, Margaret Thatcher squandered away the precious oil resources discovered in the North Sea, while Govt. of Norway used these resources as assets out of whose income the standard of welfare services were improved.

Neo-liberal philosophy downgrades the role of government in creating the legal framework, regulating the private enterprise so as to ensure that it works within the framework of common good, penalizing illegalities and financial scandals building up essential infrastructure, caring for those whom market does not take care of and using natural resources for social benefit. As Ha-joon Chang of Cambridge University, teacher of economic history has shown, rich countries did not develop on the basis of policies that they now force upon the developing countries.

With neo-liberal ideology generated by Micro economics, it can hardly be called "Soul Economics" rather it is "dismal economics" a title conferred on Economics by Thomas Carlyle. The mainly technical contributions of modern day economists like the Game Theory or mathematical economics with little empirical base and purely intellectual model building can do little to widen the horizon of Economics. Above all, Economies needs to be "humanized" by restoring the place of value, morality and happiness in economic theory and studies.

Broaden Economics

The academic movement to broaden the scope of economics so as to enable it to deal with the reality and make it a truly social science than a branch of mathematics has gathered strength. In June 2000 economics students in Paris called for reforms in their academic curriculum so as to broaden its spectrum. In 2001, 27 Ph.D. students of Cambridge University, UK launched the movement for "opening up Economics". In August of the same year teachers from 17 countries who had gathered in Kansas City in USA issued an international open letter to all economics departments, calling on them to reform Economics education and research. Thousands of Economists from scores of countries have also taken up the cause for broad band Economics under the banner of "Post Autistic Economics".

The present division between micro economics, macro economics, development economics, econometrics, managerial economics, institutional economics, environmental economics etc., needs to be ended. Economics needs to be blended into a more integrated presentation of the subject building bridges between different divisions of the subject.

References

Paul Ormerod, *"The Death of Economics"* John Wiley & Sons Inc., New York, 1997." A Guide to What

Edited Edward Fullbrook, *Wrong with Economics"*, Anthem Press, 2005.

The Soulful Science: What Economists Really Do and Why it Matters, Diane Coyle, Princeton University Press, 2007.

26

MYTHS AND REALITY OF CAPITALISM

Prof. Galbraith of Harvard University had been, through his copious and widely read books, a sustained critic of unbridled capitalism and its adverse consequences on the living of the common people. Thus in his celebrated book, *The Affluent Society*, he drew pointed attention to the glaring contradiction between private opulence and public squalor. In his "New Industrial State", he showed how the operations of the "techno structure" of the corporations which now dominate the economy, have completely overthrown the "conventional wisdom" of traditional economics. The "myths" sedulously fostered by the latter have no relation to the reality of the economic world. The slim volume, *Economics of Innocent Fraud*, his last offering, distills the essence of Galbraith several criticisms of the capitalist economy.

The capitalist economy now a days masquerades in some what neutral impersonal term "the free market economy". This enables it to escape from the responsibility of its historic crimes and blunders – subjugation of workers by the owners of the means of production, monopolistic abuses, roles of European arms and steel combines in engineering world wars and cyclical booms and busts ravaging the economy.

Galbraith exposes a series of myths attributed to the market economy.

The myth is that in the market "consumer sovereignty" prevails.

The reality in the market is that the consumer sovereignty has been impaired by the manipulation of consumer demand through advertisement, salesmanship with the help of the powerful medium of Television and mislending product differentiation.

The myth is that the economy rewards work in proportion to discomfort experienced in course of work. The reality is that those who do not have to do physical work and enjoy it are the best paid.

The myth is that the market economy consists of innumerable producers including small business and family agriculture. In reality, it is dominated by big corporations.

The myth is that the corporations are governed by the decisions of shareholders and their representative Boards of Directors. The reality is that the corporations are managed by its "bureaucracy" who award munificent compensation to themselves despite falling profits and stock market prices.

The myth is that the economy consists of two sectors – the private sector and the public sector. The reality is that on expanding part of what is called public sector is for all practical purposes in the private sector. Military expenditure (eupheminously termed defence expenditure) by government is determined by military industry complex. Even foreign and military policy of government is determined by it.

The myth is the upturns and downturns of the economy can be forecast by "consultants" and experts with the help of economic and statistical analysis. The reality is that they are unpredictable. Sometimes well published predictions by consultants are intended to serve personal gain.

Federal Reserve system especially under Alon Greenspan was endowed with the capacity to use monetary measures such as modification of Bank rate to manage the economy. In reality Central Bank action had minimal effect and had no decisive role.

The myth had been that the standards of corporate finances are maintained by professional auditors and accountants. The reality is that they had been parties to corporate scandals.

The myth is that corporate scandals can be avoided by

appropriate regulation. The reality is that public official including those of Security and Exchange Commission can be unduly compliant and corporate influence does extend to regulators.

The myth is that the economic well being of the people is measured by the GDP. The reality is that the negative social effects of the so called productive activity like pollution, destruction of environment, the neglect of citizen health and education, threat of military action and mass destruction are not taken into account. No wonder human progress is marked by unimaginable cruelty and death caused by wars.

It is these myths and frauds which are the basis of the structural adjustment programme, the so called economic reforms, which were imposed on the developing countries by the international economic organizations viz. The World Bank, The IMF and The WTO under the influence of the global capitalism led by USA and its allies.

In these days of uncritical acclaim of globalization by economists and the rest, the "Bad Samaritans", a book by the Cambridge University economic historian Ha-Joon Chay a Nurkse comes like an eye-opener.

The "Unholy Trinity" of the World Bank, the IMF and the WTO and the financial institutions under their control or influence of those whom the author rightly describes as "Bad Samaritans". They have taken advantage of the weaknesses of the developing countries, and imposed on them the so called package of economic reforms of liberalization, privatization and globalization otherwise known as the "Structural adjustment programme i.e. The SAP imposes fiscal discipline, strict money policies, deregulation, dismantling public projects and programmes, reduced role of the state, low tariffs and removal of barriers to private investment, all aimed at making them a part of the free market world economy.

In fact, it is a self-serving strategy of the rich countries led by USA intended to impose their dominance on the world economy through un-fettered operation of their multinational corporations even though it is detrimental to the economic interests of the common people of the developing countries. The rich countries have systematically tried to hide their real purpose by justifying their strategy of globalization in a self righteous manner as based on sound principles of free market economies which they advocate for the developing countries though they themselves had found it necessary to give a go by to these principles and resort to economic protection in their own early stages of development. In tendering their advice to the developing countries they do not find it necessary to pay any attention to the well being of the common people of the developing countries, nor the sovereign right of the governments of these countries to chalk out their own policies. They have sedulously fostered myths of rationality and sanctity of the principle of the free market economy though they are inconsistent with economic reality. This has been facilitated by the recent upsurge of new-classical economics under the leadership of the Chicago School of Economics – Milton Friedman and his followers – which has virtually banished Keynesian Economics and the counterveiling fiscal policies advocated by it as also the newly born Developmental Economics formulated by economists like Raghan Nurkse and Roscustein Roden to evolve a positive strategy of development for the developing countries.

Free Trade Vs. Protection

The "Official" history of globalization has spread the myth that the rich countries of which Britian was the first owed their economic development and prosperity to free market and free trade liberal *laissez fair* policies, low barriers to the international flow of goods and labour and principles of sound money (low inflation) and balanced budgets. The facts are otherwise. The protectionist policies initiated by the first Prime Minister of Britain, Robert Walpole (1721-42), continued until the middle of the 19th century. It helped British manufacturing industries to establish themselves. At the same time it banned cotton textile imports from India, destroyed Irish woolen industry and banned the construction of new steel mills in America as also manufacture of high technology products. It wanted colonies to be producing primary commodities to supply raw material at low cost to British manufactures. Once British industry becames internationally competitive, Britain adopted the free trade policy since it was in her interest. In 1846, Corn Law was repealed and tariff on many manufactured goods was abolished.

It was not long before America realized the harmful effect of British policy. As the first Finance Minister of USA, Alexander Hamilton, in his report on the state of manufactures submitted to US Congress, pointed out a backward country like USA should protect its industry in "infancy". He was the first, not Freindrich List of Germany, who coined the word. Since USA needed a big progress of industrialization, USA progressively raised import tariffs to an average of 45% by 1800. When President Lincoln of the Republic Party came to power, he raised tariffs to the highest level in US history. Tariffs on manufacturing imports remained at 50% until World War I. Following the onset of Great Depression in 1929, came in 1930 the Smoot Hawley Act which raised tariff even higher. It was with the help of those protectionist policies that the US became the fastest growing economy. USA was the most protectionist country in the world right up to 1930. It was only after Second World War that the US with it's industrial supremacy unchallenged that it liberalized its trade and started advocating the cause of free trade. But it is still aggressive in taking non-tariff measures when necessary; for example, without liberal federal funding for R & D, US would not have been able to maintain its technological lead over the rest of the world in key industries like computers, semi-conductors, life sciences, the internet and aero space. It was only after they became world's dominant industrial powers that Britain and USA themselves practiced free market economics. However, they forced non-western countries like India, China and Japan to practice free trade even though their economies needed protection.

Other countries which followed the foot steps of Britain and USA on the path of industrialization were France, Germany and Japan. The myth is that they were homes of protectionism. But the truth is they had lower tariffs than Britain and USA.

It was only after realizing after 1945 that the "hands off" Policies of the State were responsible for its relative economic decline and defeats in two world wars, that the French state took to much more active role in the economy through "Indicative planning", nationalization of key industries and active role of the state owned banks in channeling investment in strategic areas. Countries like Finland, Norway, Italy and Austria which were relatively backward at the end of World War II used similar strategies like high tariffs, State owned enterprises (SOE) and directing back credit to strategic industries.

Japan which led the "miracle economic" in East Asia after World War II did not do so through a neo-liberal policy. Though it did not keep industrial tariffs at a high level, it controlled import through foreign exchange regulation. Exports were promoted to earn foreign exchange needed to buy up better technology from abroad. Its MITI (Ministry for Industrial Trade and Industry) became well known for its orchestrated drive for industrial development programmes. Through directed credit programme, it subsidized credit into key sectors. Foreign investment was barred in key industries Foreign companies were required to transfer technology and had to buy specific proportions of inputs locally. There were strict ceilings on foreign ownership upto a maximum at 49 per cent.

An outstanding example of development in key sectors in Japan was the Toyota Automobile. It started as a manufacturer of textile machinery. It moved into car production in 1933. The Japanese government kicked out General Motors and Ford in 1939 and with money from government of Japan bailed out Toyota. After 25 years of trying, it slowly established itself as a car manufacturer. Today Toyota's luxury brand Lexus has become an icon for globalization.

Korea's economic growth over the last four and a half decades has been spectacular. From being one of the poorest countries of the world, it has come on par with some European countries like Portugal and Slovenia in terms of per capita income. A myth has been propagated that to achieve this miracle Korea pursued a neo-liberal economic strategy. The reality was different. Korea used measures like tariff protection, subsidies and various forms of government support to nurture new industries. Government owned all banks and directed credit for them.

Big projects were undertaken directly by state owned enterprises – POSCO the steel maker being the best example. Korean Government controlled foreign exchange to use hard earned foreign currencies for importing vital machinery and inputs. Korean government controlled foreign investment as well.

Taiwan used a strategy very similar to that of Korea. It used state owned enterprises more extensively while being somewhat friendlier to foreign investment than Korea.

Singapore is cited as an example of development achieved through free trade and foreign investment. But it is not all laissez faire. Government's role is considerable by way of investment in infrastructure and education targeted to particular industries. It has one of the largest state owned enterprise sectors in the world including the Housing Development Board. Even Hong Kong cited as an example of free economy had all land in ownership of Government in order to control the housing situation.

The more recent economic stories are of China and India. They also show the importance of strategic role of State rather than unconditional integration with the global economy.

It is a myth that development took place through free trade and free market policy. Virtually all successful countries used some mixture of protection, subsidies and regulation in early stages of development.

Despite this, the World Bank and the IMF imposed, as a part of "conditionality" of their aid, neo-liberal policies on the countries of Latin America and Africa. From 1980's when Latin America embraced neo-liberalisation, it had been growing at less than one third the rate from earlier days of protectionist Policy; Chile's experiment with neo-liberalisation led by so called Chicago Boys (a group of Chilean economist trained at the University of Chicago – the leading centre of neo-liberalisation) was a disaster; while African countries saw a fall in living standards a damning indictment of neo-liberal orthodoxy of the World Bank and IMF which have been practically running these economies.

Following the launching of WTO in 1995, the rich countries

made a concerted effort to push the developing countries into free trade through its regime as well as through bilateral and regional free trade agreements forgetting that industries in several developing countries would not survive if exposed to international competition before they had the time to improve their capabilities by mastering advanced technologies and building effective organization. No wonder massive trade liberalization proved harmful to several developing countries. For example, whole swathes of Mexican industry built during the period of import substitution were wiped out. In Ivory Coast the chemical, textile, shoe and automobile industries collapsed. The agricultural sector in Mexico was also hit hard by subsidized US products especially maize. Trade liberalization has reduced growth rates. The Theory of Comparative Cost on which free trade policy is based, may be conducive to efficiency in the use of resources in the short run, but not for economic development in the long run. There is a great deal of hypocracy in the advocacy of free trade by the rich countries. In the Doha negotiations (2001) USA and the EU introduced the proposal dubbed NAMA (Non agricultural market access) which wanted the developing countries to open up market for their agricultural products. The rich counties give out subsidies of $ 100 billion every year. In return for cutting tariffs by developing countries, they were not ready to reduce their subsidies substantially. Also while the USA has an overall tax rate of 1.6%, the tax rates raised for the products of a large number of developing countries – 4% for India and Peru and 14-15% for poor countries like Bangladesh, Nepal and Cambodia. The so called level playing field gives one sided benefit to rich countries, through non-trade policies like TRIPS which strengthened protection to Patents and other intellectual property rights. Subsidies are allowed for R & D, extensively used by rich countries. The rich countries give huge subsidies in the name of "reducing regional inbalances". Thus, in the name of the myth of free trade, the rich countries have in reality erected a new international trading system rigged in their favour.

Foreign Investement

Like TRIPS, TRIMS was devised as yet another instrument

devised to rig the system in favour of the rich countries. TRIMS (Trade Related Investment Measures) restricts the ability of WTO member countries to regulate foreign investors. It bans countries from laying down local content requirements, export requirements or foreign exchange balancing requirement. This has enabled MNCS to be foot loose, though their decision makers are still mostly home country nationals. The argument of the neo-liberals is that foreign firms won't come into a country unless it offers attractive market. Indeed developing countries were encouraged to enter into competition to offer concessions to MNC, to attract investment. The argument is misleading. China gets 10 per cent of World FDI not because of the concessions it offers but because of good infrastructure, cheap labour force and growing market.

Nor is foreign investment needed for a country's development as is shown by the examples of Finland which classified projects with more than 20 per cent foreign investments as dangerous. Liberalization of foreign investment came only in 1993 as a condition of access to EU in 1995. Despite its anti-foreign investment policy over half a century, Finland became a success story, its mobile phone company Nokia became an icon.

Liberal economists praise the benefits of free international movement of capital. It fills the saving gap and spreads best practices of corporate governance. But this view needs critical examination. Foreign capital has three components – grants, debts, (government and corporate bank) and investment (Portfolio and FDI) in the view. Neo-liberal economics asserts that foreign aid does not work, foreign trade does. But this is not true. Bank debt and portfolio investment are notoriously volatile. For example, in 1997 Asian crises, they turned negative. Also in the case of Russia and Brazil in 1998 and Argentina in 2002, they came and went at the wrong time. As a result, developing countries opening capital markets at the urge of "Bad Samaritans", have experienced frequent financial crises. Direct investment is more stable and often brings advanced organisation, skills and technology but through FDI, MNCS often shift most of their profits to a paper company registered in a tax haven. They create demands on foreign exchange through their import requirements. They also resort to "transfer pricing". Foreign direct investors also sometime resort to "asset stripping" of under valued enterprises bought during a crisis.

The US had a terrible record of dealing with foreign investors. US Federal Government strongly regulates foreign investment particularly in relation to acquisition of natural resource like land and mining rights. Despite this, US was the largest recipient of foreign investments. UK, France and Germany also imposed performance requirements on FDI. Thus, the neo-liberal argument that regulation of foreign investment harms growth prospect is a myth and is an example of selective historical amnesia. In recent years Singapore and Ireland succeeded by actively encouraging FDI but even they did not adopt *laissez faire* approach as recommended by "bad samaritans". FDI may help developing countries only as a part of long term development strategy.

SOE's Vs. Privatisation

Neo liberal thinkers have spread the myth that State Owned Public Enterprises do not work, since people do not take care of things that are not theirs. Public enterprises secure finances from the government treasury and fritter them away. This was the justification for massive privatization programme resolutely implemented by Margaret Thatcher in Britain in early 1980's.

It is forgotten that private enterprises like big corporates have dispersed share ownership and are run by hired managers as in the case of state owned enterprises. Key private enterprises in trouble also get subsidies and government bail outs as in the case of Rolls Royce nationalized by Conservative government in 1967 and British Leyland and British Aerospace by Labour Government in 1977. The Swedish ship building industry was nationalized by it's first right wing government in 44 years.

SOEs like private companies have to work in a market environment. SOEs are often success stories like the Singapore airline. Government linked companies in Singapore not only operate public utility industries like telecommunication, power and transport but also ship building, shipping, banking, engineering and semi conductors. 85% of housing is provided by publicly owned entities.

Housing and Development Board Korea also provides another example of successful public enterprise in the form of POSCO (Pohang Iron and Steel Co.). Within 10 years of starting production in 1973 (financed by Japanese Bank after being rejected by World Bank in late 1960's), it became one of the most efficient steel producers. Taiwan has had a very large SOE Sector accounting for 15% of national output.

China has also come up with a unique type of hybrid form of ownership called Town and Village enterprises formally owned by local authorities but which operate as if they are privately owned by local political leaders.

The economic success of many European countries such as France, Italy, Austria, Finland and Norway was achieved with very large SOEs sector at the forefront of technological modernization. Brazilian state owned company Petrobras is World class firm with leading edge technologies. EMBRAER, Brazilian manufacturer of "regional jet" has become a world class firm.

German car masker Volkswagen has the State government of Lower Saxony as its largest share holder with 18.6% shares. Large scale projects with long-gestation period and enterprises which are natural monopolies can best be taken up by the State. Also people in remote areas can be provided essential services only by state enterprises. Disinvestments of SOEs is not always easy. Privatization must be done at the right scale, at the right time, at the right price and to the right buyer. The sale of Cochabamba water system in Bolivia to the American company Bechtel in 1999 which resulted in immediate tripling of water rates is a bad example of privatization. SOES performance can be improved without privatization by providing competition.

Patent Protenction by Trips

TRIPS extended the duration, widened the scope and heightened the degree of protection to patent rights to an unprecedented extent making it difficult for developing countries to acquire the new knowledge they need for economics development as well as essential drugs. Much needed medicines have become very expensive e.g. HIV/AIDS drugs which most African countries need. When these countries acquired generic products from India, pharmaceutical companies grouped together and took them to court though after public uproar, they withdrew the law suit.

The argument that patents are necessary to provide incentive to private companies to invest in research for development of new drugs and vaccines is not entirely valid. Material incentives are not only things that motivate people to develop new ideas and products and promote discovery and inventions. Scientific curiosity and desire to benefit humanity have been of greater importance. Through history, Government research institutions and universities have done lot of research motivated by profit from patent monopoly. Actually patents block knowledge flows into technologically backward countries which is needed to develop their economies. Switzerland had no patent law till 1888. They borrowed a lot of chemical and pharmaceutical technologies from Germany. Netherlands abolished patent law of 1869 in 1871. Philips the Dutch electronic company exploited the absence of patent law to produce light bulbs on the patents "borrowed" from the American inventor Thomas Edison. Today's rich countries, when they were backward themselves in terms of knowledge blithely violated other people's patents, trademark and copyrights. And now the same rich countries are strengthening the protection of intellectual properties through TRIS to a historically unprecedented degree. They are lengthening the terms of IPR protection so that the developing countries pay more for new knowledge. The American system has only encouraged the theft of traditional "knowledge" like the curative use of turmeric (haldi).

Actually patent infringement suits have become a major obstacle to technological progress by making, producing new ideas more expensive because existing ideas are important inputs to producing new ideas. The World Bank estimated that following TRIPs agreement, the increase in technology license payment will cost developing countries an extra $ 45 billion a year which is nearly half the total foreign aid given by rich countries. Thus, IPR has become a rent extracting device. In the interest of developing countries, patent life should be shorter, license and royalty fee lowered and parallel imports allowed or compulsory licensing made easier. Also an international tax law on patent royalty should be imposed to provide technological support and developing countries.

Fiscal and Monetary Discipline

The IMF has insisted on strict monetary and fiscal discipline to be observed by the developing countries before expecting any financial support. Inflation should be tightly controlled and should never exceed 3 per cent, since it is bad for economic growth. Low inflation is a prerequisite for investment. Controlling inflation is the primary responsibility of Central Bank which should be politically independent. The Central Bank should strictly ensure capital adequacy norm to be followed by all banks. The government should live within its means, since budget deficit causes inflation. All these stipulations are not quite realistic. During 1960-70 Brazil had high inflation but it was one of the fastest growing economies. In 1960's inflation rate in South Korea was much higher than in several L.A. countries considered as profligate. Some times moderate inflation is conducive to dynamic economy and rapid growth. Moderate inflation is not harmful.

IMF imposed strict monetary discipline on South Africa and prevented it from generating rapid growth needed for promoting employment. Despite the monetary discipline or because of it, the unemployment rate in South Africa is very high. IMF insisting on the Central Bank of the developing countries to follow the single object of inflation contral overlooks the fact that the US Federal Reserve Bank itself defines its objections as "pursuit of maximum employment, stable prices and moderate long term interest rates". Such is the gap between preaching of the developed countries and the reality in the developing countries.

During the Asia crisis of 1997, advice of the bad Samaritans prevailed on Korea and Indonesia to cut spending despite high rates of unemployment and depressed economy. Cut in interest rates and increase in deficit spending would have boosted their economies and prevented distress. This is what Keynesian Economies would advice but Milton Friedman Economies would not allow it.

Corruption

Under the World Bank leadership of the former US Deputy Defence Secretary Paul Woofowitz, corruption was identified as the biggest obstacle to development. Loan disbursements to several developing countries were halted on grounds of corruption. In fact it was a convenient justification for reduction in aid commitments. Corruption is also used as an explanation for the failure of neo-liberal policies promoted by the World Bank over the past two and half decades. Most of today's rich countries including Britain, France, and US successfully industrialized despite the fact that they were spectacularly corrupt.

A country has to rise above poverty before it can significantly reduce venality in the system. It is argued that deregulation and privatization would reduce corruption by depriving policy makers and bureaucrats the opportunities to extract bribes. Hence a new public management system which advocates introducing market forces in government is advocated. These include (1) Performance related pay and short term contracts. (2) Contracting out and (3) exchange of personnel between private and public sectors. In reality, these reforms increased rather reduced corruption by creating new opportunities for bribes. Civil servants with short term contracts cultivate private business with an eye on future employment prospects. Hence following liberalization policies, corruption has often increased.

Culture

Some developing countries are condemned by the rich countries for their "culture" which makes them lazy and easy going. But there traits attributed to a people are not immutable. Japanese are nowadays considered to be hard working. But they were in the past condemned as easy going, living chiefly for the present. Before their take off in mid 19th Century, the Germans were described by the British as "dull and heavy" people. Francies Fukuyama in his 1995 book "*Trust*", attributed to lack of trust in the cultures of China and Korea which makes it difficult for them to run large firms. These infact are utter prejudices. The habits of a people are not unchangeable. Culture changes with economic development as is shown by economic history of many countries like Japan and Germany. Culture can be changed deliberately through persuasions, changes of policies and institutional building.

Democracy and Free Market

Neo-liberals postulate that democracy and free market are natural partners in promoting economic development. Francis Fukuyama, a senior policy maker in US State Department, in his speech at University of Chicago in 1989 titled – "Are we approaching the end of history?", claimed that free markets and free people are a part of an inseparable project of modernity and progress and represented the end point of mankind's ideological evolution and final form of human organisation.

There is no question of a "third way". Fukuyama's claim turned out to be a myth because it was fundamentally illogical.

There is a basic contradiction between democracy and free market. Democracy gives equal rights to each person while markets give weightage to the rich people. Hence democratic decisions usually subvert the logic of the market.

No wonder "Bad Samaritans" here recommended policies that actively seek to undermine Democracy. They have promoted the concept of "minimal state" – reduction in the scope of government activity and depoliticisation of the economy by establishing politically independent policy agencies like independent Central Bank, independent Regulatory agencies and even independent tax office.

These policies infact amount to undermining democracy by diminishing the scope of democrat control.

In her powerful indictment of neo-liberal policy, comprehensively documented, by Naomi Klein the best selling author of "*No Logo*" has shown how the radical advocates of capitalism sought to impose neoliberal policies on the developing countries of the world by subverting democratic institutions and supporting authoritarian rulers and military dictators.

The intellectual epicenter of radical capitalism and neoliberal policies of marketisation, privatization, deregulation, globalization based on free trade and free movement of capital and minimal state was the Chicago School of Economics led by Milton Friedman. He formulated the theory that "Crisis is the mother of change" – crisis in any form – economic, political or military. Advocates of free market should not hesitate to create a crisis situation since it provides them with the opportunities to push through their neo-liberal policies. The goal should be to see that "new-liberalism" rules the world.

When a crisis situation arises anywhere in the world, the neo-liberaliser should push through the whole gamut of new-liberal policies at one go irrespective of consequences on the well being of the people. This comes to be known as the "shock therapy" administered by the "Chicago Boys" in Chile and other Latin American Countries as also in China, the "Berkley Boys" in Indonesia and the wonder boy of Harvard Jeffrey Sachs who administered it in Bolivia, Poland and Russia. The ruthlessness of the "Shock therapy" is analogous to the electric shock treatment administered by CIA to the detenues in Guantnamo Bay and Abu Gharib prisons to extract confessions and "shock and awe strategy" of the American army used in their attack on Iraq. The idea is that the individual or the country at the receiving end should be completely benumbed, and disoriented and should lose the will and the capacity to resist.

Klein's extensive documentation of the "economic shock therapy" should open the eyes of the economic reformers" who indiscriminately support the neoliberal policies. Like the Tsunami waves the "neo liberal policies" hit the fragile economies of Latin American and African countries as well as the economies of Russia and Poland shattered by the breakdown of communism leaving a trail of human distress and misery. In somewhat different circumstances of China and South Africa the application of the neo-liberal policies had the same consequences viz. gross inequality and human misery. In all these countries people were cowed down by authoritarian governments using ruthless power to crush resistance.

IMF and World Bank

The IMF and the World Bank were at the forefront in thrusting the neoiberal agenda on the developing countries approaching them for help in times of financial need. After World War II these institutions were set up for a specific purpose – the World Bank to provide investment funds for long term economic development and the IMF to provide short term funds to fill in temporary gaps in the balance of payment. After Ronald Reagen took over as the US President, he supported by Margaret That cher who took over as the conservative Prime Minister in Britain, totally changed the mission and role of these institutions. They were now to spread the free market economy in every part of the world. Every assistance would have an attached 'conditionality' in the shape of the Structural Adjustment Programme (SAP) which was indiscriminately insisted upon irrespective of different situations. "One size fits all" became the rule. The disciples of the "Chicago School" who held commanding positions in there institutions spread the gospel of "market fundamentalism" through the SAP – cut public expenditure, eliminate all subsidies, privatize all public enterprises and services, deregulate the economy, remove or drastically reduce tarrifs, open the economy for foreign investment in all forms and make the currency convertible on capital account.

Britain

Margaret Thatcher set the example of "conservative radicalism" (another name for neo-liberalization) by using the "crisis situation" created by the entirely avoidable war with Argentina on the issue of control over Falklands island. By winning the war, she stirred up the suppressed jingoistic imperial frenzy of her people which enabled her to boost her sagging popularity. She then went ahead full steam with her programme of breaking the strength of the Trade Unions, dismantling the Welfare state and privatizing the enterprises nationalized by the Labour Government which came to power after World War II viz. British Railway, British Telecom, British Gas, British Airways. For achieving these ends she did not hesitate to use force to put down resistance in a manner entirely inconsistent with the tenor of British democracy at home.

Chile and Other L.A. Countries

Margaret Thatcher had derived inspiration from Gen Augusto Pinochet of Chile. On Sept 11, 1973 in a bloody *coup detat* he overturned the rule of democratically elected and popular socialistically inclined President Salvedor Allende. The Army attacked the Presidential Palace and killed the President. Thousands of citizens were arrested. People were terrified. Peaceful socialist revolution ended. Next day the "Chicago Boys" transmitted by wire "The Brick", a plan for "liberalisation" of the economy to be executed by the military *junta*. According to Orindeo Letlier, Chilian leader in exile, Milton Friedman shared responsibility for Pinochet's crimes. As per the enforced plan, borders were flung open to foreign imports pulling down barriers that had protected Chilean manufactures. Government spending except on military was cut completely. Price controls were eliminated on all commodities including bread and cooking oil. Inflation reached 375%. Common people suffered because much of the family income was spent just on buying bread. Foreign companies made a killing on speculations. In March 1975 Miton Friedman and Arnold Harberger of Chicago University flew to Santiago to offer advice. They recommended further "Shock treatment". Chicago Boys were appointed to head the Central Bank and other government departments. Four hundred state owned companies were privatized. The shock treatment led to the contraction of the economy by 15%. Unemployment rate rose from 3 to 20 per cent. Social security system was privatize-Public schools were replaced by vouchers and chartered schools. Billions of dollars were taken from the pockets of wage earners and placed in the hands of capitalists and land owners. The middle class was wiped out. By 1982 with hyperinflation, unemployment and exploding debt, Pinochet was forced to make radical course correction.

Following Chilie, Chicago School counter resolution quickly spread to Brazil which was already under US supported military Junta and several Friedman's Brazilian students held key positions. Friedman travelled to Brazil in 1973 and declared the economic experiment there a miracle.

In Uruguay the military staged a coup in 1973 and decided to go the Chicago route. The effect on Uruguay's previously egalitarian system were immediately visible. Real wages dropped by 28 per cent.

In 1976 Junta seized power in Argentina from Isabel Peron. Chicago Boys landed in key positions in Argentina. Argentina became a hospitable place for multinationals. Strikes were banned, workers could be fired at will. Price control was lifted which sent cost of food soaring. Wages lost 40 per cent of value. Those who resisted the reforms "disappeared".

Argentina, Brazil, Uruguay and Chile are the four states in LA's "Southern cone" which were show cases of development. The UN Economic commission for LA, based in Santiago and headed by economist Rault Prebisch from 1950 to 1963 has trained economists in development theory. They were working as policy advisers to these countries.

They began to look like developed countries of Europe and North America than parts of the third world. Uruguay had a literacy rate of 95 per cent and offered health care to all citizens. Developmentalism was a success. LA's "Southern Cone" became a symbol for poor countries around the world. The US multinational in these countries were required to redistribute their wealth through corporate taxes and workers salaries. In the sixties and seventies, the left was the dominant culture of LA nurtured by the poetry of Pablo Nenula and folk music of Victor Jara.

All this changed during Junta rule. They became laboratories of Chicago experiment. In all these countries terror was the central tool of free market transformation. American multinational companies supported the terror apparatus.

CIA provided training to Argentineans, Brazilians and Uruguay Police in interrogation techniques. According to CIA manual. 150,000 citizens including social and community workers went through the torture machines, many died. This was the Chicago School model of new-liberalisation.

Bolivia

For 21 years till 1985 Bolivia had been living under some

form of dictatorship. In 1984 Ronald Reagan administration funded an unprecedented attack on its coco farmers. This cut the source of half of the country's export revenue, triggering an economic meltdown. Inflation went up to 1400 per cent. It was in these circumstances that Bolivia entered into 1985 historic elections. Jeffrey Sachs then at Harvard University claimed that he could turn around the inflationary crisis in a day. He was invited to develop anti-inflation economic plan. Sachs advised "sudden shock" therapy to cure hyper inflation crisis. Gonzalo Sanchers de Lozada (known in Bolivia as Goni) who had studied at the University of Chicago shaped the bi-partison economic plan prepared according to Sachs's therapy. Bolivia's entire state centred economic model was to be dismantled. Food subsidies were to be eliminated; price control, cancelled; government spending drastically cut. As a result of the shock therapy a small elite grew far wealthier, while large portions of the working class was discarded from the economy altogether. Full time jobs were eliminated. Thousands of kids were undernourished. Families were forced to live in tents. When there were demonstrators against these economic measures and labour leaders went on hunger strike, quasi-fascist measures were used to force the plan.

Post Dictatorship LA

Argentina – Junta collapsed in 1983 after the Falklands war. Raul Alfohsin was elected as the new President. Washington insisted that the new government should pay off the debt amassed by the generals to fight the war $ 456 to IMF, US Import Export Bank and private banks. In Uruguay, the Junta had left a debt of $ 5 for a population of 3 million. In Brazil the junta which had seized power on 1964 promising financial order took the debt from $ 3 billion to $ 103 billion in 1985. In these countries as in Chile, the money borrowed by generals went to military spending as also to corruption. Gen. Pinocte had 125 secret foreign bank accounts. US government had approval of these loans to the corrupt military regimes. The dramatic increase in interest rates by US (Voleker Shock) increased the debt burden. The fall in prices of export commodities like coffee, coco and tin devastated the economics of these countries. Added to this was the currency shock by speculative transfer of funds. In the dire financial position in which they found themselves, the LA countries had to accept the SAP of the IMF and the World Bank dominated by the Chicago Boys (Bad Samaritans) – privatization, deregulation and drastic cut in public expenditure.

The hyper inflation crisis forced out President Alfonson of Argentina. He was replaced by Carlos Menem, a Peronist. However, he came under the influence of the Chicago boys who were given top economic posts. In the early nineties, Argentina rapidly sold of the riches of the country – 90 per cent of all state enterprises were sold to private companies – Citi Bank, Bank Boston etc after firing workers. In the crisis created by hyperinflation, Menem made drastic charges relating to privatization, deregulation and opening the economy. Cheep imported goods flooded the country, jobs were lost and people were pushed below the poverty line.

Poland

The same doctor Jeffrey Sachs who administered "shock treatment" which caused acute distress to Bolivia, was also invited after the collapse of communism to deal with the economic crises situation in Poland and Russia where he gave the same treatment with the same consequences.

In Poland the widespread "Solidarity" labour movement led by Lech Walasa forced the well entrenched communist regime to slowly liberalize. Thanks to Gorbachev, President of USSR, elections were held which brought the solidarity to power. But solidarity leaders could not fulfill the promise of workers' cooperatives or councils replacing the communist oligarohy in running the enterprises. Instead Jeffrey Sachs forced them to accept for free market capitalist economy as a condition of getting the IMF loan which was badly needed to prevent economic catastrophe. Sachs claimed that he was the first to write down a comprehensive plan for the transformation of a socialist economy to market economy. His plan included privatization of state industry, a convertible currency, shift from heavy industry to consumer products, creation of stock exchange and capital market, and steep budget cuts, all at once. The consequences: soaring prices, rising unemployment, deeper debts, deindustrilisation and poverty forced the Solidarity to give up the "reforms" halfway and later give up power as well when in 1993 elections left parties including former communist, won 46 per cent of seats in parliament, a resounding rejection of shock therapy.

Russia

Winds of change started blowing over the Soviet Union with Gorbachev's programme of "glasnost" (open society) and "perestroika" (economic reconstruction). Gorbachev was thinking of replacing the centrally planned socialist economy with some sort of socially oriented market economy on the Scandinavian model. But the Western leaders let him down. The IMF refused to provide the support which he needed for reconstruction of the economy. This rebuff to his efforts weakened his position. The old guard communist leaders who were suspicious of his reforms staged a coup. At that moment of crisis, Yeltsin, the head of the Russian Federation, a constituent of Soviet Union, successfully challenged the coup leaders and the coup fizzled out. Gorbachev temporarily returned as the President of the Soviet Union. But political power had passed to Yeltsin after the triumphant show down. Yeltsin managed to dissolve the union itself making Gorbachev's position untenable. He had to resign. Yeltsin became the powerful head of the Russian Federation. He was determined to dismantle the communist economic system. He invited the aid economist Jeffrey Sachs who again recommended "the shock therapy" and promised to arrange aid from the IMF and World Bank. But Sachs could not keep his word. In the meanwhile to implement "shock therapy", Yeltsin made Parliament give him a free hand, absolute power to reform the economy. But shock therapy caused havoc ushering in "gangster capitalism" or "casino capitalism" under which upstart oligarchs seized control over national and public enterprises which were sold even without tender at throwaway prices. The immense public wealth built during the Soviet era was simply frittered away. Yeltsin appointed Yegor Gaider and his associates to implement the "Chicago School programme" of privatization and liberlization. They brought about sudden changes to make resistance impossible. In the very first phase of rapid privatisation, 22,500 state enterprises were privatized. Price controls were lifted. Communist state became a corporation state. The new "oligarchs teamed with Yelstsin's Chicago Boys stripped the country of everything of value Russia's. Public riches were auctioned off far a fraction of their worth. An oil company of the size of France's total public ownership was sold for $ 88 million. Norsik nickel which produced a fifth of nickel of the world, was sold for paltry $ 170 million. This was not all. There was massive corruption. Yeltsin's ministers transferred large sums of public funds to private bank accounts abroad. The Harvard Professors invited as consultants were discovered profiting from the free market which they were supposed to help creating. They exemplified greed which was supposed to be the engine for rebuilding the Russian economy. Oligarchs became billionaires shamelessly flaunting their affluence while the people suffered because of loss of jobs and means of living. There was further collateral damage from the shock therapy. Bu 1998 more than 80 per cent of Russian farms had gone bankrupt and 70000 state factories closed creating an epidemic of unemployment. A third of population fell below poverty. There was dramatic decline in Russian population. Still sound "reformers" like Yegor Gaider and Chubaish pressed on with the so called reforms. Yeltsin own family prospered through this plunder of public wealth. Naturally there was widespread resistance. Parliament tried to curb the absolutely power given to Yeltsin for a year to enable him to deal with the economic crisis. Yelstin's answer was to render it impotent and abolish the constitution. Parliament almost unanimous decided to impeach the President Yeltsin who sent army to encircle Parliament. In the military assault 500 people lost their life. He held fresh elections and won but his time was over. He handed over power to Putin, his chosen successor and an old KG hand, on the condition of being given legal amnesty from all punishment because of his misdeeds. Putin retained the change towards free capitalist economy but took punitive action against the oligarchs found to be indulging in economic misdeeds.

China

When Mao Tse Tung, the founding father of communist China

died, Deng Xia Peing whom Mao had exiled during his disastrous "cultural revolution" managed to succeed him as the head of the communist party. He was determined to change the communist system of social ownership of all the means of production and central planning in favour of a capitalist, corporate, market economy, yet firmy holding the reins of power in the communist party under his leadership. He invited Milton Friedmen in 1980 to China to tutor hundreds of top level civil servants and party economists in the fundamentals of free market economy. Under his guidance started the programmes of privatization of public enterprises and opening up the economy for foreign investment. He also removed price controls and allowed the market economy to functión. The change gave a tremendous boost to the China's economy. For years China had a steady economic growth rate near or above 10%. The public enterprises under the communist were mainly taken over by the party functionaries whose family enormously benefited. Land was taken over for infrastructure development without paying compensation and little care was taken for rehabilitation of the uprooted people. There was forced migration from the rural area to provide labour power for enterprises in the urban area and "special economic zones", a Chinese innovation. China became a "sweat shop" of the world. Every multinational located their contract factories in China.

Job security was eliminated creating waves of unemployment. On the other hand party officials fattened themselves turning into business tycoons taking illegal possession of public assets. Competition and nepotism spread in party layers. Yet visiting Shanghai in 1988, Friedman and his wife were so dazzled that they said that mainland China was looking like Hong Kong. Yet in the face of lowering wages, rising prices and unemployment due to layoffs, protests spanned in the whole range of Chinese society. Billionaires flaunted their wealth while common people suffered. There was rising employment and no safety for mine workers who died in large number in accidents.

The countryside was denuded of natural resources while urban areas and rivers were polluted. Rising inequalities and widespread dissatisfaction amongst the common people posed a real threat to the future of the Chinese economy.

Student leaders held public demonstrations at the Tiananmen square demanding democratic freedom. But Deng was not ready to grant such freedom. He harshly put down the student demonstrations with the brutal use of force by the Red Army. People's liberation Army indiscriminately fired into the crowd and thousands died and were injured. The students revolt was crushed. This gave full freedom to Deng to go ahead speedily with the "economic reforms. He became China's General Pinochet.

Asian Countries

After India, Indonesia was the next big country to attain independence. Sukarno the nationalist leader became the first President. He sent out foreign companies and nationalized the natural resources of the country. This was not to the liking of US and their associate capitalist countries and their multinationals. They were determined to end Sukarno's rule. They hatched a plot to unseat Sukarno with the help of Gen. Suharto in 1965. The General unseated Sukarno and seized power and remained undisputed leader for several years. He parcelled out the immense natural resources of the country including oil, to multinational companies of the several ex-imperial powers in which his family had a big slice. The people greatly suffered when Suharto fully implemented the neo-liberal economic reforms under the guidance of the "Berkley Boys" i.e. economists of Berkley University. Prices rose, so did unemployment and standard of living of the common people went down. But there could be no resistance because people were terrorized by brutal and indiscriminate massacres and oppression by the army in which a million people lost their lives. The entire Indonesian left was annihilated.

Ultimately the long suffering people revolted and the dictator had to give way to elected governments. But the dictator in spite of all his preverbal corruption and brutality was left scot-free and died at a ripe old age.

Asian Meltdown, 1997

South Korea, Thailand, Taiwan, Malaysia were all applauded by the World Bank and IMF as "Asia dragons" which thrived because of their free economies and booming export factories.

But they all came in the grip of an economic crisis which none of the "experts" of the IMF had anticipated. The crisis dubbed as "Asian Flu" was caused by sudden outflow of money facilitated by the capital account convertability of their currencies. A huge sum of $ 600 billion disappeared from stock market of Asia. Families saw their savings disappear. Thousands of small businesses were shut down. There was a wave of suicides. Once the crisis came upon these countries, the IMF started attributing it to their "crony capitalism" i.e. rampant nepotism, favouritism and corruption in their banks and business houses. When these countries (except Malaysia) approached the IMF and World Bank to salvage the situation, they refused any bailout and initiated that the market should be left to correct itself and imposed uncompromisingly the SAP i.e. huge deep budget cuts and low social spending, lay off of public sector workers, privatization of basic services and removal of all restrictions on trade and investment. A huge privatization programme had to be taken up under which several public and major enterprises went into the hands of the multinational companies. Local brands were placed by multinationals. Klein describes it as a veritable "Asia loot". Korean Samsung was broken up and sold in parts; Volvo got heavy industry division; SC Johnson and Sons the Pharmaceutical division and GE the lighting division; Daewoo's car division valued at $ 6 billion was sold to GM. for just $ 400 million. Local firms were wiped out by multinationals. Several South Korean Banks were privatized . The adoption of these measures under compulsion was looked upon as loss of economic sovereignty and national humiliation. The SAP turned crisis into a catastrophe. As per ILO, 24 million people lost their jobs, unemployment soared. Ideology of unfettered capitalism advocated by the IMF and World Bank were held responsible for the fate that fell upon the Asian countries.

South Africa

After 27 years in jail in the Roben island, Nelson Mandela was released in November 1990. The Apartheid regime preferred to negotiate with him for the transfer of power bowing to the relentless pressure of the outside world. The negotiators led to the transfer of political power to the black majority. Mandela became first President after the transfer of power. But the transfer of political power remained illusory because under the terms of negotiations maneuvered by the whites, economic power firmly remained in the hands of the white minority. Emancipation of the black was born in chains. The Central Bank became independent and the former white Minister remained as Finance Minister, who in the name of fiscal discipline tightly controlled the purse and made little provision for the welfare programmes. National Freedom Charter of ANC, drafted before the end of apartheid, under which land had to be redistributed so that the black could became owners of land, remained on paper, 10% of white continued to own 70%. Houses had to be built for the poor and enterprises like gold mines had to be nationalized. None of these programmes could be implemented as per the terms of the negotiated agreement. The poor Africans remained poor in their slums while the whites lived in the splendour in their fabulous mansions with black servants working for them. South Africa remains an extremely unequal society. President Mandela and Thabo Mbekei failed to fulfill the programmes of ANP for the black people.

Both Mandela and Mbekei thought after they assumed political power, that ANC Charter of Freedom must be surrendered at the alter of the market economy. After a series of secret meetings with white corporate executives, the neo-liberal shock reform were introduced in South Africa – more privatisation, cut back in government spending and labour "flexibility". Mbekei started calling himself a Margaret Thatcher ! But his announcement of the new programmes failed to attract long term investment. His government failed to give compensation to apartheid victims and their families in the name of "truth and forgiveness". On the other hand, his government continued to pay the debts incurred by the previous apartheid regime which took away all funds which could have been used for the welfare of people. Since 1994, the year ANC took power, the number of people living on less than a dollar a day has risen from 2 million to 4 million in 2006. The unemployment rate for black doubled from 23 to 48%. One million black people have been evicted from farms and 2 million lost their houses. The number of shanty dwellers has grown by 50%. Promises of freedom were betrayed.

Conclusion

The entire thirty year history of the Chicago School experiment has been one of collusion between authoritarian states and large corporations and massive corruption. The history of neo-liberalism has been a "second colonial pillage", IMF and World Bank were a party to this after they betrayed their original objectives and became a tool of Washington consensus.

US's Disaster Capitalism

Ever since Ronald Reagan of the Republican Party was elected President of US, extremely conservative economic ideology advocating unbridled capitalism and free market was preached by Milton Friedman and his Chicago School has become the ruling economy ideology of USA, going by the name "Washington Consensus". Under the Presidency of George Bush (Junior), it has reached its acme. This was manifested in the privatization of even "core" functions of government, maximum deregulation, cut in expenditure on people welfare programmes and promotion of neo-liberal policies all over the world.

The prolonged Iraq war from 2003 till today was an example of the extreme ideology. Defence Secretary Donald Rumsfield brought the corporates into the heart of the US military. Logistic functions relating to the war were handed over to private companies like Halliburton with which Vice President Cheney has been intimately connected. Health care and housing for soldiers was privatized. All the security functions were discharged by Black Water including the security of the US military base and its seat of governance (Paul Bremmerls Green Zone area). Of course production and supply of weapons and material were handled by private companies. The contracts for Iraq oil exploitation were prepared by private firms. The selected contractors, whether for oil exploitation or construction in infrastructure project sub-contracted, since they themselves had no operational base. The local Iraqi public sector enterprises were left outs so were the local professionals. The Defence Minister, Donald Rumsfeld was a strong advocate of this approach of slim military, supported by a huge network of corporations. Billions of dollars spent on Iraqi war want to the coffers of these private corporations.

The department of Home Land Security set up after 9/11 handed over $ 130 billion to private contractors to develop and install detection equipment and cameras against unproven threats. War on Terror, an un-vinafle proposition, has become a permanent fixture of the global economic architecture. In the name of security, Bush Administration fulfilled the corporate mission of merging political and corporate interests.

The same approach was adopted in dealing with the calamity of Hurricane Katrina which hit New Orleans in Sept 2005. The poor people were left homeless as their public housing was washed away. So were the public schools where their children studied. Milton Friedman saw in this the opportunity for privatization of housing and schooling system. Here again the private contractors failed in housing the poor.

The poor were provided with vouchers to be paid to the owners of the private schools which had a good business opportunity to make money. The money making got the better of provision of public services like education and health to the poor. No wonder New Orleans rehabilitation programmes did no good to the poor.

Iraqi war and Hurricane Katrina, both disasters, have been good opportunities to corporate business for making money.

Israel, the mini USA in the middle east, has discovered that the "perpetual" war with Arabs whether in Palestine or in Lebanon is conducive to its dynamic economy. Rise of insecurity the world over has been an opportunity to Israel to develop "security industry" in a big way. This is what Klein calls "Disaster Capatalism" of today.

Revolt against NEO-Liberalization

The theory rather myth of neo-liberalisation that the market is always efficient and right and public service is always inefficient and public intervention and regulation always wrong has not worked well in reality. In fact, it has proved a disaster to the well being of the common people who have not benefited from the so called "trickle down effect" As this realization has grown, a reaction against neo-liberalism has set in.

Latin America

Countries after countries have thrown out military rulers and their neo liberal "democratic" successors. They have elected left of the Centre Governments, Hugo Chavez in Venezuela, LuladeSilva in Brazil, Rafael Corea in Equador, Krichner in Argentina, Michelle Bachlet in Chile and Evo Morales in Bolivia.

They have (1) renationalized the ownership and management of natural resources for their use for public benefit and public service. In Venezuela, Chavez gave top priority to cooperative enterprise by offering incentives. By 2006 there were 100,000 company in the country employing more than 700,000 workers. (2) Started social welfare programmes discontinued during military regime and their neo-liberal successors. (3) They have asserted their economic sovereignty and refused to go to the IMF and world Bank for assistance, since they are no longer willing to accept their conditionalities. As a result business of both these institutions has diminished. They don't want to listen any longer to their "expert advice" of "shock therapy". In 2005, LA countries accounted for 80% of IMF's lending portfolio. In 2007 it was reduced to 1 per cent. IMF's worldwide lending portfolio has fallen from $81 to 15 $ 11.8 IMF. It has become a pariah and has started withering away. (4) They have countered US domination by building regional organisation of Latin American countries. Under the auspices of the organization there is barter between the health services provided by Cuba and petrol supplied by Venezuela. Such barter exchange have been found to be of mutual advantage.

(2) Russia – Under Putin, Russia is trying to build its own strength and is no longer prepared to go down before US. Well connected businessmen like Mikhael Kudorovsky, former head of oil giant Yuko or Boris Bevezovsky who made billions from privatization are either in jail or in exile.

(3) China - Growing inequality, rural – urban divide,

environmental pollution and rural revolts have created challenges before the Communist regime. The recent incident of contaminated milk has exposed the weaknesses of the regulatory regime of China. Hereafter party authoritarianism would not work. The China communist rules will have to respond to the woes of the common people. There were 87,000 protests in China in 2005 involving 4 million workers and peasants.

(4) South Africa - The Mbeke government did little for the common black people. Unrest amongst them has grown. His recent unseating is indication of the winds of change blowing over South Africa.

USA itself has not escaped reality. Enron's Ken Lay was convicted of financial conspiracies and died in jail. The recent "financial meltdown" has thoroughly exposed the hollowness of unbridled capitalism. Major companies like FanniMae and Freddy Mac, and AIG had to be nationalized. Some others like Lehman Brothers faced bankruptcy. Naoml Kleh has described the public take over of financial institutions as "Socialism for the rich" while capitalism has been for the poor to rob them of their savings, houses and jobs. These financial disasters have shown that market is not always right and public regulation is not redundant. Unbridled capitalism can lead to disaster.

References

1. "The Economics of Innocent Fraud" by John Kenneth Galbraith, Houghton Milfni Company, Boston New York 2004

2. *Bad Samaritans – The Guilty Secrets of Rich Nations and the threats to global prosperity by* Ha-Joon Chay, published by Random House Business Books 2008, price 8.99, pages 276

3. Naomi Klein – *The Shock Doctrine* – the rise of Disaster Capitalism – Allen Lane, 2007, pp. 558 price £12.99

27

PARTICIPATIVE ECONOMICS

Capitalism rules triumphant roday all over the world in the era of globalisation. It has been left with no rival or alternative after the collapse of communism in the erstwhile Soviet Union and other eastern European countries. Soviet Union has disintegrated and many eastern European countries have joined NATO and have whole heartedly accepted American leadership. Marxism is dead and its battle cry, "workers of the world unite" no longer inspires. It was in this context, that the American writer Francis Fukuyama had announced the end of history. History had ended in the sense that search for alternative to capitalism had ended.

But Fukuyama might have spoken too soon. Capitalism has not solved all the economic problems of humanity nor is it a system without severe failings. Michael Albert quotes the words of John Maynard Keynes, the leading economist of the early 20th century who said "capitalism is not a success. It is not intelligent. It is not beneficial. It is not just. It is not virtuous and it does not deliver the goods. In short, we dislike and we are beginning to despise it." But when we wonder what to put in its place we are extremely perplexed !. Michael Alebert's *Participative Economics* is an attempt to answer the question raised by Keynes – 'What to put in place of capitalism?'.

It is not as though Albert's is the first attempt to provide an alternative to capitalism or to highlight its shortcomings. Such attempts have been made from early years of capitalism when industrial capitalism first came to be established in Great Britain during the period 1760 to 1820. It was marked by exploitation of the working classes in the form of 'iron law of wages' that existed at subsistence level and long hours of work. The worst exploited were women and children. A large hearted capitalist Robert Owen sought to find an alternative in the form of a cooperative community. The textile workers known as Rochdale Pioneers set up consumer cooperative shops to escape the exploitation of shops run by capitalist owners. The emancipated farmers of Germany organized credit cooperatives under the leadership of Raiffeisen in order to escape the exploitation of money lenders. The cooperative organization was an alternative to capitalist enterprise. While the latter was based on shareholding, the farmer was based on membership. Cooperative organizations were associations of members that were to be managed democratically on the basis of 'one member one vote'. Membership was based on participation in appropriate manner. Cooperatives were economic democracies based on the principle of self help and mutual help; not profit or charity but service was to be the goal of cooperative enterprises. In cooperatives there was no scope for profit to be appropriated by the owner of capital. On the other hand, the surplus was to be used for the distribution of dividend to members in proportion to participation, for the generation of resources for further development and for common use. It was expected that cooperatives could be established in myriad activities of economic life and the cooperative visionaries dreamt of a cooperative commonwealth. These hopes have not been realized and instead of emerging as an alternative system, cooperatives remained as islands in capitalism. In order to survive and succeed in the capitalist system, cooperatives perforce have to adopt the principles of management of capitalist enterprise.

Inequality, disregard for social cost and social benefits, instability caused by ups and downs of business cycle and unemployment came to be recognized as the failings of capitalism even as it established its hold on the entire economic system. There were two alternatives – either to mend capitalism or to end it. The idea of welfare state or social democracy emerged in many European countries. The welfare state used the state's resources to provide comprehensive social securities to citizens from hazards to the earning capacity caused by sickness or accidents, unemployment or old age. John Kenneth Galbraith in his book, *The Affluent Society* drew attention to yet another failing of capitalism, viz. promoting private opulence at the cost of public squalors and made a case for massive state investment in public goods. Keynes and many other economists showed that unemployment, chronic to capitalism was caused by deficiency of demand and advocated that the counterveiling power of the state must be used to boost consumption and investment in order to revive economic activity.

Socialism aimed at ending capitalism and replacing it by social ownership of means of production. Marx had predicted that socialist economic system would first come into existence in a country of most advanced capitalism, which would collapse as a consequence of inner contradictions. Socialism did come into existence but not in the most advanced capitalistic country as predicted by Marx. It came into existence in Russia after the October Revolution of 1917, which had a backward capitalist economy. After Second World War Socialism spread to many Eastern European countries which came under Russian domination and to China. The socialist economies were managed by central planning. The planners decided what to produce, how much to produce, when to produce, where to produce and for whom to produce. Economists like Ludwig Von Mises and Fredrick Von Hayek had predicted from the very beginning that centrally planned economy would be incapable of taking rational economic decisions and would therefore be unworkable. Moreover, imposition of planners' decisions on all consumers and producers would be a road to serfdom. It took 70 years for their prophecy to come true. The Soviet Union economy started stagnating and could not withstand competition with capitalism and collapsed in Soviet Union and other eastern European countries. The road to its replacement by capitalist economy has proved to be tortuous and painful. In contrast, the Chinese Communist Party while retaining its hold on political power started from the year 1979 to reform the communist economy and today has virtually dismantled it and replaced it by capitalist economy and succeeded in attaining impressive high rates of growth.

A Possible Alternative

With the collapse of the alternative model, corporate capitalism fully assisted by the international institution, viz. IMF, World Bank and the WTO and supported by the governments of the affluent countries known as G7 has started a comprehensive process of globalisation. However, at a time when no government is in the position to halt or restrain the process of globalisation, different people's movements have come forward to oppose globalisation. The participants in the movement are a variety of institutions and NGOs which have come together under the auspices of the World Social Forum. They have successfully held demonstrations against the meeting of the G7 Countries, WTO and the financial institutions held at various places in the world. The movement has forcefully pointed out that corporal globalisation has subordinated the welfare of the whole population of the developing countries and of ordinary peoples in the developed countries to the advantage of western corporate capitalism. It has promoted global trade at the expense of local economic activity. It has led to environmental degradation and indiscriminate exploitation of natural resources to the detrimental sustainable development. It has fostered authoritarian political state structures to put down popular movement's. It has threatened diversity and traditional lore. It has aggressively violated the values of equity, diversity, solidarity, self-management and ecological balance. It has created huge difference in wealth and income and shifted financial resources from productive activities to speculative profit seeking. The popular movements aimed at fighting all these ills of global capitalism and bettering the lives of the disenfranchised and exploited population around the globe. It stands therefore for economic justice.

But it is not enough for the popular movements to oppose global capitalism. It has to provide an alternative. In this book, the author who has been associated for several years with the popular movements has tried to present a comprehensive and coherent blue print of a "participative economy". The logic of participative economy requires the end of the basic institutions of capitalism, viz. (i) private ownership of means of production (ii) allocation of resources for private profit at the cost of the needs of the people, and (iii) hierarchical decision making without the participation of the disenfranchised working class.

Participative economy builds on an alternative set of institutions. The following are the characteristics of the participative economy as conceived by the author. First there would be social ownership of the productive assets so there would be no class of private proprietors or of capitalist owners. Nor, secondly, would there be a separate class of coordinators, managers or decision makers. This is because the work organization in a participative economy would be entirely different. There would be balanced job complexes to replace the present division of labour where the coordinating class performs only the task of decision making while the working class is engaged in the drudgery of debilitating and depressing task of routine work, the day to day grind without any access to information or knowledge of the overall goals. Everyone would have his or her share of routine task and decision making. Thirdly, the reward system would also be entirely different. In the capitalist economy the reward system is based on ownership of property, bargaining power, difference of circumstances or different characteristics of individuals. On the other hand, in the participative economy the reward would be for effort and sacrifice. This is despite the fact that there may be differences in talent or in education or training. Training and educational opportunities would be socially provided and would be available to all. Similarly, healthcare and social amenities like public parks would be free for all, special needs of people like the handicapped would also be taken care of. Thus, the reward system would aim at justice for all. Fourthly, the participative economy would be self managed through decisions by workers and consumers councils helped by cooperative communication and facilitation boards. The decisions would be based on indicative prices reflecting social opportunity costs and benefits. They would be arrived at through a process of successive iteration and approximation to a balance between demand and supply.

The author has given a detailed picture of how the system would function and how consumers and producers could participate cooperatively in planning and coordinating joint endeavours without central planning and without markets. The councils would function at various levels and would take both production and investment decisions. The author has illustrated the working of the system of the participative economy with various work units like a publishing house, a steel plants or a city planning office. The consumer councils would take decision not only about the consumer needs of individual families but also of collective consumption needs like airports, roads, fire stations, etc. The producers councils would not only do work planning but also take decisions regarding job transfers, overtime work, etc.

The author has tried to meet possible objections to his concept of participative economy. One possible objection is the ideas of reward in proportion to efforts or sacrifice. Effort and sacrifice are difficult to measure. The author shows how this can be done and at the same time points out that the economist's concept of marginal productivity is also in practice difficult to measure. He does not agree that the proposed reward system would not provide necessary incentive if allocation duties, responsibilities and rewards are fair as contemplated in participative economy. It would promote a strong sense of social duty and no additional external motivation would be necessary.

The author has claimed that the participative economy would remove the shortcomings of capitalist economy. It would promote equity, diversity, solidarity, mutual concern and empathy. It would eschew the typical tendencies of individualism and egoism leading to taking undue advantages of fellow citizens. It would end the dichotomy between owners and workers, buyers and sellers. It would internalize the external costs like pollution and therefore lead to greater efficiency as measured by social costs and benefits. In a participative economy there would be widespread opportunities to fulfill needs and desires. There would be economic security for all. There would be no monopoly of ownership and coordination, no domination of political and economic elite, and no autocratic decision making by privileged individuals. There will be improved conditions of work, dignity for all and improved quality for life. There will be greater expenditure on public goods and reduced military expenditure; because of economic security, there would be no compulsive need for accumulation.

Michael Albert's participative economy is indeed an ambitious utopia. But how will it be brought into existence? In the past attempts in that direction have been made but have not been successful. Polish economist Oscar Lange had provided a detailed blueprint of market socialism. Erstwhile Yugoslavia had experimented economic decision making through workers' councils. But neither the blueprints nor the experiments have been a practical success.

The coming into existence of participative economy would require a socio-economic revolution to end private ownership; a social psychological revolution for people to accept balanced job systems as well as self-management and socio-organizational revolution to end hierarchical decision making. Who would bring about these revolutions and where? Perhaps the NGO's who gathered together at the World Social Forum could make a small beginning in their own area of influence. In that endeavour, the book can provide them with a sense of direction. One of the demonstrators at the siege of Genoa in 2001 carried a placard 'capitalism should be replaced by something nicer'. The participative economy is that 'something nicer'. The logic of participative economy rejects the proposition that an economic system expressly working for the promotion of common good is not workable. It shows how this can be accomplished provided revolutionary changes can be brought about to serve as the foundation of the participative economy.

28

RELEVANCE OF GANDHI'S IDEALS IN THE AGE OF GLOBALISATION

In the economic sphere, capitalism has emerged triumphant as we approach the end of the twentieth century. The basis of the capitalist ideology was laid down by the classical economists whose socio-psycholigical assumptions were embodied in the concept of the 'economic man' and his 'rational behaviour' governed by the motivation of pursuit of self-interest or hedonism. This led to the emergence of what R.H. Tawney called the 'acquisitive society' in which participants in economic activity were pitted against each other – the producers against the consumers, the factory owners against the workers.

The political counterpart of the competitive economic system was provided by the party system in a democracy whose goal was acquisition of power for its own sake. Hobbes talked of 'natural order' in which life was 'solitary, poor, nasty, brutish and short'. The State came into existence to enforce some order. But the State became a leviathan, a repository of power. Acquisition of control over the levers of power became the 'be all and the end all' of political activity.

Marxism provided an alternate ideology. It has now become a 'god that failed'. But it too was based on conflict between two classes-one owning the means of production and the other who had nothing but their labour to sell. The State was an instrument in the hands of the dominant class. However, the system was destined to collapse as a result of its inner contradictions and gave way to the dictatorship of the proletariat. In practice, it became the dictatorship of a ruthless individual.

Both capitalism and socialism violated to nature in their blind pursuit of material achievement. Environmental damage inflicted by the economic programmes in China was found to be even worse than in the countries of unbridled capitalism. The collapse of the socialist economies have brought out the conflict between different people within a nation state. That conflict could not come into the open so long as a strong socialist state existed.

Francis Fukuyama has talked of the end of history. Capitalism and democracy, he argues, are the culmination of economic and political evolution and no further advancement would be possible. He further urges that there would no bloody conflict between countries with established systems of capitalism and democracy since none of these countries would think in terms of physical control over each other. He notes that all the conflicts after World War II have taken place in Asia or Africa, not in Europe or America.

Fukuyama might have spoken too soon. Oklahoma has shown that there could be indigenous terrorism even in the US. The US has not been able to solve its problems with Japan through negotiations. And it has now started a no-holds –barred confrontation with Iran. In a uni-polar world, US wants to impose its will over all the countries but this may not be possible without conflict.

Obviously the world wants a different ideology if the seeds of conflict are to be eliminated. The UNESCO Constitutions states that all wars start in the minds of men. So do peace and harmony. This is what Gandhian ideology stands for. In sharp contrast to capitalistic and Marxist approaches, it explicitly rejects the concept of economic man and seeks to raise the human being to a higher level of spiritual existence.

Mindless materialism is not the goal of life. Of course, the essential needs of the human being should be met, but they can be provided for without environmental degradation or exploitation of other people. The economic system can be built on the basis of co-operation rather than competition. The owner of business and industry can act as a trustee of society. Individuals can live for the good of the community, economic activity and resources conserved for the public good. Violence can be avoided and tolerance and broad-mindedness can become a way of life for the individual and society.

These essential propositions of Gandhian ideology are of even greater relevance today than during Gandhi's own lifetime. They cannot be dismissed as utopian ideas. Vinoba Bhave's Bhoodan movement and Pandurang Shastri Athavale's Swadhyay movement have shown that radical social and economic reconstruction can be based on the changes in the minds of men, that the 'haves' and even the criminals can be transformed into socially committed people. These movements demonstrate how Gandhian ideology can be applied effectively in bringing about far-reaching and durable changes in individual and social life.

industry can act as a trustee of society. Individuals can live for the good of the community, economic activity and resources conserved for the public good. Violence can be avoided and tolerance and broad-mindedness can become a way of life for the individual and society.

These essential propositions of Gandhian ideology are of even greater relevance today than during Gandhi's own lifetime. They cannot be dismissed as utopian ideas. Vinoba Bhave's Bhoodan movement and Pandurang Shastri Athavale's Swadhyaya movement have shown that radical social and economic reconstruction can be based on the changes in the minds of men, that the 'haves' and even the criminals can be transformed into socially committed people. These movements have demonstrated how Gandhian ideology can be applied effectively to bring about fundamental, non-violent changes in individual and community life.

INDEX

R

V

W

Y

Z